Preaching and Social Issues

Praise for *Preaching and Social Issues*

"The wisest advocates for justice seek mentors who can offer sound advice on discerning entry points for preaching and teaching on issues that affect those whom God loves. With this book, Dr. Schade invites us into her homiletics classroom, office hours, and collegial relationships to benefit from collective knowledge and skills. What riches there are here for those of us seeking productive preaching paths! What you'll find are tools for sound preaching that consider the local context, the moment, the preacher's heart, and Gospel imperatives. A worthy addition to any preacher's bookshelf." —**The Rev. Kerri Parker, Executive Director, Wisconsin Council of Churches**

"Leah Schade's decades of noteworthy experience addressing social issues through Christian proclamation weds trusted pastoral and homiletical praxis to data-driven insights. Scholars, students, and pastors will find *Preaching and Social Issues* to be a timely treasure. There is no preaching resource more essential in this hour for equipping responsible heralds of the gospel of Jesus Christ. Schade confronts the endemic alienation between socio-political topics and preaching, and through painstaking research, charts a clear course forward. Offering practical instructions, tethered to the irrefutable theological principles of justice, love, and mercy, *Preaching and Social Issues* elucidates critical and compelling content that promises to galvanize preachers who understand this unprecedented and dangerous time and the need for prophetic urgency." —**Tyshawn Gardner, Associate Professor of Preaching, George W. Truett Seminary, Baylor University**

"For religious leaders in today's fraught and contested political and religious climate, especially those who must lead their communities in worship each week, Leah Schade's important work, *Preaching and Social Issues*, could not have come at a better time. Charging and guiding preachers not to avoid but rather to confront, albeit carefully and with practiced nuance, the major issues of the day, Schade gives well-researched examples of preachers, scholars, and parishioners and the ways they have engaged the preaching task, the listening responsibilities, and ethical needs of their local communities and broader realities alike. Readers of this well-organized, well-written, and thorough text will be rewarded with strong, evidenced-based guidance on preaching with gentle but firm integrity, robust but measured energy, and above all pastoral care and genuine love for their charges. Thank you, Professor Schade for conceiving and delivering this important volume to all of us!" —**Efrain Agosto, Boskey Visiting Professor in Latina/o Studies, Williams College**

"Gospel-talk about social issues by pastors of congregations in a polarizing society requires consideration, study, and skill. Rev. Dr. Leah Schade presents Gentle, Invitational, and Robust options that allow preachers to bring a Christian heart and mind to the intersection of any congregation with society. Schade offers data about congregational life and shares the work of several scholars of social gospel preaching. I advise readers to put on an ecumenical hat and take time for careful study." —**Rev. Gregory Heille, Professor of Preaching and Evangelization, Aquinas Institute of Theology, editor of *Preaching Racial Justice***

Preaching and Social Issues

Tools and Tactics for Empowering Your Prophetic Voice

Leah D. Schade

Foreword by Lisa L. Thompson

AN ALBAN BOOK
ROWMAN & LITTLEFIELD
Lanham • Boulder • New York • London

Published by Rowman & Littlefield
An imprint of The Rowman & Littlefield Publishing Group, Inc.
4501 Forbes Boulevard, Suite 200, Lanham, Maryland 20706

www.rowman.com

86-90 Paul Street, London EC2A 4NE

Copyright © 2025 by The Rowman & Littlefield Publishing Group, Inc.

All rights reserved. No part of this book may be reproduced in any form or by any electronic or mechanical means, including information storage and retrieval systems, without written permission from the publisher, except by a reviewer who may quote passages in a review.

British Library Cataloguing in Publication Information Available

Library of Congress Cataloging-in-Publication Data

Names: Schade, Leah D., author.
Title: Preaching and social issues : tools and tactics for empowering your prophetic voice / Leah D. Schade.
Description: Lanham, Maryland : Rowman & Littlefield, [2025] | Includes bibliographical references and index.
Identifiers: LCCN 2024022490 (print) | LCCN 2024022491 (ebook) | ISBN 9781538187609 (cloth) | ISBN 9781538187616 (paperback) | ISBN 9781538187623 (ebook)
Subjects: LCSH: Social justice–Biblical teaching. | Social justice–Sermons. | Christianity and politics.
Classification: LCC BS680.J8 S36 2025 (print) | LCC BS680.J8 (ebook) | DDC 251–dc23/eng/20240807
LC record available at https://lccn.loc.gov/2024022490
LC ebook record available at https://lccn.loc.gov/2024022491

∞™ The paper used in this publication meets the minimum requirements of American National Standard for Information Sciences—Permanence of Paper for Printed Library Materials, ANSI/NISO Z39.48-1992.

Dedication

I dedicate this book to my past, present, and future students and ministry colleagues. You are why I do this work. You have been a blessing to me, and I hope this book is useful and a blessing to you.

Contents

Foreword		xi
Acknowledgments		xv
1	Preaching and Social Issues: Introduction and Overview	1
2	The Challenges of Preaching and Social Issues: Findings from Surveying Preachers in the Red–Blue Divide	17
3	What's Your Path to Prophetic Preaching? An Assessment Tool	39
4	Gentle, Invitational, and Robust: Three Approaches to Addressing Social Issues in Preaching	63
5	Ethical Foundations for Preaching and Social Issues	83
6	Why the Church Needs to Address Social Issues: Biblical and Theological Foundations	105
7	Homiletical Conversation Partners for Addressing Social Issues	127
8	Three Social Issues for Applying Ethics, Scripture, and Theology for Preaching	151

9	Two Sermons on Social Issues Based on Philippians 2:1-13	175
10	Case Studies of Preachers Addressing Social Issues	197
11	Practical Advice for Preaching and Social Issues	219

Bibliography	241
Scripture Index	249
Topical Index	251

Foreword

The interconnectedness of our public and more private relationships are readily at the forefront of the hearts and minds of many. But even those not frequently thinking of these relational dynamics experience them daily. Their trickle-down effects are experienced in the economy and inflation; housing and food insecurity; access to health care and living aid; depletion and pollution of our ecological resources; or most acute encounters of violence, harm, and premature death.

Everyday occurrences mark both subtle and seismic shifts in our daily encounters and shared futures. Down to the final minutes of penning this foreword, our media circuits have reported an incessant stream of global, national, and local issues. The following is only a glimpse of two-weeks in time in 2024:

- *April 1*—Seven World Central Kitchen aid workers were killed in central Gaza from Israeli airstrikes after unloading one hundred tons of food for famine relief in the region.
- *April 3*—U.S. Secretary of Transportation visited Shiloh, Alabama, amidst a civil rights probe into state highway construction and their flooding impacts on historically Black landowners.
- *April 4*— After a one-month siege of Port-au-Prince, the crisis worsens in Haiti.

- *April 7*—Over the six months of the Israel–Hamas war, 33,000 Palestinians have been reported killed.
- *April 8*—A total solar eclipse crossed North America, and crowds gathered in its path.
- *April 9*—The Arizona Supreme Court placed restrictions on reproductive health care measures that banned all abortions outside of life-saving measures, upholding an 1864 pre-state and pre-women's voting rights law.
- *April 10*—The Tennessee State Senate passed a bill that would allow teachers to carry concealed handguns in K–12 schools.
- *April 11*—Jim Wallis sat for an interview with ABC News about his new book, *The False White Gospel*, which seeks to unpack Christian nationalism and its threat to both faith communities and democracy.
- *April 13*—Iran launched three hundred drones and missiles at military targets in Israel as a retaliatory action for an Israeli airstrike on an Iranian embassy compound in Syria on April 1.
- *April 14*—Over forty deaths by gun violence were reported over a weekend in Chicago.
- *April 15*—Severe famine continues in Sudan after one year of civil war.
- *April 16*—The U.S. Supreme Court began hearings that could overturn felony obstruction charges for over three hundred people involved in the Washington, DC, Capitol Building riots on January 6, 2021, including a former U.S. president.

The above list does not nearly capture all of the happenings of our world, let alone those tucked away in our personal lives. However, just as we are prone to skimming past these bullet points to get to this very sentence—the point of it all—we are prone to fast-forwarding through the ongoing cycles of life happening around us. We often miss that the point of it all resides in the details. We miss the tangibly consequential ways our neighbors' fate is bound to ours. Our private lives are not unscathed by public happenings, though some live more removed from this scathing than others.

In *Preaching and Social Issues*, Leah Schade is summoning Christian preachers to slow down and pay attention to the details. These details include those of the wider world, of their communities, of their preaching practice, and maybe most importantly, of one's internal motivations. As a reader, you'll be gifted with the expertise of one who researches and teaches about preaching and the morass of our human relationships, beliefs, and competing values. Schade leads as a scholar, synthesizing a wider conversation about preaching that attends to personal and collective welfare, ethical frameworks, biblical and theological frameworks, and supportive interpretive avenues.

While Schade leads as a scholar, her practitioner's awareness carries the pulse of the book—helping preachers probe their internal heartscape and that of their communities for faith-filled risk-taking. Schade offers tactics and techniques for more informed decision-making in Christian preaching that is accountable to both faith and the outcomes it makes possible in the wider world. The broader applicability of the approaches offered here is made salient through case studies that emerge from the background social crises of migration, systemic racism, and White Christian Nationalism. Familiar or not with Schade's previous books, *Preaching in the Purple Zone* and *Creation-Crisis Preaching*, we're joining a conversation in its evolution and reaping the benefits of its insights.

The pages ahead operate on a few underlying assumptions. For one, faith has a role to play in the outcomes of the world in which we live. For two, faith can be an impetus for either the regeneration or greater deterioration of our societal relationships. For three, for many preachers who want to attend to difficult conversations in their contexts, their will to do so is not the problem; *how* to attend to these issues is the obstacle.

In 2021, I published *Preaching the Headlines*. The book came after eight years of working through its ideas in an eponymous graduate course with groups of curious laity, clergy leaders, concerned citizens, and organizers across various religious affiliations and traditions. Our primary task in the endeavors of learning and questioning was to help Christians and others determine "what might be said," out of fidelity to Christian faith traditions, that informs "what one might do" to contribute to more democratically just relationships in the day-to-day. In other words, *how does preaching participate in cultivating self-leadership within everyday people of faith*? And more so, *how does preaching cultivate self-leadership in ways that lead to greater accountability in our personal and collective capacity for flourishing?*

These are questions we have long contended with in attending to preaching as an act of prophetic care, as the late homiletician and practical theologian Dale P. Andrews described it. We continue to ask these questions and search for accessible resources that support the evolution of responses in contemporary contexts. There is no corner on this market. Schade's book is an additional timely resource in our urgent collective efforts toward a more sustainable democratically flourishing existence.

Preaching and Social Issues deftly ushers preachers along pathways for intuiting their wisdom in determining *how* to preach about faith and the world at hand for the specific listeners before them.

Lisa L. Thompson
Cornelius Vanderbilt Chair
and Associate Professor of Black Homiletics and Liturgics
Vanderbilt University
April 16, 2024

Acknowledgments

I am indebted to many people and organizations that have contributed to this book in different ways. My colleagues at Lexington Theological Seminary gave me invaluable feedback on draft chapters and the overall scope of the book. Jon Barnes, Denise Bell, Sharon Ellis Davis, Wilson Dickinson, Lon Oliver, Esther Shanti Parajuli, and Dolores Yilibuw—thank you for your thoughtful engagement and suggestions for strengthening the book. A special thanks to Emily Askew and Jerry Sumney, who allowed me to share their sermons and have been my pedagogical colleagues, as well as dear friends, for nearly a decade. Thanks also to President Charisse Gillett and Dean Loida I. Martell for their unwavering support of my scholarship.

Many students at Lexington Theological Seminary worked with the Assessment Tool and offered feedback on its earlier version. Three of them—Jeffrey Birch, Bridget Hill, and Tamara Mills—used the tool for their sermons and have generously allowed me to share their work in this book. I'm also appreciative of Dikiea Elery and Mariah Newell, who permitted me to use their powerful sermons to illustrate key concepts. And to Father Jude Thaddeus Langeh—I am in awe of your courage, scholarship, and innovation and humbled by your willingness to experiment with this book's tools and methods in your context of Cameroon.

The Wabash Center for Teaching and Learning in Theology and Religion awarded me a grant in 2019 through their Pedagogies for Social Justice and Civic Engagement to undertake my project, "Dialogue in the 'Purple Zone': Pedagogies for Civil Discourse in Online and On-site Settings." I am grateful to the team of people who served as training leaders—Ron Allen, Emily Askew, Amanda Wilson Harper, Gregg Kaufman, and Jerry Sumney. Thanks also to the project participants: Bill Barker, Becky Brown, Lisa Caldwell-Reiss, Jacque Compton, Julie Cory, Sandy Gruzesky, Cindy Franks, Carol Devine, Polly Hawkins, Heather McColl, Joseph Pusateri, Warren Rogers, Susan Smith, Chad Snellgrove, Rob and Jeanne Stepp, Kory Wilcoxson, and Anna Hope Curwood Wills. I appreciated your willingness to take part in the training and experiment with engaging social issues in your congregations. I'm especially indebted to Stephanie Moon, who has taken the tools from that training and used them with her congregation continually, allowing me to study how preaching and social issues can happen in a congregation over time.

Bishop Ruben Saenz of the United Methodist Church invited me to work with clergy and congregational leaders in the Great Plains Conference and supported my research by encouraging his conference to participate in surveys, conferences, and dialogue projects. Thank you to Portia Cavitt, Jeff Clinger, Loren Drummond, Kara Eidson, Grace Gichuru, Marshal Johnson, Amy Lippoldt, Bonnie McCord, Morita Truman, and Brad Wheeler for learning—and then teaching to others—the sermon–dialogue–sermon process. Thanks also to Nancy Lambert and Delores Williamston for their organizational and relational skills and expertise.

Three people have been especially helpful in my research on ministry, preaching, and social issues. Amanda Wilson Harper, Wayne Thompson, and Katie Day—I would be lost without your expertise, methodological skills, and technical guidance on designing, implementing, and analyzing the surveys and ethnographic data. Amanda and Wayne also gave particular input on chapters 2 and 3. I am thankful for your generosity of time and assistance!

Gregg Kaufman, Ekaterina Lukianova, Elizabeth Gish, and David Allred—each of you has been a vital conversation partner and catalyst for my work on preaching and social issues, especially regarding dialogue in our divided and contentious society. You have shaped my work with your questions, observations, perspectives, and modeling of how to have productive community deliberation in faith-based settings. Your camaraderie has meant a great deal to me.

In 2020, I cofounded a network of pastors and faith leaders called the Clergy Emergency League, which provides support, accountability, resources, and networking for clergy to prophetically minister in their congregations and the public square. I have learned so much from our meetings, workshops, author and book discussions, and online exchanges about the difficulties clergy face when trying to preach about social issues. Many of you worked with an early version of the Assessment Tool and offered feedback about the instrument. And to the members of our Steering Committee—Stephen Fearing, Robert Franek, Carolyn Smith Goings, Joelle Henneman, LaVinnia Pierson, Pamela Griffith Pond, Nelson Rabell, and Lauren Grubaugh Thomas—words are not enough to express my appreciation for your support, encouragement, and commitment to justice.

The Academy of Homiletics has been my primary academic guild since 2010, and I am so appreciative of the collegiality, critical feedback, and professional support that I have received both from the organization and from individuals within it. The Preaching and Culture Workgroup were early conversation partners with me as I was sifting through survey data on ministry, preaching, and social issues and considering the meaning and ramifications of my findings. Ron Allen, O. Wesley Allen Jr., Suzanne Duchesne, Eunjoo Mary Kim, Gregory Heille, John McClure, Alyce McKenzie, and Karyn Wiseman were especially helpful and supportive of me as an early-career scholar. As a member of the Executive Committee, I have appreciated the collegiality and leadership of Teresa Fry Brown, Susan McGurgan, Debra Mumford, Courtney Murtaugh, Hank Langknecht, Rob O'Lynn, Joni Sancken, Richard Voelz, Andrew Wymer, Sunggu Yang, and Chelsea Yarborough, as well as David Jacobsen, Kenyatta Gilbert, and Donyelle McCray, who saw potential in me that I had not yet recognized. I'm also indebted to the many homileticians whose work I draw on for this book, including Lisa Cressman, Tyshawn Gardner, Carolyn Helsel, Lucy Atkinson Rose, Frank Thomas, Leonora Tubbs Tisdale, and Lis Valle-Ruiz. I'm especially grateful to Lisa Thompson for her profound words in the foreword as well as her own scholarship and pedagogy on preaching and social issues.

A writer's work remains a private thing until a publisher takes a chance to bring their words to the world. I have been blessed to work with Rowman & Littlefield on four books, including this one. For *Preaching and Social Issues*, I have been guided by the editorial prowess of Richard Brown and his team. Your professionalism, flexibility, and encouragement have been a gift to me.

Discussions about social issues often begin around kitchen tables and in family living rooms, and this has certainly been the case with me and my family of origin, as well as my family through marriage. Carl and Peggy Jacobs are my parents, and from them I learned the importance of engaging the intersection of faith and politics from an early age. Jim and Carolyn Schade are my in-laws, who have readily discussed with me the headlines and the challenges of the church. All four of you have provided me insights and ongoing discernment over these many decades.

When my brain was weary and my patience wore thin as I wrote this book, I could always rely on my husband, Jim, and my children, Rachel and Benjamin. You lifted my spirit, checked in with me, fed my body and soul, and filled my lungs with laughter. I give thanks to God every day for you individually and for us collectively as a family, my Gooses!

CHAPTER 1

Preaching and Social Issues
Introduction and Overview

I have taught preaching to seminary students and led countless workshops on preaching for clergy for nearly a decade. One of the questions I hear most frequently is, how can we address social issues in our sermons? Or can we address them at all? Given the polarization that exists in society, which carries over into churches, preachers wonder how they can proclaim the gospel in a way that invites and builds up a congregation rather than divides or diminishes it. Is it even possible to talk about topics of public concern in a sermon? While these questions are especially on the minds of early-career preachers, even some seasoned pastors can feel hesitant to broach contemporary issues for fear of blowback that can derail their ministry.

What Do We Mean by "Social Issues"?

Ronald J. Allen has identified six characteristics of a "social issue": "It is public. People are aware of it, or should be aware of it. The issue affects the community as a community, that is, it creates social consequences. It affects the well-being of the society. Many social issues are systemic. Social issues may call for the community to invoke a common understanding or behavior in light of the issue."[1]

Here are the characteristics I have in mind:

- The issue affects people and communities at many levels (personal, family, institutional, governmental, cultural, and global).

- Decisions made about this issue at any one of the levels have an impact on at least one other level.
- There are a wide range of opinions about how best to deal with the issue.
- Emotions about the issue tend to be very strong for some people.
- There are a variety of factors involved in explaining why the issue is a "problem."
- There is a great deal at stake for certain parties, depending on how decisions are made at the personal, family, institutional, business, governmental, economic, policy, and global levels.
- There is usually a perceived debate about "rights" versus "responsibilities" regarding the issue.
- The issue is in some realm of public debate and has some bearing on politics and public policy.
- Examples may include (but are certainly not limited to) climate change, gun violence, health care, immigration, systemic racism, and women's access to reproductive health care.

Some issues are more controversial than others, depending on the current headlines; the political makeup of the congregation and community; and the national, international, and planetary forces that are observed or experienced on the local level. What is a hot topic for one pastor and congregation may not be for another. And what is controversial at one point in time may not be as polarizing a few years later. Further, there are many public issues that do not garner media attention but are nevertheless affecting people and communities and would benefit from a church's bringing their biblical and theological lenses to the topic.

But no matter the social issue and the degree to which it interests or affects a congregation or community, I take it as a basic premise that churches must be attentive to the issues that affect the people of God. It follows, then, that preachers have a moral, ethical, and vocational obligation to speak to these issues from a biblical, theological, and ethical perspective to bring some kind of community discernment to bear.

With this in mind, I want to be clear about what I mean when I talk about addressing social issues in sermons. I am talking about bringing a topic of public concern into conversation with the Bible and theology—not "political" preaching in the sense of pushing a partisan agenda. As Lisa Cressman states, "Our calling is to preach the gospel, and how the gospel sets the world—with its issues—to rights. The gospel doesn't call us to take a 'position.' The gospel calls us to position ourselves to love Jesus first and most, and tend his sheep" (referencing John 21:16).[2] If there is an issue that is hurting people, causing inequity, injustice, or the suffering of people or God's Creation, then the church—including preachers—are authorized to address it, just as the prophets and Jesus did in the Bible. "The sermon needs to ask the question why: Why are [the sheep] not being tended? Who and what is being loved more than these?" urges Cressman (John 21:15).[3]

Of course, when we ask these questions, some people are going to become uneasy, uncomfortable, defensive, and maybe even angry. There is a lot at stake around issues such as racial justice, gender equality, women's reproductive health care, and the environment, for example. Disputes around things such as identity, safety, money, and freedom shape the underlying values, dynamics, and influences that surround these issues. All of this can create a fraught situation for the preacher who wants to bring the gospel to bear on the contemporary issues of our time.

Nevertheless, as Lisa L. Thompson reminds us in her book *Preaching the Headlines*, "Faith is not neutral. Preaching is a practice of faith. Neutrality in preaching is not attainable."[4] In other words, preachers are called to make faith claims about the issues that affect people's lives and do so without fear of violating false ideas about being "neutral." "Preaching goes awry and misses the mark either by not naming what is at stake in the claims being made or by not naming why people of faith should be concerned based on the values they claim," she writes.[5]

While Thompson cautions that preaching that engages the issues of the day should not be a "political stump speech," she rightly notes that "unless a message candidly addresses life on the ground and moves to the collective concerns of life together, it succumbs to being an insular message hovering in the clouds. These messages never attend to faith as a dynamic and significant influence on the way we live and operate in the world."[6]

To be clear, many preachers are already doing this work of "candidly addressing life on the ground" in their sermons. Those who preach among a people who are living through the realities of racism, sexism, poverty, xenophobia, or homophobia, for example, already have considerable experience speaking truth to power about the issues that affect the lives of their congregation. At the same time, even pastors who regularly address certain topics may be hesitant to address others that their congregation might deem taboo. For example, a preacher may have no problem talking about the ways in which gun violence threatens their community, but talking about women's access to reproductive health care is a topic they avoid because they know their congregation is divided on that issue. Similarly, we cannot assume that a pastor who regularly preaches about the need for equity for LGBTQIA+ persons will be similarly emboldened when it comes to addressing the needs of the Spanish-speaking migrant population in their community, especially if their congregation is ambivalent about the changing demographics of their neighborhoods.

This book, then, is for preachers who are looking for strategies to address any social issues that would qualify as the proverbial "third rail" in their context. This term refers to a highly charged topic that, like the electrified rail of a train system, can be dangerous because of its potential for provoking strong reactions, backlash, or political consequences. My intention is to equip preachers with tools to understand themselves, their congregations, and the relationships between them and then to bring Scripture, theology, and ethics into a productive homiletical conversation about the issues with their congregation.

At the same time, this book takes the position that there is no *one* way to address social issues in preaching. What "speaking up and speaking out" looks like for one preacher in their church might be very different for a preacher in another situation. Addressing social issues should not require anyone to be nailed to a cross or sacrifice their health, sanity, or job—unless they so choose. Nor should preachers allow themselves to compromise or capitulate to the forces that want to silence their public theology and pastorally prophetic voice. Sometimes our ministerial vocation requires us to preach about "the thing that must not be named" in order to bring it to light and bring faithful discernment to bear for the sake of our neighbors in need and the healing of our world. As Thompson says, "Something different happens when the power of the unspoken is removed. When people are truthful and honest about how they really feel, we can stop pretending like nothing is wrong."[7] Once something is named or a taboo topic addressed aloud, the community can then open it up for exploration, examination, and interrogation using ethical, biblical, and theological tools.

Ministry in the Midst of Political Volatility

Everything that both Cressman and Thompson have said about the necessity of addressing the issues of the day in preaching is most certainly true. So my question is, how can a pastor talk about these issues when just the mere mention of certain topics in some congregations is enough to elicit angry emails, personal confrontations, or threats to withhold financial giving or to leave the church entirely? Or even more extreme, what if the pastor faces intimidation, demands for their resignation, or even violence from the growing number of hate groups that scour the internet looking for clergy and churches to target?

These kinds of threats may seem far-fetched to some. But, in fact, cases of intimidation of clergy are on the rise. I'll share just a few examples.

- In a preaching workshop I was leading during the Trump administration, one female pastor who served in a rural congregation shared that she felt called to address the issue of racism and police violence in one of her sermons. After the sermon, she came home to the parsonage later that day to find a skinned animal on her porch. The message she interpreted from this disturbing act of intimidation was, stop preaching about race or this is how you'll end up.
- Another female pastor in that same workshop recounted that after she preached a sermon about racism, one of her male parishioners in her rural congregation showed up unannounced on her porch, shotgun in hand, with the excuse that he was there "just to check on her." She felt understandably afraid for her safety and soon left the congregation.
- A pastor serving a church in California that is open and affirming to the LGBTQIA+ community often preaches in support

of social justice issues. In December 2022, he shared a post on Facebook that a hate group called the Proud Boys threatened the church and in April 2023, the church was vandalized with broken windows and doors. The Proud Boys left a sticker on one of the railings. A few months later, an anonymous bomb threat led to police sweeping the church building and the pastor's car to check for explosives.

- An Episcopal priest in Colorado often preached on topics such as LGBTQIA+ rights, immigration, and nonviolent resistance to oppression during the Trump years. She discovered that she had been "doxed" on the internet by an "Antifa watch" group that published personal information about her, including pictures of her and her spouse.
- A portion of the social justice–themed Easter sermon by the pastor of a small Lutheran church in North Dakota was shared by the Twitter account "Woke Preacher Clips" in 2023. The pastor then became the target of Fox News's Tucker Carlson, who twisted the words of the sermon and took them out of context in what amounted to a completely fabricated headline and commentary about what the preacher said.

Granted, these are the extremes of what can happen to a pastor who preaches the gospel and is accused of "wokeness" or simply being "too political" for the taste of the congregation. But they are real, and many pastors have faced their own versions of pushback in the congregations they serve. I'll talk about this more in chapter 1 when I share the data my team and I have been collecting from our three surveys of preachers from 2017–2023 about how they are navigating preaching and social issues.

For now, I want to share with you a story from the first congregation I served when I was beginning my ministry in the early 2000s. While neither my safety nor my job security was at risk, I did find myself at the center of a political maelstrom around the topic of climate change (then called global warming). Navigating that complex situation taught me some early lessons about addressing social issues in preaching and ministry.

My First Experience with Navigating a Social Issue in a Purple Congregation

From 2000–2009, I served as the associate pastor of a suburban ELCA Lutheran (Evangelical Lutheran Church in America) congregation near Philadelphia, Pennsylvania. Wanting to help people connect their faith with their love for God's Creation and to respond to the growing environmental crises, I had started an EcoMinistry Committee. In 2007, we decided to show the documentary *An Inconvenient Truth*, a film that conveyed Al Gore's message about global warming. Our little committee decided to open this to the community, which was excited about this event. We had planned a potluck supper prior to showing the film and posted flyers around the town. We had also secured a guest speaker, one of the activists trained by Gore's Climate Reality Project (CRP), to lead a question-and-answer session after the film.

But two weeks before the event, conservative members of the congregational council convinced their fellow members to vote for censoring the film on the grounds that it was "too political" for a church to show. I was shocked and angry. But I wanted to find a way for this event to go forward since it had already been advertised and the committee had worked so hard to make it happen.

So I approached the council member who had spearheaded the censoring effort and asked, "What would it take for you to allow us to show this film?"

The person said that if a speaker who represented "the other side" of the climate debate could have equal time at the event, they would permit the film to be shown. While I cringed at this idea, I took this person up on the offer. At their own expense, they flew in someone from the Heritage Foundation (HF), a conservative think tank, to be the additional speaker.

What would have been a small gathering of like-minded people from the church and community turned into a huge, politically diverse event. Word quickly spread that these two speakers were going to go toe-to-toe after the film regarding the truth about global warming. In this congregation of both red-state and blue-state parishioners, and in a community that was politically "purple," the event drew a large crowd. The committee was thrilled that people who normally would never watch such a film attended just so they could see "their guy" refute and rebuke the "Al Gore guy."

After the dinner and film, the two men shared why they were there that evening. The gentleman from the CRP said he was not being paid—he was a volunteer. "I'm doing this because I'm concerned about this planet and because I want my children and grandchildren to have a positive future."

In contrast, the gentleman from HF launched into a diatribe about the amount of money it would cost to transition away from fossil fuels. In fact, most of his arguments were all about money and why global warming wasn't real.

Their introductions set the tone for their responses during the question-and-answer period. By the end of the evening, it was clear who the "winner" was. The warmth, authenticity, patience, and calmness of the gentleman from CRP was in stark contrast to the cold, corporate, frantic hostility of the gentleman from HF. As the evening came to a close, many people crowded around the man from CRP to ask more questions and learn about what they could do to address the climate crisis. Meanwhile, the HF man packed up his things alone, except for the conservative council members who stood nearby.

And then something interesting happened. After the HF gentleman left, those council members motioned me over. "We still don't believe in global warming," they said, "but Al Gore did make a good point about the need to protect clean water. If you ever want to preach about that, you won't get any pushback from us."

I was shocked, and this time in a positive way. We had found common ground or, rather, common water.

So when it came time to preach on the Sunday celebrating the Baptism of Jesus in January, my sermon was about protecting the waters of baptism. And I encouraged the congregation to "give up the bottle" for Lent—bottled water, that is. The EcoMinistry later gave out reusable water bottles for Lent imprinted with the church's logo to help keep single-use plastic bottles out of landfills and waterways. It was an effort the whole congregation could get behind—conservatives, progressives, and independents alike.

This was one instance of preaching and social issues that taught me a great deal about what it means to listen to those who differ from me politically while also not giving up on addressing an important issue just because some folks thought it was "too political." I learned what it can look like to "thread the needle" between progressives and conservatives within the same congregation. And this situation was one that sparked my interest in how a preacher can use different strategies to preach about issues of public concern so that people will stay engaged instead of storming off in a huff.

Where I Stand Now

As I write this, nearly two decades have passed since that incident in my first congregation. There were many more learning experiences for me about preaching and social issues in that church as well as others I have served. Currently, I teach preaching and worship at Lexington Theological Seminary, an accredited graduate theological institution of the Christian Church (Disciples of Christ). Consistent with the Disciples' historic commitment to Christian unity, the Seminary is intentionally ecumenical with students, faculty, staff, and trustees of various denominations. We have students from across the denominational spectrum serving churches with varying political shades of red, blue, and purple. Many of them have sought guidance from me for approaches to sermons about contemporary issues. Because of their willingness to experiment with the tools, strategies, and tactics I offer in this book, I have learned a great deal. Some of their stories and sermon examples are included in this book to give readers models of how to apply these concepts in a variety of preaching contexts.

A commitment to diversity, equity, inclusion, and justice is part of my core values in my teaching, preaching, and personal life. I occupy a social location that includes being a White, cisgender, heterosexual married female in my fifties who, at the time of this writing, is the mother of a teenager and a young adult. I am temporarily healthy and able bodied. I speak and write the dominant language of this country (English). I have had the benefit and privilege of growing up in a middle-class household and having access to resources that allowed me to fulfill my academic and vocational aspirations. All of this means that there are aspects of social location that I know from experience, while there are others for which I have no experience. However, I seek to be an ally to people from historically underrepresented and marginalized communities. Therefore, I am committed to recognizing, learning from, and valuing difference and incorporating that difference into the courses I teach, the research I conduct, the books and articles I write, and my professional and personal relationships. I seek to create space and time that is welcoming and provides equal access, equal voice, and equitable treatment for all. I invite all readers of this book to contribute to this effort of diversity, equity, inclusion, and justice as well.

What Does It Mean to Empower Your "Prophetic" Voice?

What do we mean when we talk about "prophetic preaching"? We begin by examining the term *prophetic*. The term *prophet* originates from the Greek word *prophetes*, meaning "one who comes before another to speak," where *pro* signifies "before" and *phenai* signifies "speak." The Bible illustrates the continual presence of prophetic messages throughout the history of God's people. Prophets, broadly speaking, are concerned about the biblical concepts of *mishpat* and *tsĕdaqah*, the Hebrew words for justice and righteousness, respectively. In both Hebrew and Christian Scriptures, prophets speak on behalf of God and God's people, particularly advocating for those who are most vulnerable to oppressive systems and leaders. Examples include Isaiah, Jeremiah, Amos, Joel, John the Baptizer, Jesus, and John of Patmos.

While there isn't a singular definition of *prophetic preaching*, it generally involves expressing God's concern for the oppressed, condemning those who abuse power, and envisioning a new future aligned with God's justice. When discussing the term for her book, *Prophetic Preaching*, Leonora Tubbs Tisdale clarifies that she is not speaking of preaching that predicts the future in apocalyptic terms. Rather, she describes this type of preaching as "cutting edge and future oriented (yet not future predicting), and addresses public and social concerns."[8] Kenyatta Gilbert distinguishes prophetic preaching as a "voice" that "expresses unrelenting hope about God's activity to transform church and society in a present-future sense based on the principle of justice."[9] While homileticians define it in different ways, for our purposes, I am referring to a socially engaged homiletic that does the following: focuses on ethics; calls for justice; engages in social critique; and boldly unmasks the systemic sin that subjugates and controls individuals, communities, and the larger society. All of this is in service of the gospel of Jesus Christ to transform brokenness into healing, violence into peace, scarcity into abundance, and fear into love.

Prophetic preaching is not limited to any particular style or personality type. For instance, a prophetic preacher could deliver an impassioned sermon on a social justice issue that may fire up their congregation—either to enact God's justice and righteousness or, in the opposite direction, to remove the pastor from the pulpit and the congregation because of their discomfort and anger at the challenge. But there is more to prophetic preaching than an in-your-face, finger-wagging approach. Preaching about social issues is something *any* pastor can find a way to do within whatever context they minister and depending on their personal style and mode of sermon delivery. This is because, as Dale Andrews pointed out, prophetic preaching is actually a form of pastoral care. In fact, this idea has come to be called "prophetic care."[10]

In my book *Preaching in the Purple Zone*, I likened the task of prophetic care to that of bridge-building:

> "Prophetic care" is a way of understanding prophetic preaching as an *expression of pastoral care*. Rather than seeing the two aspects of ministry in contrast or even opposition to each other, [Andrews] saw pastoral care and prophetic proclamation as inextricably fused. When pastors care for their people, they call out sin (including systemic sin) for the way it harms individuals, families, communities, the nation, and the planet. And when they are prophetic, it springs from their deep and empathetic—even suffering—love for God's people. All of this is done, he explained, in the spirit of *bridge-building*—seeking ways to span the seemingly uncrossable polarizations between people of different political orientations, religions, races, ages, genders, physical/mental abilities, and socioeconomic strata.[11]

To help you find the right "materials" for this bridge, the proper place to "site" the bridge, and how to invite people to meet each other—and

God—on that bridge, in this book I suggest three approaches to a prophetic sermon. These approaches are what I call Gentle, Invitational, and Robust. When used in conjunction with biblical, theological, and ethical frameworks, you should be able to find at least one strategy within these approaches that will enable you to build a bridge of prophetic preaching in your context. As Thompson writes, "No border exists between pastoral care and the pursuit of justice, setting the world right-side up and calling out the chasm between the world as it is and could be."[12]

Overview of Preaching and Social Issues

In this chapter, I have defined what I mean by "social issues" and discussed how ministry in this time has been affected by the increase in political volatility. I then shared some of my own story about preaching and social issues as well as my demographic intersections and commitment to diversity, equity, inclusion, and justice. I also clarified how I am using the term *prophetic* in this book.

In chapter 2, we'll begin by looking at research that my team and I have conducted about preaching and social issues to get an overview of some of the challenges preachers face. Chapter 2 will also explore the contours of what I call *preaching in the purple zone*, a term I use to describe the tension of ministering within the "red–blue divide" of U.S. politics. Drawing on longitudinal research from three thousand clergy and one thousand congregation members from 2017–2023, I'll discuss barriers that preachers encounter when preaching about social issues with moral and theological imagination. The data will also provide some insights into the factors that can appear to impinge on the willingness of preachers to exercise their prophetic voice as well as what contributes to prophetic courage for preachers to address social issues.

In chapter 3, you will find an assessment tool for gauging risk and capacity for preaching about social issues. This tool will help you think about your approaches to preaching and social issues using a questionnaire that assesses three dimensions: (1) your own vulnerabilities and strengths, (2) the characteristics of the congregation you serve, and (3) the quality of relationships within the congregation and between the congregation and yourself. Then, I suggest three approaches to a sermon addressing a social issue: Gentle, Invitational, and Robust. I strongly recommend that you take the time to do the assessment exercise before going further in the book so that you can think about how the three approaches apply to your context.

In chapter 4, I lay out three different strategies for each of the approaches for a total of nine different sermon tactics. I have used these tactics in my own sermons; my students, as well as fellow clergy, have tried them as well, with encouraging results. Altogether, they provide a preacher with multiple options for sermons that deal with contemporary topics. This chapter will include ideas for crafting sermons that address social issues drawing on the three approaches. I close out the chapter with tips and advice for preparing spiritually, relationally, and pragmatically to preach on social issues.

Chapter 5 establishes the ethical and moral foundations for addressing social issues in sermons. I will elucidate Frank Thomas's concept of a "dangerous sermon," delineate the various "working gospels" he identifies in the United States, and summarize the two predominant moral worldviews he observes in this nation. Then, we'll look to the work of social psychologist Jonathan Haidt, who identified six moral foundations that people use to determine what is right and wrong. These moral matrices can help preachers identify the values that motivate the choices people make when it comes to ethical dilemmas, which, in turn, can provide framing for a sermon addressing a social issue.

These ethical foundations dovetail with and inform the biblical and theological foundations for why the church needs to address social issues. In chapter 6, I'll explore the work of biblical scholars from three hermeneutical standpoints—historical critical, Latino/a, and womanist—for their insights and critical lenses for interpreting Scripture, especially when it comes to preaching and social issues. We will see why the Bible is a political document, in the sense that it addressed the social issues of its day. Thus, Christians, and especially preachers, are authorized to bring God's Word to bear on how we understand and respond to contemporary issues in our own time.

The work I'm doing in this book stands on the collective shoulders of many scholars of preaching who have developed important foundations for homiletical approaches to social issues. So, in chapter 7, we'll start with John McClure's four categories of ethical approaches to preaching, onto which we'll overlay Haidt's moral foundations. Then, we'll examine three strands within homiletics—conversational/collaborative, African American, and postcolonial—for guidance on how to approach social issues from a homiletical perspective. We'll also see how these homileticians utilize different strategies within the Gentle, Invitational, and Robust approaches to preaching and social issues.

In chapter 8, we'll apply these ethical foundations, biblical and theological frameworks, and homiletical strategies to three social issues. The first will be immigration, the second will be systemic racism, and the third will be Christian nationalism. With each of these issues, we'll explore ways that a preacher could address them with their congregation from the Gentle, Invitational, and Robust approaches.

Then, in chapter 9, we will examine two sermons that illustrate some of the principles for preaching about contemporary issues. Each of the preachers used the same text but had different audiences and topics. The text is Philippians 2:1-13, and the sermons were preached by two of my colleagues at Lexington Theological Seminary, Jerry Sumney and Emily Askew. I'll provide an in-depth analysis of their exegetical work, theological claims, ethical foundations, and homiletical approaches and strategies. This chapter will show readers how the process of preaching about social issues can come together in a comprehensive way.

Chapter 10 will include examples of six preachers who utilized various tools in this book for crafting sermons addressing social issues, including three who used the Assessment Tool to better understand themselves and their ministerial context to employ the Gentle, Invitational, and Robust strategies. These preachers include a diversity of perspectives, standpoints, and intersections, including gender, race and culture, sexual orientation, age, length of time in ministry, and denomination. Also, the congregations in which they preached their sermons represent a variety of geographic, socioeconomic, demographic, and political standpoints. What these case studies will show is that when a preacher thinks deeply and strategically about the ways in which ethics, Scripture, and theology frame our approach to the important issues of our time, they can courageously proclaim God's Word. And they can do so in ways that challenge injustice and advocate for the vulnerable while building up the community of Christ and strengthening the resolve of a congregation to put their faith into action.

In chapter 11, the final chapter, I will present advice for avoiding pitfalls in preaching about social issues as well as suggestions for spiritual, liturgical, collegial, and pastoral practices to support this aspect of your preaching ministry. Then, recognizing that a preacher can receive negative pushback, even when they have given a well-prepared and solid sermon, I present twelve steps for responding to criticism in a healthy and constructive way.

But I also discuss what can happen in the worst-case scenarios when parishioners or pastors discern that it's best to leave the congregation. When is it time to graciously release a person who is not supportive of a congregation's mission to engage with social issues? Conversely, how does a pastor discern when it's time to leave a church if their values are not in alignment with their congregation, or the situation is too toxic, or there simply is no forward motion toward a gospel-centered ministry? This chapter will include examples of parishioners and pastors who made the decision to leave and what we can learn from this leave-taking that might eventually lead to closure; healing; or in some cases, surprising new life and energy for ministry. I'll conclude the chapter with some final words of advice and encouragement for your preaching journey.

Ultimately, the goal of this book is to offer strategies, tactics, and tips to support and equip preachers who choose to address a social issue in a sermon. My hope is that you will feel supported in your preaching vocation and equipped for the task of bringing the Bible, theology, and ethics into conversation with the issues that affect your congregation and community, Creation, and those most vulnerable.

Notes

1. Ronald J. Allen, "Preaching on Social Issues," *Encounter* 59, no. 1/2 (1998): 59, as cited in Tyshawn Gardner's *Social Crisis Preaching: Biblical Proclamation for Troubled Times* (Brentwood, TN: B&H Academic), 7.

2. Lisa Cressman, *The Gospel People Don't Want to Hear: Preaching Challenging Messages* (Minneapolis, MN: Fortress Press, 2020), 97.

3. Cressman, 97.

4. Lisa L. Thompson, *Preaching the Headlines: Possibilities and Pitfalls* (Minneapolis, MN: Fortress Press, 2021), 11.

5. Thompson, 12.

6. Thompson, 12.

7. Thompson, 95.

8. Leonora Tubbs Tisdale, *Prophetic Preaching: A Pastoral Approach* (Louisville, KY: Westminster John Knox, 2004), 3.

9. Kenyatta Gilbert, *The Journey and Promise of African American Preaching* (Minneapolis: Fortress Press, 2011), 81. Gilbert notes that the prophetic voice in preaching is distinct from—but interwoven with—the "priestly" voice (focusing on moral and ethical formation) and the "pastoral" voice (focusing on wisdom for a congregation's vision and mission).

10. See Phillis-Isabella Sheppard, Dawn Ottoni-Wilhelm, and Ronald J. Allen, eds., *Preaching Prophetic Care: Building Bridges to Justice, Essays in Honor of Dale P. Andrews*. Eugene, OR: Pickwick Publications, 2018.

11. Leah D. Schade, *Preaching in the Purple Zone: Ministry in the Red-Blue Divide* (Lanham, MD: Alban Books, 2019), 182.

12. Thompson, *Preaching the Headlines*, 17.

CHAPTER 2

∼

The Challenges of Preaching and Social Issues

Findings from Surveying Preachers in the Red–Blue Divide

"The church should stay out of politics, and politics should stay out of the church!" This is the kind of erroneous cliché preachers sometimes hear from those who wish that the pastor would keep quiet when it comes to addressing social issues in the pulpit. When I served as a parish pastor in congregations, I often heard the maxim not to mix religion and politics. This sometimes would happen when I preached a sermon that talked about protecting the sanctity of God's Creation from fracking in Pennsylvania. Or when I suggested that Christians should think about the implications of Jesus and his family as refugees in Egypt as we consider immigration policy in our country. Or when I challenged people to name what aspects of a capitalist economic system were in alignment with the biblical vision of the Realm of God. Inevitably, there would be one or two individuals who would pull me aside (or send an email or anonymous note) to insist that it was not appropriate to "talk politics" in church.

Interestingly, however, I would also come upon these same individuals talking politics as they sat at the table in the fellowship hall with their friends before worship began, or over cookies and punch in the narthex, or in a church parking lot conversation after a worship service. They would openly criticize the current president. Or carp about "the government." Or debate a local hot-button issue, such as whether a polluting business should be allowed a building permit in the community.

So I began to suspect that regardless of whether *preachers* choose to engage contemporary issues in their sermons, their parishioners are, in fact, discussing these topics. And that they are discussing these issues at church specifically. While some may insist that the church is not the place to discuss such things, it seemed to me that these discussions happen regularly, either informally or in church meetings, education forums, and fellowship gatherings. These were my hunches, but I wanted to verify them. So, over the span of seven years, I surveyed clergy and congregations regarding their attitudes and opinions on social issues. What I learned has shaped my teaching and preaching in important ways and informed one of my earlier books about what it's like to preach about social issues in the "purple zone."

Surveying Preachers and Congregations in the "Purple Zone"

In 2016, I began work on a book called *Preaching in the Purple Zone: Ministry in the Red-Blue Divide* to help preachers address justice issues through a process that I call the sermon–dialogue–sermon method (more about that in chapter 7). Social scientists studying religion have found that there is a myriad of reasons pastors and church leaders do not engage in dialogue or engagement around social issues, ranging from avoiding dissension, to steering clear of denominational or congregational schisms, to sidestepping their own discomfort.[1] I suspected that the stories preachers told me about the pushback they sometimes receive when they preached a "dangerous sermon," as Frank A. Thomas calls it, were not merely isolated incidents.[2] But I knew I needed quantifiable data to get a clearer picture of the landscape when it comes to preachers addressing social issues.

Because the 2016 election both exacerbated and created new social and political divisions that affected churches, I launched what would become a repeated cross-sectional study about preaching, ministry, and social issues. The survey was designed to represent mainline Protestant pastors serving congregations in the United States. The questions focused on topics such as the difference the presidential election made in preachers' willingness to address social issues in the pulpit, reasons why clergy either engage or avoid social issues in their sermons, and what kind of training and support pastors seek to foster healthy dialogue about public issues in their congregations.

In 2017, I gathered responses for the surveys using what's called a "convenience sample" and "snowball" distribution through various channels, such as social media, denominational emails, state councils of churches, seminaries, and preacher groups and networks. I received responses from just over 1,200 preachers in forty-eight states as well as Washington, DC, and Puerto Rico. The responses were anonymous and included clergy from more than twenty different denominations. This gave me a snapshot of what preaching was like during and after the election season at that unprecedented time in U.S. history.

Wanting to continue this study after the 2020 presidential election, I worked with two researchers, Rev. Dr. Amanda Wilson Harper and Dr. Wayne Thompson, who helped me design another survey in early 2021. For that one, we received just over 2,600 responses and were able to compare and contrast what we saw happening four years prior. And we didn't stop there. Because of the volatility of the 2022 midterm elections, we decided to send out yet another survey in early 2023 so that we could track changes, patterns, and trends in light of the political, religious, and social upheavals happening at the time. For that survey, we garnered just over nine hundred responses. The results of these three survey waves have given us important insights into what it's like to be a preacher during a time of social stress, such as the rise of Christian nationalism, Trumpism, political polarization, racial reckoning, conspiracy theories and disinformation, gender, sexuality and LGBTQIA+ issues, climate and environmental crises, and the COVID-19 global pandemic.

Increasing "Brittleness" in Congregations

This study has taken place during a time when congregations are becoming more "brittle." This is a term I draw from Lisa Cressman's book *The Gospel People Don't Want to Hear: Preaching Challenging Messages*. Cressman observes that when congregations are stressed, they are more "brittle," meaning that they are emotionally fragile and less receptive to being transformed by the gospel. What are signs of a brittle congregation? "The people are anxious, they rarely laugh, and they are probably exhibiting symptoms of grief, including anger, lashing out, withdrawing, isolating, waxing nostalgic, circling the wagons, overreacting, bargaining, making much ado about nothing, targeting you or another leader (or a problem) as *the* problem, and/or displaying passive-aggressive behaviors," she explains.[3]

This means that when preachers try to address social issues, it may turn into what Thomas calls a "dangerous sermon," which he describes as a sermon that challenges "unjust moral orders and dominance hierarchies and the resulting misallocation of freedom, resources, assets, and legitimacy."[4] Such a sermon "disrupts the legitimacy of the oppressive moral order that operates smoothly, efficiently, and often silently in the economic, political, cultural, and religious structures of a given society."[5]

My team and I were especially interested in measuring the ways in which brittleness in congregations affected the level of "danger" that preachers perceive and experience when attempting to preach a sermon with moral imagination and prophetic courage. As Wilson Harper states, "The church has a long history of advocating on behalf of social and political justice issues, yet today's pastors and church leaders are often met with criticism or avoidance when introducing current issues are often seen as partisan or political within their congregations. In a world that is described as increasingly more divisive and culturally and politically polarizing, social justice issues are increasingly seen as partisan or political."[6]

Preachers who *do* decide to address an issue of public concern go about it in various ways. While some jump right into the fraught waters of "political" preaching, others skirt around the edges. Still others feel comfortable addressing less controversial issues while avoiding those that might result in negative pushback. In whatever ways a preacher chooses to engage (or not) contemporary topics, most have a sense of where the "danger zone" is in their context for certain topics, such as climate change, immigration, racism, gun violence, or poverty. As we'll discuss in this chapter and throughout the book, the data my team and I have collected gives us insights into what it's like to preach during this polarizing time. This, in turn, can inform strategies and tactics for addressing social issues in preaching.

But first, I want to give some caveats about the data we collected in these surveys. Keep in mind that these questionnaires involved self-reporting by clergy. This means that we encounter the classic problem of researchers eliciting "socially desirable rather than objective responses from their subjects," as Clifton F. Guthrie has described it.[7] He rightfully noted that "Asking preachers via surveys about their own preaching can be like asking folks to calculate their own tax deductions: there is always the temptation to claim too much."[8] While this is certainly true, I want to emphasize that our surveys were not intended to yield data on the *content* of the preachers' sermons. Rather, we were testing for *attitudes*, *perceptions*, and *expressions of underlying feelings and concerns* of clergy regarding preaching and social issues. The surveys were designed this way so we could track changes in these attitudes, perceptions, and feelings over time.

The other thing to note is that we did not have the same set of respondents for each survey, which means that while the completed samples are roughly comparable, they do reflect some variation. This is a limitation of the research suggesting some caution in making inferences about changes we observed across the three survey waves. Nevertheless, we have tried to account for that limitation by triangulating similar patterns across different topics regarding preachers' willingness to preach about social issues.

Now, let's begin with the basics about the demographics of the respondents and the types of congregations they served.

The Types of Preachers We Surveyed and the Congregations They Serve

In terms of respondent demographics, the gender distribution across the three survey waves was fairly even, ranging from 52 to 48 percent between male and female. Sexual orientation hovered between 83 and 86 percent heterosexual and 6 and 13 percent LTGBTQIA+. Racial representation ranged between 82 and 89 percent White and 7 and 16 percent other races and ethnicities. And in terms of age, we noticed an increase in the number of pastors older than fifty after the first survey (46 percent in 2017 and 65 percent in 2021 and 2023).

When it came to the kinds of churches the respondents served, I'll highlight three characteristics: denomination, setting (rural/small town, suburban, or urban), and worship attendance.

Denominations

While most respondents (67 percent) were mainline Protestant, we did get measurable representation from Evangelical traditions as well (7 percent). And among the "other" respondents (16 percent), we saw Roman Catholic, Orthodox, nondenominational, Unitarian Universalists, those who held dual standing in two different denominations, and various other affiliations. Altogether, more than twenty different denominations and nondenominational traditions are represented across the three surveys. This diversity of traditions strengthens our confidence that the sample population is a good representation of mainline Protestant clergy while also including perspectives of Evangelicals and other traditions.

Ministry Status, Setting, and Worship Attendance

About half of the respondents indicated they had been in their congregation three years or less. At the same time, the number of respondents reporting that they were employed full-time in their congregations dropped significantly over the six years, from 75 percent in 2017 to 66 percent in 2021, and down to 47 percent in 2023. Approximately 30 to 40 percent of respondents served in rural or small-town settings. The number of those serving suburbs came in second at 25 to 30 percent, followed by those serving in urban areas, 10 to 25 percent.

Worship attendance has been trending downward for decades.[9] Especially after the onset of the COVID-19 pandemic in 2020, according to Lifeway Research, "Protestant pastors reported that typical church attendance is only 85% of pre-pandemic levels."[10] Our surveys show similar reporting about diminished church attendance and correlates with decreased financial giving and stability.

Also notable was the number of pastors who expressed concern that their congregation might not be able to sustain its ministry and have to close its doors. In 2021, during the height of the COVID-19 pandemic, about one-fifth of respondents were worried that their church might close. By 2023, 56 percent of respondents said they were either somewhat or very concerned that their congregation would not be able to sustain its ministry beyond the next three years (i.e., unable to keep the building open and/or pay for a minister). The number was higher, and understandably so, for those with attendance less than one hundred. Just over 70 percent of those pastors were very or somewhat concerned about their church closing. This aligns with data from Lifeway Research showing that church closures have accelerated since the pandemic.[11]

These numbers about lower church attendance and increased church closures correlate with data indicating a broader exodus from Christianity since the 1970s. A study by Pew Research showed that the number of Americans who identified as Christian in 2020 was 64 percent and is expected to drop below 50 percent by 2070.[12] In contrast, the number of Americans who said they were Christian in 1972 was 90 percent.

But as much as all of the above factors may contribute to a preacher's hesitancy to address social issues, one of the strongest was the mismatch between the preacher's political leaning and that of their congregation.

Differences in Political Leanings between Clergy and Congregations

Figure 2.1, from the 2023 survey, illustrates some important political contrasts between preachers and those in the pews. Most respondents (80 percent) considered themselves progressive/liberal, while around 8 percent were moderate, and 12 percent were conservative. But when asked to estimate the political leanings of their congregations, there was a marked difference. According to the assessments of the pastors, 41 percent of their congregations were moderate, 30 percent were conservative, and 29 percent were progressive/liberal. Other studies, such as the one conducted by Public Religion Research Institute in 2023, have also shown that mainline Protestant clergy tend to lean more progressive and Democrat compared with their parishioners.[13]

Such ideological differences can make for tense situations regarding preachers wanting to address social issues in sermons. If some people in the congregation believe that the pastor does not align with their values or stands in judgment of their political position, they may be defensive, get offended, or become hostile when they hear a sermon that they believe is challenging or critiquing the political positions with which they are aligned. As a result, some pastors attempt to veil their political leanings, take a neutral stance, or simply avoid social issues altogether for the sake of avoiding controversy. Rather than risk alienating anyone on either side of the red–blue divide, they strive to maintain unity within the Body of Christ so that the congregation can continue to do the work to which they are called.

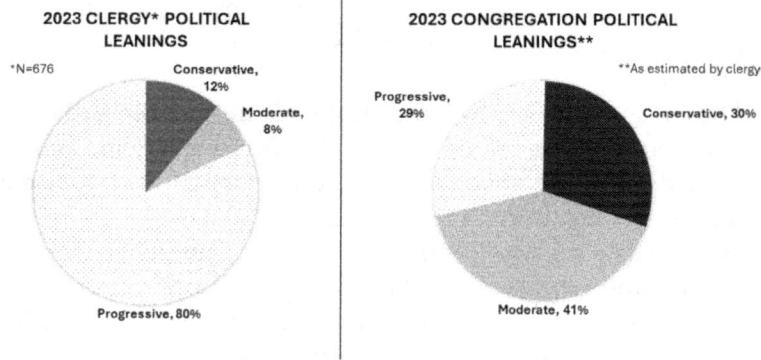

Figure 2.1 Clergy and Congregation Leanings, Ministry, Preaching, and Social Issues Survey, 2023, Leah D. Schade, Amanda Wilson Harper, Wayne Thompson, unpublished survey data, conducted Jan.-March 2023.

In fact, in the 2021 survey, when asked to indicate their reasons for avoiding social issues in preaching, respondents chose "maintaining unity and avoiding divisiveness" more frequently than any other reasons, including the fear of people leaving the church or withholding their financial giving or because of a belief in the separation of church and state.[14] Half of all respondents said maintaining unity and avoiding divisiveness was either "very" or "somewhat" important when deciding whether to address social issues in sermons.

However, a position of neutrality in the pulpit is becoming increasingly difficult to maintain. This is due to many factors, including the fact that the most strident voices sowing division among the body politic, especially those touting Christian nationalism, are forcing the hand of preachers who would rather stay out of the political fray. But more than that, simply quoting Jesus is now enough to be accused of pushing a "liberal agenda." As Wilson Harper found, "Social justice issues can seem controversial [and] divisive . . . and many issues Jesus references in the gospels are even misinterpreted as partisan."[15]

For example, as Russell Moore, a former official in the Southern Baptist Convention, explained in an interview with National Public Radio, multiple pastors have told him that when they preach about "turning the other cheek" from Jesus' Sermon on the Mount, people come up to them and say:

> "Where did you get those liberal talking points?" And what was alarming to me is that in most of these scenarios, when the pastor would

say, "I'm literally quoting Jesus Christ," the response would not be, "I apologize." The response would be, "Yes, but that doesn't work anymore. That's weak." And when we get to the point where the teachings of Jesus himself are seen as subversive to us, then we're in a crisis.[16]

This rejection of Jesus' teachings of nonviolence, grace, and love is not something that is happening only in Evangelical churches. A study conducted by the Public Religion Research Institute and the Brookings Institute in 2023 found that one-third of Americans are either "adherents" or "sympathizers" with the Christian nationalist belief that political violence is not only acceptable but necessary for maintaining power.[17] So, if you're a progressive Christian minister serving a church where a third of your congregation is opposed to the teachings of Jesus because of their own alignment with Christian nationalist values, it's no wonder that you are receiving pushback when you try to preach the gospel.

RANK REASONS FOR HESITANCY IN ADDRESSING SOCIAL ISSUES IN PREACHING

What makes you nervous about the idea of addressing social issues in a sermon? Look at the list below and rank them in order from 1–9, 1 being the highest level of concern, 9 being the lowest.

____People may stop attending worship services

____People may stop speaking to me

____People may withhold their financial giving

____People may stop volunteering

____People may leave the church altogether

____I might receive angry words, letters, or emails

____I'm worried about threats or intimidation

____I might be asked to resign

____I might be fired or let go from my position

Now read on to see how respondents in the surveys answered these questions.

Preaching in the Red–Blue Divide Since 2016

As my team and I looked at the three surveys, we paid attention to the factors that we identified as increasing brittleness in congregations. These included perceptions of divisiveness (both within the congregation and the surrounding community), congregational strife, levels of clergy stress and burnout, and demographic factors that may contribute to a pastor's vulnerability when addressing social issues in preaching. Let's look at each of these factors in turn.

Perceptions of Divisiveness Increase

Survey respondents reported an increase in the level of divisiveness within their church in 2023 compared to 2021, from 25 to 35 percent. In some denominations, the level of divisiveness was even higher. For example, 38 percent of ELCA (Evangelical Lutheran Church in America) Lutherans and 43 percent of United Methodist Church (UMC) pastors reported that their church was very or somewhat divided in 2023.

But even more significant were the perceptions of divisiveness in one's *community*. In 2021, 48 percent of all respondents said their community was very or somewhat divided. That number jumped to 69 percent in 2023 and rose to 74 percent for those serving in suburbs. So, even if a minister is mostly in agreement with their congregation politically, they may find themselves at odds with other local clergy and congregations or with members of the community at large who take issue with their stance on social issues.

As one survey respondent said, "I have never felt physically unsafe from any members of my congregation, past or present. But I have felt unsafe as a result of others in the community who have heard my preaching and/or my stance on social issues." Add to this the fact that violent extremists are increasingly setting their sights on congregations and clergy and it's natural that there may be a chilling effect on the parish pastor's desire to address social issues. This is exactly the intention of those violent actors, including clergy themselves who call for attacks on their colleagues. As one respondent reported, "The FBI issued a warning about our church being targeted for violence because a neighboring pastor preached to burn our church down."

All these factors we have discussed so far can contribute to high levels of stress for clergy. In the 2023 survey, we asked respondents whether their stress was low, moderate, high but manageable, high enough that they're planning to leave their current ministry setting, or so high that they're planning to leave ministry altogether. Thirty-eight percent of respondents reported high but manageable stress, with 9 percent planning to leave their church, and 2 percent planning to leave the ministry as a vocation. Altogether, this means that half of respondents reported high stress levels, in other words, brittleness. And when the pastor and the congregation are stressed, they may be more hesitant to bring more controversy to the system with sermons about a contemporary issue.

Prophetic Courage and the Realities of Vulnerability
Despite these brittleness factors, in each successive survey, we saw an increase in the number of clergy who said that they "frequently" preach on social issues. In 2017, that number was 30 percent, which increased to 55 percent in 2021 and rose to 70 percent in 2023. What might account for this shift invites closer analysis. It is possible that the change is due to differences in the samples, but our data suggest that the marginal distribution of political preference and voting behavior among our clergy respondents was modest. Thus, our hypothesis is that clergy were more willing to address controversial issues in the 2021 and 2023 surveys in part because of greater salience for some issues in the broader sociocultural context. Our hunch is that this increase in frequency might be attributed to the "Trump effect," in that clergy felt morally and ethically obligated to address the many violations of norms during the 2016–2020 administration as well as the harmful policy decisions that targeted what Christians might call "the least of these," or those vulnerable in society.

For the survey respondents, two main reasons emerged as their rationale for addressing social issues: (1) connecting the Bible and faith with issues that affect people's lives and (2) providing ethical and theological perspectives on an issue. In 2021, 88 percent said that "connecting scripture and faith with issues that affect people's lives" is the most important reason. A close second, at 85 percent, is because they believe "Jesus and the Bible speak about social issues." And three-quarters of respondents said they address social issues in their sermons to "provide moral, biblical, or theological perspective on an issue."

ASSESSING GUIDING PRINCIPLES FOR ADDRESSING SOCIAL ISSUES

Here is a list of six possible reasons for addressing social issues in a sermon. Think about these on your own and discuss them with a group of preaching colleagues or your preaching mentor. Which would you rank highest and why? Which would be lowest and why? Are there other reasons that would compel you to talk about a contemporary issue in a sermon? Also, consider sharing this list with parishioners and asking how they would rank these reasons for a preacher's addressing social issues in their sermon.

What Are Appropriate Reasons for Preachers to Address Social Issues?

- Because Jesus and the Bible speak about social issues
- When lectionary readings address an issue
- When God places an issue on the preacher's heart
- To provide moral, biblical, or theological perspective on an issue
- When asked by the bishop, ecclesial leader, or larger church body to address an issue
- To connect the Bible and faith with issues that affect people's lives

Given these results, it was not surprising to see that in the 2021 and 2023 surveys, nearly all respondents indicated that when it comes to the church's role in the public square, they favor engagement over avoidance. Ninety-three percent strongly or moderately agreed that the church should host educational dialogues about social issues and faith, and 92 percent strongly or moderately agreed that churches should put their faith into action through advocacy and social justice. Similarly, when it comes to engaging social issues with their congregations, 96 percent either strongly or moderately agreed that clergy should help congregants think about social issues biblically and theologically. This indicates that clergy, broadly speaking, lean heavily toward having their congregations and themselves engage in social issues.

At the same time, however, a little more than a third of respondents in 2021 and 2023 said that they would like to address social issues in their preaching and teaching but *feel inhibited*. When we factor in things such as gender, length of time in a church, congregational setting, and race, we see certain constellations of characteristics that indicate which clergy feel most inhibited when it comes to addressing social issues in a sermon. Those characteristics include less than forty years old, female, clergy of color in White congregations, clergy in smaller churches with smaller budgets, clergy in rural churches, or clergy who are new to their congregations or new to the ministry overall. If any of those factors intersect, the inhibition increases. For example, pastors who are younger than forty, female, and serving a rural church are less likely to feel confident in addressing issues than their White male colleagues in their fifties or sixties serving suburban or rural churches.

What, then, are the characteristics of preachers who are *most likely* to address social issues? Those characteristics include White, more than forty years old, male, serving larger congregations with larger budgets, having seniority, and tenure greater than ten years. Again, this is probably not surprising when we consider the ways in which our society privileges certain demographics over others. What we saw in these surveys is that those preachers who had the most social privilege in terms of gender, race, economic status, and markers of authority demonstrated more confidence in addressing social issues compared to those pastors who occupied positions of lesser privilege.

So, for example, senior clergy serving multistaff congregations are in better positions to take risks because they enjoy more job security than solo pastors or those in assistant pastor or other kinds of clergy roles.

These senior pastors are more likely to be serving congregations in urban areas with more affluent, better educated parishioners who may be more receptive to sermons about social justice and systemic oppression. By comparison, clergy who are in the earlier stages of their careers or serving smaller congregations located in more conservative settings appear to be more hesitant to address social issues.

ASSESS YOUR REASONS FOR *AVOIDING* SOCIAL ISSUES IN PREACHING

Here is a list of six possible reasons for avoiding social issues in a sermon. Think about these on your own and discuss them with a group of preaching colleagues or your preaching mentor. Which would you rank highest and why? Which would be lowest and why? Are there other reasons why you would avoid talking about a contemporary issue in a sermon? Also, consider sharing this list with parishioners and asking how they would rank these reasons for a preacher to avoid addressing social issues in their sermon.

What Are Reasons That Preachers Should Avoid Addressing Social Issues?

- Maintain unity and avoid divisiveness.
- If there is no clear or overt biblical position on the issue.
- People may stop giving financially.
- People may stop attending worship or leave the church.
- Spiritual issues are more important than social issues.
- Preaching on the issue won't make a difference.

Barriers and Negative Pushback When Preachers Engage in Social Issues

To better understand what aspects of ministry might hinder a preacher's engagement with social issues, we gave respondents a list of different options and asked how much of a barrier they were. In all three surveys, the option most frequently chosen was "opposition or negative pushback from congregants." Another important factor was "feelings of burnout." Managing conflict in congregations is burdensome for pastors and affects their selection of sermon topics. If they are concerned that their sermon addressing a social issue may either produce or sustain conflict, they may opt for avoiding it. As the adage goes, the Christian gospel may be about changing lives, but churches are often about keeping the status quo.

But it's not just fears about what might happen that can cause preachers to think twice before they approach social issues in the pulpit. Many have directly experienced negative reactions to their sermons when they dared broach certain topics. When we asked in each survey what types of negative pushback they experienced after preaching about a social issue, the same two responses topped the list each time: (1) angry words, letters, and emails and (2) some stopped attending worship services. Approximately half of all respondents said these things had happened to them because of a sermon they preached.

Others reported that some parishioners withheld financial giving, refused to speak with them, stopped volunteering, or left the congregation entirely. And though it is a much smaller percentage, around 3 to 4 percent of respondents reported that some in the congregation had called for their resignation or that their employment was terminated due to their preaching about social issues. Although these numbers might be lower compared to other negative repercussions, the consequences for these preachers are emotionally, professionally, and spiritually stressful.

Perhaps most alarming is the percentage of preachers who reported that they have been threatened or feared for their safety or wellbeing due to a sermon that they preached or because of their engagement with social issues. In both 2021 and 2023, that number was 10 percent.[18] Recall from chapter 1 the anecdotes about clergy being threatened, intimidated, and doxed (personal information shared on the internet) and enduring both online and in-person attacks. In the surveys, we learned of even more disturbing examples, including gunshots fired at a church housing an undocumented family, long-standing members banding together to subvert the pastor and report them to their judicatory leader, verbal threats from a parishioner carrying a concealed weapon, and online death threats. Notably, these threats were experienced by pastors of various genders, races, denominations, and locations. Put differently, should violent extremists detect a message advocating love, acceptance, justice, and peace emanating from either a pulpit or a congregation, the identity of the messenger becomes inconsequential; what becomes imperative is the suppression or eradication of the source.

With all these stressors and threats against clergy, it stands to reason that having a strong support system—in addition to one's own personal faith—is vital for buoying the pastor when they face the lion's den for preaching prophetic truth. So we also asked where clergy are finding support and encouragement.

Where Are Preachers Finding Support for Engaging Social Issues?

Ministers named the following sources that provided the most encouragement and support (in order of importance): (1) family, (2) clergy groups or networks, (3) congregational leaders, and (4) their denomination or central church office.[19] Some noted that even having just one or two supportive people in the congregation was enough to give them the encouragement they needed to preach about an issue.

Others found their best support outside of the congregation. For example, some listed local, state, or national organizations and their seminary, divinity school, or Bible college as sources of assistance. As one respondent said, "My seminary cohort is the source of my greatest support." Similarly, another said they have a "small friend group from seminary [that] is the biggest support. We encourage each other and listen when someone needs to get the frustration out."

What Do *Parishioners* Say about Engaging Social Issues at Church?

While my team and I found our data about preachers both fascinating and informative, we knew we needed a perspective from those who listen to sermons. So we also surveyed groups of parishioners. From 2019 to 2020, I directed a grant project, titled "Dialogue in the 'Purple

Zone': Pedagogies for Civil Discourse in Online and On-site Settings."[20] One aspect of the program was bringing together a pastor and lay leader from ten Disciples of Christ (Christian Church) congregations for training in a sermon–dialogue–sermon process and moderating deliberative dialogue.

Of the nine congregations that completed the project, one was located in a rural area, five were in small or midsize towns/cities, and three were in suburban areas. Three mid-central states were represented—Kentucky, Ohio, and West Virginia. We designed congregation questionnaires to collect initial data. Also, one of the grant research consultants, Amanda Wilson Harper, conducted one-on-one interviews with each of the clergy and each lay leader. Both the questionnaire and the interviews helped us to establish a baseline on their attitudes about the role of the church in the public square, how they define social justice, and how they assess the level of divisiveness in their congregation.

Two key insights emerged from these initial interviews and questionnaires. First, when asked if they felt prepared by their seminary training to engage in hard conversations with their congregation about social justice and public policy issues, every one of the pastors in the cohort said that they did not feel equipped. In fact, this was one of the reasons they agreed to take part in the training—they knew they needed support and resources for social justice engagement, so this opportunity came at just the right time for them.

We also noted that even during the height of COVID-19, the upcoming election season, and social unrest around justice issues throughout the nation, congregants reported that engaging social issues was important for them. For example, in both years, 83 percent strongly or moderately agreed that "working for social justice is an extension of my faith." Further encouraging data from the survey was the response to a question about whether the church should "help members discuss social issues and host community dialogues." The number who agreed or strongly agreed in both years remained high at 86 to 87 percent. Even more heartening was the increase in the percentage of those who agreed or strongly agreed that their church should "work to make changes in community and society." In 2019, that number was 87 percent, and in 2020, the number rose to 92 percent. It may be the case that the sermon–dialogue–sermon process conducted in these congregations is related to this increase.

I found similar patterns when surveying parishioners in UMC congregations in Nebraska and Kansas in 2020 and 2021 as part of my consulting work with the Great Plains Conference. In that survey of parishioners in ten different congregations, we found that 85 percent of respondents agreed that the church should encourage dialogue and discussion about social issues from a faith perspective. Sixty-eight percent agreed that the church should help members discuss social issues and host community dialogues (though that number is twenty points lower than the Disciples of Christ [DOC] parishioners we surveyed). And 73 percent agreed that the church should work to make changes in community and society (though, again, that number was twenty points lower than the DOC respondents).

But no matter whether congregants think the church should formally address issues of public concern, one thing we learned from the congregation surveys is that they themselves are often doing so and they are having those conversations *at church*. Yet few of them feel equipped to have these conversations in a healthy and constructive way.

Conclusion: Parishioners Are *Already* Talking about Social Issues—So Let's Meet Them There

In our 2019 survey of the ten DOC congregations, we found that 73 percent of congregants said they observed people talking about current events while in the church building. Similarly, our 2020 survey of ten UMC congregations in Nebraska and Kansas found that 59 percent reported seeing people talk about current events at church. Thus, the reality is that Christians *already* talk about social issues at church, whether or not they think that the preacher should do so. In fact, those who say that the church should stay out of politics when it comes to, say, protecting God's Creation from pollution, are often the same ones who are fine with their church pushing to stop gay marriage or hanging signs that say "God Bless America"—both of which are political actions and statements.

At the same time, respondents in both denominational surveys acknowledged that social issues are often a cause of division and even separation. Fifty-two percent of DOC respondents and 42 percent of UMC respondents said they knew about people leaving the church because of disagreements about social issues. With this in mind, preachers must be strategic when helping their listeners think about the ways in which faith can inform and shape the relationship between the church and social issues and to do so in ways that are both faithful to the gospel and upbuilding to the Body of Christ. To help with this task, you will find the Assessment Tool in chapter 3. This will help you determine whether you should take a Gentle, Invitational, or Robust approach.

Notes

1. See: Amanda Wilson Harper, "Strengthening Congregational Communities: Social Justice Engagement through Deliberative Dialogue," *Social Work & Christianity* 7, no. 3 (2020): 85–99, quoted in Paul A. Djupe and J. R. Neiheisel, "Clergy Deliberation on Gay Rights and Homosexuality," *Polity* 40, no. 4 (2008): 411–35; Evangelical Lutheran Church in America, "Talking Together as Christians about Tough Social Issues," 1999, https://download.elca.org/ELCA%20Resource%20Repository/Talking_Together_as_Christians_About_Tough_Social_Issues.pdf; Paul A. Djupe and L. Olson, "Public Deliberation about Gay Rights in Religious Contexts: Commitment to Deliberative Norms and Practice in ELCA Congregations," *Journal of Public Deliberation* 9, no. 1 (2013): 1–27.

2. See Frank A. Thomas's *How to Preach a Dangerous Sermon* (Nashville, TN: Abingdon, 2018); *Surviving a Dangerous Sermon* (Nashville, TN: Abingdon, 2020); *The God of the Dangerous Sermon* (Nashville, TN: Abingdon, 2021).

3. Lisa Cressman, *The Gospel People Don't Want to Hear: Preaching Challenging Messages* (Minneapolis, MN: Fortress Press, 2020), 52–53.

4. Thomas, *How to Preach a Dangerous Sermon*, xviii.

5. Thomas, xviii.

6. Wilson Harper, "Strengthening Congregational Communities," 88.

7. Clifton F. Guthrie, "Quantitative Empirical Studies in Preaching: A Review of Methods and Findings," *Journal of Communication and Religion* 30 (2007): 73.

8. Guthrie, 76.

9. According to Gallup, church attendance levels in 2023 were about 10 percentage points lower than what Gallup measured in 2012 and most prior years. Jeffrey M. Jones, "U.S. Church Attendance Still Lower than

Pre-Pandemic," Gallup, published June 26, 2023, accessed January 5, 2024, https://news.gallup.com/poll/507692/church-attendance-lower-pre-pandemic.aspx.

10. Adam Gabbatt, "Losing Their Religion: Why US Churches Are on the Decline," *The Guardian*, published January 22, 2023, accessed August 15, 2023, https://www.theguardian.com/us-news/2023/jan/22/us-churches-closing-religion-covid-christianity.

11. Gabbatt.

12. Pew Research Center, "Modeling the Future of Religion in America," published September 13, 2022, accessed August 15, 2023, https://www.pewresearch.org/religion/2022/09/13/modeling-the-future-of-religion-in-america/.

13. Public Religion Research Institute, "Clergy and Congregations in a Time of Transformation: Findings from the 2022–2023 Mainline Protestant Clergy Survey," published September 13, 2023, accessed January 5, 2024, https://www.prri.org/research/clergy-and-congregations-in-a-time-of-transformation-findings-from-the-2022-2023-mainline-protestant-clergy-survey/.

14. This parallels findings from the 2017 survey where I identified *fear* as a major factor inhibiting preachers from addressing social issues, namely, "fear of hurting or dividing their congregation, and fear about compromising their ability to effectively minister, fear about receiving negative pushback for being 'too political,' and fear about loss of members, money, and their own positions." Leah D. Schade, *Preaching in the Purple Zone: Ministry in the Red-Blue Divide* (Lanham, MD: Alban Books, 2019), 21.

15. Wilson Harper, "Strengthening Congregational Communities," 89.

16. Scott Detrow, Gabriel J. Sánchez, and Sarah Handel, "He Was a Top Church Official Who Criticized Trump. He Says Christianity Is in Crisis," NPR, published August 8, 2023, accessed August 13, 2023, https://www.npr.org/2023/08/08/1192663920/southern-baptist-convention-donald-trump-christianity.

17. Public Religion Research Institute, "A Christian Nation? Understanding the Threat of Christian Nationalism to American Democracy and Culture," published February 2, 2023, accessed August 14, 2023, https://www.prri.org/research/a-christian-nation-understanding-the-threat-of-christian-nationalism-to-american-democracy-and-culture/.

18. We had not asked a question about threats or intimidation in the 2016 survey because at that point, we had not perceived that this was a common experience among preachers. That began to change during the Trump administration, the January 6 insurrection, and growing social protests.

19. While it was not as high on the list of barriers, approximately 15 percent of respondents did list lack of support among clergy colleagues or from their

denomination as barriers to their engagement with social issues and reported feeling professionally isolated.

20. This research was funded by the Wabash Center for Teaching and Learning in Theology and Religion as part of their Pedagogies for Social Justice and Civic Engagement program.

CHAPTER 3

What's Your Path to Prophetic Preaching? An Assessment Tool

In 2021 during the height of the COVID-19 pandemic, I was moderating a clergy discussion on a teleconference meeting. We had gathered to consider how they might address the growing threat of police violence against people of color and nonviolent protestors who were advocating for reforms. One of the pastors was a White man with many years of experience in the church who had a passion for speaking publicly and boldly from the pulpit about justice issues.

"You just have to take the bull by the horns and preach the truth!" he admonished the group after some expressed hesitancy about directly addressing issues of race and police violence. "You can't let your fear keep you from preaching the gospel! Look at me—I've been doing this for decades. If people get upset, that's on them. We have an obligation to preach justice."

On the screen I could see people shifting uncomfortably in their chairs. One woman responded, "It's not that simple. You don't know what it's like to preach while female. Or preach while Black. Or preach in a small church where, if one family gets angry, they could leave and take a quarter of the congregation with them."

Another person added, "I have a family to support. If the church decides to end my call because they think I'm being too political, my kids and spouse will suffer. We don't all have the protections that you have."

What I heard in this exchange was the reality that despite a preacher's desire to address social issues, there are factors that may mitigate their ability to do so, or at least to do so directly. Often, these factors are beyond the preacher's control, such as their gender, sexual orientation, setting, financial and job security, skin color, or culture. Also, congregational factors may be beyond their control, especially if they are placed in a congregation by a denominational office instead of having a call process of mutual discernment between the clergy and congregation. But even in churches where pastors have a choice as to where they serve, there may be factors that are not immediately visible that can affect the congregation's ability to receive challenging sermons. For example, there may be unresolved conflict that predates the pastor's arrival, a series of deaths in the congregation that may shake their faith and leave them emotionally raw, or a pandemic that may expose previously hidden political divisions.

With all of this in mind, it's important not to generalize or make assumptions about a preacher's prophetic courage. There are many things to consider if you're planning to address a contemporary issue that some might deem "political." One thing I have learned after working for nearly a decade with preachers—including those who are seminarians, early career, long established, and retired but still active—is that the full constellation of personal, congregational, and relational factors needs to be considered in each situation. This is why I developed the Assessment Tool to help clergy gauge their risk and capacity for addressing social issues in sermons.

How the Assessment Tool Was Developed

I developed this Assessment Tool after years of working with preachers and realizing that different factors affect their willingness to preach about social issues. I thought it would be helpful for preachers to systematically think through their own potential as well as their congregation's capacity for engaging social issues in sermons and to quantify that in a concrete way.

I consulted on the questions in the Assessment Tool with two social science experts, Dr. Wayne Thompson, professor emeritus at Carthage College, and Rev. Dr. Amanda Wilson Harper, assistant professor at Tarleton State University. Then, I field tested the Assessment Tool with students in courses I taught, clergy in workshops I led, and in large gatherings of pastors at denominational gatherings. I also received helpful feedback from homileticians as well as my colleagues at Lexington Theological Seminary, all of whom helped me to refine the instrument. While neither exhaustive nor perfect, I believe the tool is useful for gauging risk and capacity for addressing social issues in sermons.

As we saw in chapter 2, there is more than just anecdotal evidence about these factors. The data my team and I have collected from our research on ministry, preaching, and social issues has shown that certain clusters of variables appear to influence a preacher's willingness—or hesitancy—in addressing social issues. The likelihood that a preacher will address social issues appears to be affected by three factors:

- The preacher's vulnerability, risk, and capacity for addressing social issues
- Congregational characteristics and community context
- The relationships between the pastor and congregation and among congregation members with each other

Let's take a closer look at these three factors.

The Preacher's Vulnerability, Risk, and Capacity for Addressing Social Issues

What makes some preachers more vulnerable than others when it comes to addressing social issues in sermons? What are the things that can mean more risk to some pastors than others? What factors can contribute to having a higher capacity for tolerating risks and vulnerabilities when preaching?

The Effects of Social Privilege—or Lack Thereof

Our surveys of clergy revealed that there were certain aspects of social location that correlated with preachers who indicated a higher willingness to address contemporary issues in their sermons. Those who were senior clergy, male, White, middle aged (fifty to sixty years old), or serving in larger churches (three hundred or more members) with substantial budgets were the most likely to address social issues in sermons. This is not surprising given the many ways in which social privilege affords more respect for male pastors, pastors who are White, and pastors who have years of experience. For instance, senior clergy serving multistaff congregations appear to be in better positions to take risks. This is because they often enjoy more job security than solo and assistant pastors or those in other kinds of clergy roles. Also, senior pastors are more likely to be serving congregations in suburban or urban areas with more affluent, better educated congregants who may be more receptive to sermons about social justice and systemic oppression.

By comparison, clergy who are earlier in their careers, or with less job security, indicated a lower willingness to engage with social issues. Similarly, those serving congregations that are smaller and located in more conservative settings were also less willing. As well, those preachers who occupy intersections of demographics, such as female, clergy of color, and LGBTQIA+, are afforded less social privilege. Not surprisingly, they also demonstrated more hesitancy than their male, White, cisgender, heterosexual counterparts. Again, this is probably not surprising. Preachers who are younger than most of the members in their congregation may find that they are afforded less respect than their older colleagues. And having less experience as a minister or being new to a congregation is a good reason to tread lightly when addressing issues that may be controversial since you're not sure where the political "land mines" might be.

As for gender, female preachers overall showed more hesitancy to address social issues in preaching than their male colleagues. It appears that some congregants feel more emboldened to critique females, be dismissive of them, or even bully them into silence when hearing about topics that they find uncomfortable or challenging. Female respondents in the survey reported this kind of pushback from parishioners at a higher frequency than their male counterparts. If the female is also a person of color, speaks in an accent that the congregation believes to be "foreign," or is a lesbian or transgender, the risk to them is even greater. And as you may recall from the opening story in chapter 1, female clergy may be specifically targeted and their safety and well-being endangered if they choose to address a social issue.

Personal and Professional Factors

But even clergy who appear well positioned to have the protections of privilege may have reasons for steering clear of "third rail" topics in their sermons. For example, if they have the metaphorical bruises and scars from past church conflict—or if the church is currently embroiled in some kind of controversy—they may be wary about adding further stress to themselves and the congregational system by tackling a controversial social issue.

Along the same lines, if a pastor does not feel that they have the support of congregational leaders, colleagues, family, or denominational leaders, they may avoid addressing hot topics in the pulpit. Without a solid network to give them reliable and constructive feedback, a pastor may feel isolated and unsupported and, thus, unwilling to jeopardize their mental and spiritual health by taking on a "political" issue in their preaching.

And, of course, one's energy level for ministry can vary no matter whether one is new to a church or has been there for decades. These energy levels can be affected by any number of personal, professional, and relational factors, such as health issues, relational strife, levels of burnout, and the unremitting demands of one's congregation and/or denomination.

In the Assessment Tool, you'll find that the questions in part A can help you gauge your capacity and limitations for addressing social issues. There's no judgment meant in any of these questions. Rather, they are designed to help you get a read on where you are personally when it comes to having the wherewithal to take on social issues in your preaching.

Congregation Characteristics and Community Context

Naturally, there is no one factor that determines a congregation's capacity for hearing social issues addressed in a sermon. But there are certain aspects that can have a bearing on that capacity. For example, smaller churches with attendance less than one hundred people may prefer that their pastor avoid social topics so as not to disrupt close-knit relationships or cause people to leave and jeopardize the congregation's ability to sustain itself. On the other hand, if such a church has a culture of social engagement, they may encourage and expect their pastor to address social issues—or at least the ones about which they are most concerned.

Congregational Health and Vitality

Church vitality and health play a significant role in a congregation's readiness to engage in contemporary topics. For example, worship attendance correlated with a preacher's willingness to talk about hot topics regardless of their setting. Generally, the lower the worship attendance, the greater the pastor's concern about losing members if they preach about a controversial topic. But it's not just the total number in worship; it's also about the age groups who are represented. In congregations with at least 20 percent of their membership made up of children, youth, and young adults, pastors may be motivated to attend to the concerns of younger generations, such as gun violence, affirmative action, access to abortion, and climate and environmental issues.

Vitality can also be seen in churches that serve as intellectual, artistic, cultural, and musical centers for their community. Likewise, if they are regarded as service-oriented and a leader in advocacy and activism in the community, the congregation may take pride in having their pastor address social issues. Also, if a significant proportion of the congregation is engaged in faith formation, such as adult forums, Bible studies, book studies, or children and youth education, that is another indication of vitality. Rev. Dr. Margaret Krych, who was my Christian education professor in seminary decades ago, used to say that we shouldn't judge the vitality of a church merely by how many people are in the pews. Instead, ask how many *adults* (not just children and youth) are participating in faith formation, education, and service.

The Role of Gender and Sexual Orientation

One question you'll find in the Assessment Tool is about the role of women in ordained leadership within the church. You'll note that fewer points are afforded for preachers serving in churches where women cannot be ordained. This is because a church that does not allow women to be pastors has already communicated that women are of a lesser status than men. Thus, any contemporary topic that affects women in a particular way—and nearly all of them do—will likely have a built-in bias against women that would have to be overcome. But even in churches whose denomination allows women to serve as pastors, if they have not had a female minister in the history of their pastorate, they are at a disadvantage. And the first woman who serves in such a congregation will likely find many unspoken or explicit prejudices against her that may implicitly stifle her prophetic voice.

The same is true for congregations that are not open, affirming, and inclusive of people who are LGBTQIA+. Until there are secular and legal protections for all people regardless of sexual orientation or gender expression, as well as open hearts and policies in congregations, any preacher who tries to address issues such as violence against transgender people or blessing same-sex marriage will likely encounter resistance.

The Role of Race and Culture

How about the race and culture of congregations? We found that there were distinctive patterns for addressing social issues for preachers serving congregations with 25 percent or more members from historically marginalized groups, such as African American; Latino/a; Asian; or mixed races, languages, and cultures. These preachers tended to address a broader range of topics than their counterparts in primarily White or culturally homogeneous congregations. And they were more willing to address topics such as environmental racism, criminal justice reform, education, gender-based and domestic violence, and critiques of capitalism.[1]

According to our survey, African American mainline congregations are more likely than White congregations to hear sermons that tap into themes around systemic racism. They are also more likely to hear sermons about family and wellness topics where pastors focus on providing psychological and spiritual support in areas of concentrated poverty and where people are underprivileged. The Black Church tradition is prophetic and also a source of interpersonal support for concerns such as raising children and keeping families together.[2] These results support claims that Black congregations blend both comforting and challenging narratives into sermons.

Part B of the Assessment Tool has questions that touch on these aspects of church vitality, community context, diversity, equity, and inclusion. But parts A and B are not enough to get an adequate measurement of a preacher's and congregation's capacity for delivering and receiving sermons on issues of public concern. So part C rounds out the instrument by examining the *relationships* between the preacher and the congregation.

The Relationships between Pastor and Congregation and among Congregation Members

The third part of the Assessment Tool focuses on the relationship between the pastor and the congregation and the congregation members with each other. This section is important because, in addition to the pastor's individual strengths and vulnerabilities and congregation's health and vitality, the quality of the relationships add that all-important third dimension. For example, a pastor may be well established in a well-to-do congregation that has enough resources to sustain ministry for many years to come. But, if a scandal, such as financial malfeasance or sexual misconduct, has erupted that threatens the integrity of the pastoral office or the congregation, there may be little energy left to address something like gun violence or immigration. In contrast, a pastor might be new to a church struggling financially in the downtown section of a city. But, if the church has healthy church governance and is aligned politically with the preacher and the members are mutually motivated to address local issues that are affecting their community, they might be willing to have sermons that focus on issues of public concern from a biblical and theological perspective.

In other words, part C of the Assessment Tool is designed to help preachers gauge either the tension or suppleness in the relationships between them and their congregation and among the congregants with each other.

Gauging "Brittleness" and Resilience

As I explained in chapter 2, there are many factors that lead to what Lisa Cressman calls "brittleness" in congregations.[3] Dwindling attendance and finances, repairs and maintenance, a changing neighborhood, and church conflict can all affect a congregation's willingness to hear sermons that take on challenging contemporary topics. When congregations are stressed, they are more "brittle," meaning that they are emotionally fragile and less receptive to being transformed by the gospel. Part C of the Assessment Tool provides a way to quantify this brittleness, or its opposite—resilience and flexibility.

The Role of Conflict and Church Governance

One of the biggest contributors to brittleness in congregations is church conflict, whether due to external or internal factors. For instance, tensions may arise over seemingly petty things but actually point to deeper congregational dysfunction (as in the proverbial "color of the carpet" arguments). Or there may be hidden secrets and long-simmering tensions within the congregation that come out in unhealthy ways. However, if the congregation has gone through conflict that resolved in a healthy way with adequate closure, they may emerge stronger and more cohesive than before.

The functionality and health of the governing body of the congregation also contributes a great deal to its level of brittleness or resilience. Whether it's called the council, board of elders, presbyters, or some other name, nearly all churches have some group that makes decisions on behalf of the congregation between the times when the whole church meets to vote on larger issues. If that group trusts each other and the pastor, this increases the congregation's capacity to deal with conflict in healthy ways. However, if they are in the midst of flux or are mostly dysfunctional, it's likely that this either carries over into or reflects the larger congregational system, thus making the task of preaching about social issues more fraught.

Relational and Deliberative Well-Being within the Congregation

Yet another aspect of congregational health is the members' level of comfort with each other. How often do you observe people laughing together in wholesome fun? Are they able to tease each other good-naturedly and engage in enjoyable fellowship activities on a regular basis? If so, they likely have the capacity to process difficult issues because they have found healthy ways to deal with tension and can make space for difficult conversations.

Speaking of challenging conversations, a church that intentionally and regularly hosts events for healthy community dialogue or discussion about contemporary issues is much more fertile ground for preaching that accompanies these discussions. In fact, as I pointed out in *Preaching in the Purple Zone*, preaching and deliberative dialogue can go hand in hand for building stronger, more resilient, and more democratically adept congregations and citizens. In contrast, if the congregation avoids these deliberative conversations, it's likely that people will feel discomfort and even anger if a preacher delves into contemporary topics because there is no place to process the complexities that the sermon raises.

The same is true when it comes to the level of engagement in the congregation's infrastructure as well as service in the community. If participation in these aspects of congregational life is limited to a small group of people who do most of the work, both within and outside the church, this may indicate that a significant portion of the body of Christ is, in a sense, atrophying in their faith. However, if there is a regular rotation of people who share the load of planning church events, serving the community, and volunteering, this may indicate that a majority of the congregation is aware of what's going on in the community and may be more open to hearing sermons that address the issues that affect their friends and neighbors.

Also, as we discussed in chapter 2, another factor that affects a pastor's willingness to address social issues is the degree to which they are aligned (or misaligned) politically with the majority of their congregation. For example, we found that preachers wanting to address the climate crisis were more likely to do so in congregations that were more progressive, compared to their colleagues in more politically mixed or conservative congregations, who tended to avoid such issues. Progressive preachers in "purple" or "red" congregations or communities often feel they must tread lightly when it comes to social issues so as not to introduce or reveal political divisions among them.

It's a Matter of Trust

For all aspects of relationships between the pastor and the congregation and the congregation members with each other, it's about trust.

If congregants feel that the preacher genuinely cares about them, has demonstrated a willingness to listen, and exercises leadership with wisdom and prudence, they are more likely to be open to sermons that challenge them. At the same time, if the pastor trusts that the overall health of the congregation is at a level where they can work through initial discomfort with hearing about social issues in order to engage in a process of biblical and theological discernment together, then such a sermon is more likely to be heard.

Before you get started with the Assessment Tool, I want to share some caveats and cautions about how certain factors may need to be given more or less weight than others when determining your approach to a social issue in a sermon.

Caveats and Cautions for the Assessment Tool

As you work your way through the three parts of the Assessment Tool and answer the questions, here are some things to keep in mind.

- The Assessment Tool is not intended to be a scientific tool; it's only for personal assessment of one's vulnerabilities and strengths, the capacities and limitations of a congregation, and the strengths and weaknesses of the relationships within the congregation and between the congregation and the pastor.
- Note that none of the questions are meant to reflect your worth as a person or your congregation's overall character. This is neither a diagnostic tool nor a means by which to do in-depth analysis. It's simply a way to provide an overall map of the landscape for preaching about social issues for your particular situation at any particular time.
- If you think the point values are not accurate for your situation, feel free to adjust them.
  o For example, question 4, about age, is designed with the assumption that ageism (prejudice against those who are deemed either "too old" or "too young") is a mitigating factor. But if you are in your early thirties serving a younger congregation or in your seventies serving an older congregation, you

might want to adjust the points higher to reflect that your congregation sees your age as a strength rather than a detriment.
- Similarly, when it comes to race and ethnicity/culture in question 3, you may want to adjust the point values. For example, if you are a Black pastor serving a primarily Black congregation, you may decide to assign more points to yourself because your race would not be as much of an issue as it would be if you were a Black preacher serving a White congregation. Just keep in mind that since many churches post worship services online, there may be people beyond your congregation who have access to your sermon. Thus, preaching on certain social issues as a preacher of color may still involve more risk for you than for your White colleagues.

- You may need to subtract points if a particular situation is overriding other concerns.
  - For instance, one of my students scored in the Invitational range, but, because the senior pastor of her church had recently resigned, the stress level was higher than what could be reflected in the Assessment Tool. So she opted for the Gentle approach when we worked on her sermon.
  - Along those lines, you may be going through personal issues that are affecting the energy you have for ministry, much less preaching about controversial topics. For example, if you are dealing with mental or physical health issues, have new children in your household, or are going through a grief process, you may want to dial back to the Gentle approach.
- You may want to add or subtract points if you feel the total does not accurately reflect you or your congregation's readiness to address social issues.
  - For example, even though you may be a new pastor for a congregation, you may sense a strong willingness for them to want to engage with certain social issues and, thus, welcome your preaching about them. In that case, you may opt for the Invitational or Robust approach instead of the Gentle.
  - By the same token, while your score may indicate that the Robust approach would be appropriate for your context, if the

congregation is in the midst of a significant building program or capital campaign, for instance, there may not be bandwidth for addressing certain hot topics at this time. So a Gentle or Invitational approach may be better suited.
- The topic you're wanting to address may have more influence on the approach you take than the Assessment Tool would indicate. As an example, your congregation may be very willing to hear a sermon that addresses a local issue with which they are familiar and about which they have concerns. But they may be less willing to hear about a topic that some believe is controversial on a *national* level. In other words, the Assessment Tool is designed to give you a broad and general appraisal of you and your congregation's readiness to engage with a social issue in a sermon. The specificity of particular topics is something you'll need to consider in your context.

Overall, the Assessment Tool can help you "exegete" yourself, those who will hear your sermon, and the relationships among and between you. Tyshawn Gardner encourages preachers to ask the following questions: "How well do I know this congregation or the people hearing my sermon? What are the convictions, beliefs, and fears that this congregation shares about the crisis at hand? How might this congregation differ in their convictions and opinions about it? What are the demographics of the congregation?"[4] These kinds of questions and the Assessment Tool help preachers not to take anything for granted about their hearers. At the same time, they encourage sensitivity to one's own vulnerabilities as well as those in the congregation while weighing the psychological and emotional burden that the preacher and the church might be shouldering. With this knowledge and understanding, the preacher increases the chances that their sermon will be received and the Word of God will take root and grow.

Now, I invite you to set aside some quiet time to fill out the Assessment Tool or to take it online at https://thepurplezone.net/assessment-tool.

ASSESSMENT TOOL FOR GAUGING RISK AND CAPACITY FOR ADDRESSING SOCIAL ISSUES IN SERMONS

As you are thinking about if—and how—to approach social issues in your sermons and ministry, this instrument is designed to help you assess your level of risk and vulnerability as well as the congregation's capacity to receive these kinds of sermons and engage in the public square. In each question, circle the answer that best describes you or your situation. Keep in mind that this is a tool to help you gauge how comfortable you and your congregation might be with a sermon or education about an issue of public concern. This, in turn, can help you decide what approach you might take, whether you're in a high-risk/high-stress, moderate-risk/moderate-stress, low-risk/low-stress, low-risk/high-stress, or high-risk/low-stress situation. This information will help you determine what approach to take with your sermon: Gentle, Invitational, or Robust.

Note that this assessment instrument is for your own personal use. You are not required to share this with others or disclose your assessment to anyone.

You can also opt to complete the Assessment Tool online to receive your score. Visit https://thepurplezone.net/assessment-tool.

Part A—Preacher's Vulnerability, Risk, and Capacity for Addressing Social Issues in a Sermon

Note: Some of the points in part A are assigned according to how much privilege is typically afforded by U.S. society to certain demographics; however, *they are not a reflection of your worth as a person.*

1. What is your gender?
   Male/cisgender = 3 points
   Female/cisgender = 2 points
   Gender fluid/nonbinary = 1 point

2. What is your sexual orientation?
   Heterosexual = 3 points
   LGBTQIA+ = 1 point

3. What is your race/ethnicity/culture?
   Asian or Asian American = 1 point
   American Indian, Native American, or Alaska Native = 1 point

Native Hawaiian or other Pacific Islander = 1 point
African National/African Caribbean = 1 point
Black/African American = 1 point
Latina/o or Hispanic = 1 point
Another race or two or more races/ethnicities/cultures = 1 point
White/Caucasian = 3 points

4. What is your age?
   70+ = 1 point
   50–69 = 3 points
   30–49 = 3 points
   18–29 = 1 point

5. How long have you served your current congregation?
   6+ years = 3 points
   3–5 years = 2 points
   Less than 3 years = 1 point

6. How long have you been in ministry overall?
   11+ years = 4 points
   6–10 years = 3 points
   1–5 years = 2 points
   Less than a year = 1 point

7. What is your current position in the church?
   Senior pastor or co-pastor = 4 points
   Solo pastor = 3 points
   Associate pastor, youth pastor, or assistant pastor = 2 points
   Pastor emeritus, visiting pastor, or interim pastor = 2 points
   Seminarian/student pastor = 1 point

8. What has been your relationship with church conflict in the past?
   Learned healthy ways to deal with it = 3 points
   Not as healthy as I would like = 2 points
   Not handling it in a healthy way at the present time = 1 point

9. How do you feel about the level of support you receive as a minister, such as from colleagues, denominational leaders, friends, family, a counselor/therapist, or others?

Solid support = 3 points
Moderate support = 2 points
I feel isolated and alone at this time = 1 point

10. What is your current level of energy for ministry?
    Fully energized = 3 points
    Moderate energy = 2 points
    Very little energy = 1 point

SUBTOTAL PART A: _____

If you scored between 10 and 15 points, it's likely that your personal vulnerability and risk are high and your capacity for addressing social issues in preaching is low at this time.

If you scored between 16 and 24 points, it's likely that your personal vulnerability and risk are moderate and your capacity for addressing social issues in preaching is not at its highest at this time.

If you scored between 25 and 32 points, it's likely that your personal vulnerability and risk are low and your capacity for addressing social issues in preaching is high at this time.

Part B—Congregational Factors and Community Context

Note: The points in part B are assigned according to congregational factors that may indicate their readiness and capacity to be challenged by a sermon that addresses a social issue. However, *these point values are not intended to assess the overall character of the congregation.*

1. How many regularly attend worship services (both online and onsite)?
   \>300 = 4 points
   100–299 = 3 points
   50–99 = 2 points
   <50 = 1 point

2. What is the net loss of church membership over the past 12 months when taking account of gains (births, baptisms, and new members) and losses (death, moving away, or withdrawing membership)?

Net gain of 1% to 5% or more = 4 points
Loss of 5% or less, or overall breaking even = 3 points
Loss of 6% to 10% = 2 points
Loss of 11% or more = 1 point

3. How long can the church financially sustain its ministry given the current level of giving from the congregation (excluding outside sources of revenue)?
   10+ years = 4 points
   5–9 years = 3 points
   2–4 years = 2 points
   Less than 2 years = 1 point

4. What percentage of the congregation is made up of children, youth, and/or young adults?
   20% or greater = 3 points
   5%–19% = 2 points
   Less than 5% = 1 point

5. What is the setting of the congregation?
   Large metro area or suburb = 3 points
   Small or midsize city or suburb = 2 points
   Rural or small town = 1 point

6. How diverse is the congregation in terms of race, culture, language, and LGBTQIA+?
   At least 25% diversity = 3 points
   5%–24% diversity = 2 points
   Less than 5% diversity = 1 point

7. To what degree is the church a center for intellectual, artistic, cultural, musical, service oriented, advocacy, or activism in the community?
   Hosts several outside groups and vibrant, active member of community = 3 points
   Hosts one or two outside groups and sometimes engages with community = 2 points
   Little outreach or engagement in community = 1 point

8. What is the congregation's level of participation in faith formation (Christian education, adult forums, Bible studies, book studies, children's education, speaker series, etc.)?
   More than half engaged = 3 points
   About one-third engaged = 2 points
   Very few engaged = 1 point

9. What is the role of women in ordained leadership within the church?
   Women can be ordained; church has more than one female currently or in the past = 4 points
   Women can be ordained; church has only had one female minister or current female minister is the first = 3 points
   Women can be ordained; church has had no female ministers = 2 points
   Women cannot be ordained = 1 point

10. How open, affirming, and inclusive is the congregation of people who are LGBTQIA+?
    Fully open, affirming, and inclusive = 3 points
    Beginning or mild interest in becoming open, affirming, and inclusive = 2 points
    Resistant to becoming open, affirming, and inclusive = 1 point

11. How willing is the congregation to learn about, discuss, and confront racism, both on personal and systemic levels?
    Significant steps undertaken or racism is the lived experience of most in the congregation = 3 points
    Beginning or mild interest in addressing racism = 2 points
    Resistance to addressing racism = 1 point

SUBTOTAL PART B: _____

If the congregational factors scored between 11 and 20 points, it's likely that the congregation may have limited capacity for receiving a sermon about social issues.

If the congregational factors scored between 21 and 29 points, it's likely that the congregation has moderate capacity for receiving a sermon about social issues.

If the congregational factors scored between 30 and 37 points, it's likely that the congregation has a high capacity for receiving a sermon about social issues.

Part C—Assessment of Relationships

Note: The questions in part C are a general assessment of the potential for tension in the relationships between the congregation members and each other, the pastor, and within the community. However, *they are not intended to diagnose the quality of those relationships.* For those who are new to a congregation and have served less than three years, it may be difficult to answer some questions in this section. Simply answer as best you can with the limited knowledge you have at this point.

1. How many signs of strain do you observe that indicate congregational stress (i.e., members lashing out, overreacting, arguing, being passive-aggressiveness, displaying intense emotion, or withdrawing)?
   Very few signs of congregational stress = 3 points
   Two or three signs of congregational stress = 2 points
   More than three signs of congregational stress = 1 point

2. To the best of your knowledge, how recently and to what degree is/was the congregation engaged in significant conflict?
   >3 years ago, fully resolved = 3 points
   >3 years ago, not fully resolved = 2 points
   Currently engaged in conflict or engaged within last 3 years = 1 point

3. What is the level of unhealthy "secret-keeping" in the congregation (e.g., skeletons in the closet regarding misconduct or abuse, substance abuse, infidelity, domestic violence, etc.)?
   No secrets; open and transparent = 3 points
   Moderate level of secret-keeping = 2 points
   Damaging secrets that are harming congregation = 1 point

4. How healthy is the governing body of the congregation?
   Healthy, trusts each other, good relationships = 3 points

In the midst of flux or not functioning at its best = 2 points
Mostly dysfunctional = 1 point

5. What is the congregation's level of comfort with each other (i.e., how often does the congregation laugh together, tease each other good-naturedly, and engage in fun fellowship activities)?
High level of comfort, frequent opportunities for fun = 3 points
Medium level of comfort, occasional opportunities for fun = 2 points
Low level of comfort, rare opportunities for fun = 1 point

6. How often does the congregation host opportunities for healthy dialogue or discussion about contemporary issues?
6 or more times a year = 3 points
1–5 times a year = 2 points
Rarely or does not yet engage in such discussions = 1 point

7. What percentage of the congregation regularly volunteers in the congregation's infrastructure (worship and music, education, planning/hosting fellowship events, governing board, etc.)?
More than 50% = 4 points
25%–50% 3 points
10%–24% 2 points
Less than 10% = 1 point

8. Congregation's level of participation in serving the community (volunteering for local charities, advocacy/activism, working with other congregations on local projects, ministry outreach programs, etc.)?
Many are engaged = 3 points
Some are engaged = 2 points
Very few are engaged = 1 point

9. How close are the political orientations between the minister and the congregation?
Closely aligned on most issues = 3 points
Aligned on some issues but not others = 2 points
Not aligned on most issues = 1 point

10. How would you assess the level of trust between the minister and the congregation?
High level of trust = 3 points
Medium level of trust = 2 points
Low level of trust = 1 point
Not able to assess at this time = 1 point

SUBTOTAL PART C: _____

If the relationships scored between 10 and 15 points, it's likely that this congregation is very "brittle" and may be unable to tolerate a sermon that directly addresses a social issue at this time.

If the relationships scored between 16 and 20 points, it's likely that this congregation is experiencing a moderate level of stress. Preaching a sermon that addresses a social issue may be risky at this time but could be possible with appropriate strategies and approaches.

If the relationships scored between 21 and 31 points, it's likely that this congregation is experiencing a low level of stress at this time and is more likely to be open to hearing a sermon that addresses a social issue in a direct way.

TOTAL OF PARTS A, B, AND C: _____

0–49 points (Gentle): It's likely that your personal vulnerability/capacity, the congregational factors, and/or the relationships are such that preaching a sermon about a social issue may be risky at this time. If you choose to preach a sermon that addresses a social issue in this situation, try the Gentle approach.

50–75 points (Invitational): It's likely that your personal vulnerability/capacity, the congregational factors, and/or the relationships are such that preaching a sermon about a social issue could be possible, depending on the whether the issue is a "cool," "warm," or "hot" topic. If you choose to preach a sermon that addresses a social issue in this situation, try the Invitational approach.

76–100 points (Robust): It's likely that your personal vulnerability/capacity, the congregational factors, and/or the relationships are such that preaching a sermon about a social issue would carry minimal risk.

> *You and the congregation are both generally healthy and functioning well, have a strong level of trust, and can likely tolerate or even welcome a sermon that challenges them to grapple with and respond to a social issue. If you choose to preach a sermon that addresses a social issue in this situation, try the Robust approach.*

Summary of Three Approaches to Addressing Social Issues in Preaching

In chapter 4, I'll describe the Gentle, Invitational, and Robust approaches for addressing social issues in preaching. For now, here is a summary of each.

Gentle approach: Recommended for a *low-trust/high-stress* context. Focuses on naming emotions and framing them biblically and theologically. Helps the congregation process inwardly so that they can take tentative steps outward. Strategies include the following:

- Name the issue and frame it biblically
- Share your own struggles with the issue
- Stand with the congregation, voice the feelings

Invitational approach: Recommended for a *moderate-trust/moderately stressed* context. More flexibility and freedom to stretch the congregation with a challenging message but depends on the "temperature" of the topic (cool, warm, or hot). Focuses on moving beyond self-protection in order to listen to others, build bridges, find common ground, and imagine possible next steps. Strategies include the following:

- Tell stories to create empathy
- Sermon–dialogue–sermon process
- History, mission, future

Robust approach: Recommended for a *high-trust/low-stress* and *high-trust/medium- or high-stress* context. When the preacher and congregation have a healthy sense of their identity as children of God, they are less defensive and able to be humble and spiritually flexible. Focuses on creative and concrete ways to be transformed by the gospel and make a difference in the world. Strategies include the following:

- Be blunt, be bold
- Collaborate before, during, after
- Equip for justice

Note: For a sermon addressing a social issue, a preacher can use a combination of any of these strategies and blend aspects of different approaches.

Questions for Reflection and Discussion on the Assessment Tool

1. What was it like for you to fill out the Assessment Tool? Were your hunches confirmed, or did you see things in a different way than you had before? Did anything surprise you? Did you need to adjust any of the point values?
2. What did you learn that either gave you a different perspective or affirmed that your assessment prior to the exercise was fairly accurate?
3. Invite a preaching colleague to take the Assessment and compare your results. Did you feel that the results accurately capture your capacity and risk for addressing social issues?
4. How might the results of the assessment affect your approach to preaching about social issues in your context?
5. How might your results change if you were considering a less controversial topic for your sermon? Or a more controversial one? While we can't predict the future, how might things change if you took the Assessment Tool a year from now, knowing the expected trajectory of your congregation and what might lie ahead?

Notes

1. Leah D. Schade, "White Mainline Protestant Preachers Addressing Racial Issues: 2017 vs. 2021," in *Unmasking White Preaching: Racial Hegemony, Resistance, and Possibilities in Homiletics*, ed. Lis Valle-Ruiz and Andrew Wymer (Lanham, MD: Lexington Books, 2022), 70.

2. See Melvin Williams's 1974 book, *Community in a Black Pentecostal Church: An Anthropological Study* (Long Grove, IL: Waveland Press, Inc.); C. Eric Lincoln and Lawrence H. Mamiya's 1990 book, *The Black Church in the African American Experience* (Durham, NC: Duke University Press); and Hans Baer and Merrill Singer's 1992 book, *African American Religion in the Twentieth Century: Varieties of Protest and Accommodation* (Knoxville, TN: University of Tennessee Press).

3. Lisa Cressman, *The Gospel People Don't Want to Hear: Preaching Challenging Messages* (Minneapolis, MN: Fortress Press, 2020), 52–53.

4. Tyshawn Gardner, *Social Crisis Preaching: Biblical Proclamation in Troubling Times* (Brentwood, TN: B&H Publishing, 2023), 110–11.

CHAPTER 4

Gentle, Invitational, and Robust

Three Approaches to Addressing Social Issues in Preaching

Preaching in the age of pandemics, war, racial reckoning, threats to democracy, a deteriorating planet, and contentious politics is a risky proposition. Congregations are weary, wary, and wondering if there is truly any *good news* when media cycles pummel us with bad, even horrific news hour upon hour. There is existential angst when loss, world-shattering change, and death hover menacingly close. The challenge for preachers is how to help their listeners think biblically and theologically about this very real fear, pain, and suffering that accompanies the vicissitudes of our lives. As Lisa L. Thompson puts it: "You know the world could be different and should be different. But why? You know people should not be treated as though they are dispensable. But why? In the depths of your being, you know something is off course. But why? And why should it matter to people of faith?"[1] As we ask these questions, we know we must keep ourselves attuned to signs of God's grace breaking through the crucifixions of our time with a rolling-the-stone-away resurrection.

This cross-and-resurrection gospel is not easy, however; it requires something of us even as it promises something even deeper and more profound than mortal human life. As Jesus said to his disciples, "For those who want to save their life will lose it, and those who lose their life for my sake, and for the sake of the gospel, will save it" (Mark 8:35). In Lisa Cressman's words, this is "the gospel people don't want to hear" because it requires something for the ways in which we live our lives, conduct our business, navigate our conflicts, shape public policy, decide what we eat, and determine how we equitably distribute resources. The challenge is to find ways to proclaim the word of God so that people will listen instead of stopping their ears, stomping out the door, or clicking the little X in the corner of the screen.

In this chapter, I'll suggest three approaches for addressing a social issue in a sermon: Gentle, Invitational, and Robust. To make the best use of this chapter, I recommend that you first answer the questions in the Assessment Tool in chapter 3 or online at https://thepurplezone.net/assessment-tool. This will help you to gauge whether you are in a low-trust/high-stress, medium-trust/medium-stress, or high-trust/low-stress situation with your congregation. You'll then be able to make use of the strategies offered within the typology presented here.

The Gentle Approach: Strategies for Preaching about a Social Issue in a Low-Trust/High-Stress Congregation

When you have completed the Assessment Tool, you may discern a combination of personal vulnerability, congregational factors, or quality of relationships that indicates a low-trust or high-stress situation. If this is where your score lands, you'll want to address preaching about social issues with what I call the Gentle approach. This approach can be geared toward naming the feelings and emotions that can swirl around an issue and then framing them biblically and theologically. While people may be debating facts or principles on the surface, just below (and sometimes right out in front) are fears and "pain points" that come from people's experiences. The Gentle approach helps listeners reflect inwardly and, once they're ready, begin looking outward. The idea is that when we can coax the feelings out into the open and articulate them without blame or judgment, God can transform that energy into something liberating and life-giving. Here are three strategies you can experiment with when preaching about a social issue in a low-trust/high-stress situation.

- *Name the issue and frame it biblically.* At the most basic level, a preacher can simply bring the issue to the congregation's attention and show how the Bible either speaks directly to the topic or points to the questions and core values that we can bring to it. If parishioners try to say that the Bible has no bearing on contemporary issues, preachers can use historical–critical methods of exegesis to connect the biblical and theological dots between the world of the text and the world in which we live.[2] Such a sermon establishes the foundation for engaging the public issue while asking questions that invite curiosity, establish trust, and open the door for deeper engagement. Keep in mind that biblical framing can and should be applied in all sermons, not just for the Gentle approach. But for low-trust/high-stress situations, framing an issue biblically may be the only or best tactic to use.

- *Share your own struggles with the issue.* Admit your own complicity with injustice and ways in which your heart and mind have needed to be changed in order to see things a different way. Share your humanity even while you maintain some distance for prophetic critique. Acknowledge that while you don't have the answers, you are interested in the questions—especially working on those questions with others from a faith perspective.

- *Stand with the congregation, voice the feelings.* It can be tempting for preachers to think of themselves as working on the side of God as they take on the prophetic task of calling the unrepentant to account, and let the chips fall where they may. More often than not, however, this approach alienates listeners and creates hostility. Leonora Tubbs Tisdale, taking notes from Walter Brueggemann, suggests that a better approach is to stand *with* the congregation when facing the prophetic word of a biblical text, "letting the radical Word of God offend both!"[3] For this approach, using "we" language instead of "I/you" is important, especially when voicing the feelings around an issue. Why does articulating these feelings matter? Because God can work with our feelings. God can help us look inside of ourselves, locate our points of shared humanity, and simply listen to each other. In that sharing, listening, and attending is where God's Spirit can do the quiet work that leads to healing, reconciliation, and finding the next step forward.

Exercise: Gentle Approach for Addressing Immigration Using Leviticus 19:33-34

This is an exercise to try one of the strategies in the Gentle approach. We'll look at the topic of immigration and bring it into conversation with Leviticus 19:33-34 using each of the three strategies within this approach. Here is the passage:

> When a foreigner resides with you in your land, you shall not oppress the foreigner. The foreigner who resides with you shall be to you as the citizen among you; you shall love the foreigner as yourself, for you were foreigners in the land of Egypt: I am the Lord your God. (Lev 19:33-34)

- *Name the issue and frame it biblically.* Consult commentaries and take notes on what you learn about the "story behind the story" for this text. What was going on in history and for this community when this text was written? What is this text saying about who God is and what God is doing in relation to foreigners? And how might we apply our exegesis to the present-day situation of immigration?
- *Share your own struggles with the issue.* For this strategy, talk about how you have wrestled with the topic of migration and immigration. What is your personal experience with being a foreigner in a different country? If you have had the experience of not having proper documentation, what was that like for you? If you haven't had these experiences personally, what are the prejudices you've recognized and the stereotypes you've confronted in yourself? How have you felt God changing your heart and mind through your reading of Scripture and your theological and ethical discernment?
- *Stand with the congregation, voice the feelings.* What are ways you can stand with the congregation when facing the commandment of Leviticus 19:33-34? What is "offensive" about this passage? What is the scandal that confronts us in God's command to treat foreigners as fellow citizens? Could you describe different scenes of families having conversations about immigration at the dinner table? Using "we" language can articulate different perspectives while also standing with the congregation to experience and

meet the challenge of being the church in the midst of tensions around immigration.

The Invitational Approach: Strategies for Preaching about a Social Issue in a Medium-Trust/Medium-Stressed Congregation

After completing the Assessment Tool, if you see signs that indicate a medium-trust or medium-stressed situation, you may have a bit more flexibility in how you approach preaching about social issues. Note that the Gentle strategies can also be used for medium-stress congregations, but with the Invitational approach, you may be able to stretch the congregation with a more challenging message.

You'll first want to assess whether the issue is a "cool," "warm," or "hot topic" for your congregation. You'll be able to do this by having conversations with leaders and members to "take the temperature" on how controversial it may be. In this approach, the sermon can speak to the feelings of trepidation but also the curiosity and tentative courage to listen to others in a spirit of mutual respect and trust. The focus for this approach is moving beyond self-protection to hearing what it's like for those who are affected by the issue, building bridges, finding common ground, and imagining possible next steps.

Note that in both the Gentle and Invitational approaches, an inductive sermon form may be the best. In the inductive form, the preacher leads the congregation on a journey to arrive at the conclusion (as compared to deductive, which makes its claim at the beginning and then gives reasons for why the claim is true). As Tyshawn Gardner advises, "An inductive approach may be suitable when preaching about a sensitive subject to an audience that may not be well informed about the crisis at hand, or who may be resistant to the biblical application the text calls for."[4]

- *Tell stories to create empathy.* Tell the story of people's experiences who have been affected by the issue. Using vibrant words, salient images, and evocative stories can help to humanize a social issue beyond the politicized and depersonalized headlines. Narratives help to create empathy, which, in turn, allows for the transformative power of God to change people's hearts and minds. (Just be sure that the stories are not emotionally manipulative or seem to push an agenda in a coercive way.) You can also invite one or two people to share their stories, perspectives, and experiences within the sermon itself. This is a way to expand the pulpit to include other voices and bodies so that we show radical hospitality to those who are different than us (and perhaps challenge us) but also join us in the work of proclaiming God's work in the world. Do be sure to obtain permission when sharing personal stories, or change identifying details to ensure anonymity.

- *Sermon–dialogue–sermon process.* In my book, *Preaching in the Purple Zone: Ministry in the Red-Blue Divide*, I offer a three-part method of addressing social issues. First, the preacher offers a "prophetic invitation to dialogue" sermon inviting the congregation to engage in dialogue about a particular social issue. This is followed by a form of civil discourse called "deliberative dialogue" in which a faith community establishes ground rules for discussion, shares their personal stake in the social issues, weighs the benefits and drawbacks of three different approaches using a nonpartisan issue guide, identifies shared values and common ground, and brainstorms next steps for responding to the issue.[5] The preacher follows up with the "communal prophetic proclamation sermon," which integrates the insights and wisdom from the dialogue, framing it theologically and offering a shared vision of putting faith into action on the issue based on the congregation's joint discernment.
- *History, mission, future.* This strategy uses a congregation's history as well as current mission to help them envision their prophetic future. For example, one of our students at Lexington Theological Seminary was working with his church on a process to become an Open and Affirming (O&A) congregation, a designation of welcoming people who are LGBTQIA+. At the service that kicked off the initiative, he reminded them of how the congregation began as a mission to a nearby orphanage. Reaching out to those who were vulnerable and outcast was in their ecclesial DNA, so to speak, so initiating the process of becoming O&A was a natural extension of their heritage. Further, the congregation had recently welcomed a Hispanic congregation to "nest" in their church. So their mission of welcoming and accepting

others could be extended to their LGBTQIA+ siblings as well. Using this strategy, the preacher frames prophetic vision for the congregation with what they already know as their history and understand as their mission.

Exercise: Invitational Approach for Addressing Environmental Issues Using Romans 8:18-25

This is an exercise to try one of the strategies in the Invitational approach. In this case, we'll look at the topic of environmental issues and bring them into conversation with Paul's letter using each of the three strategies. Here is the passage:

> I consider that the sufferings of this present time are not worth comparing with the glory about to be revealed to us. For the creation waits with eager longing for the revealing of the children of God; for the creation was subjected to futility, not of its own will but by the will of the one who subjected it, in hope that the creation itself will be set free from its bondage to decay and will obtain the freedom of the glory of the children of God. We know that the whole creation has been groaning in labor pains until now; and not only the creation, but we ourselves, who have the first fruits of the Spirit, groan inwardly while we wait for adoption, the redemption of our bodies. For in hope we were saved. Now hope that is seen is not hope. For who hopes for what is seen? But if we hope for what we do not see, we wait for it with patience. (Rom. 8:18-25)

- *Tell stories to create empathy.* We could apply our exegesis to the present-day situation of environmental issues by noting that in Paul's time, Roman occupation meant exploitation and depletion of natural resources. They could witness Creation "groaning" to give birth to redemption while being subjected to futility. Similarly, a preacher could share different scenarios of communities that have not only been "subjected to the futility" of pollution, toxic waste, or climate catastrophes but also witnessing the "first fruits of the Spirit" through things such as ecological restoration and environmental justice.
- *Sermon–dialogue–sermon process.* For the first sermon in this process, you could invite people to think about the places in nature

they love that are "groaning" due to human activity. This sermon would make the case that the Bible invites us into dialogue about the church's role in protecting and preserving God's good Creation so that life can thrive. For the dialogue, consider using the National Issues Forum Institute's issue guide, "Climate Choices: How Should We Meet the Challenges of a Warming Planet?"[6] During the dialogue, take note of the different stories people tell, the values that they find they have in common, and what next steps they identify for protecting God's Creation. For the follow-up sermon, use vibrant words to describe the dialogue as well as the insights and wisdom that emerged from the group as a shared vision of putting the congregation's faith into action on climate change or a local environmental issue.

- *History, mission, future.* For this strategy, the sermon's introduction could begin with reminding the listeners that they have been "revealed as the children of God" through their ministries of care in the past. Then, using an expository format, the preacher could go verse by verse explaining the text and how it supports promoting care for the planet. The conclusion of the sermon would cast a vision for what God is doing to restore Creation, sustain the health of their community, and enjoy the blessings of nature's beauty and sustenance. The preacher could issue an invitation to take action on a local environmental issue as giving evidence that we are being revealed as the children of God. Thus, advocating for this local environmental issue is in keeping with their mission as a congregation.

The Robust Approach: Strategies for Preaching about a Social Issue in a High-Trust/Low-Stress Congregation

If you discern a high-trust/low-stress situation after completing the Assessment Tool, not only can you draw on the previous six strategies from the Gentle and Invitational approaches, you can also avail yourself of the strategies within the Robust approach. How do you know you're in such a situation? As Cressman describes it, the congregants are prepared to be "transformed more closely into Christ. These people are more receptive and spiritually flexible."[7] Such a congregation has the capacity to closely examine a social issue "with humility and curiosity," she says. "Secure in their identity as a child of God, they're ready to see the wrongs they have done, and the rights left undone. They have enough spiritual and emotional trust to accept Christ's forgiveness and amend their lives."[8]

A sermon using the Robust approach can be direct about the social issue and offer concrete ways that the congregation can be transformed by the gospel and work to bring about the Realm of God. For these sermons, a deductive form can be utilized (although inductive can also work). In a deductive sermon, the preacher makes a claim at the outset and then explains why this is so throughout the sermon (as compared to an inductive sermon, where the preacher gives "clues" along the way to arrive at the claim closer to the end of the sermon). As Gardner explains, "If I am preaching to instill hope to communities battered by distressing economic and environmental issues, I will be more direct and deliberate in communicating the all-sustaining power of God, as evidenced in the text, by the power of the Holy Spirit."[9]

Gardner also recommends being intentional about "posing penetrating questions to the congregation and using two to three seconds of sacred silence for them to ponder and wrestle with the ethical concerns and tensions introduced by the text."[10] Ultimately, the sermon would call the congregation to a concrete response to the issue with suggestions for putting their faith into action.

Here are the three Robust strategies:

- *Be blunt, be bold.* Be blunt about the "bad news," or crucifixion, being caused by this issue. And also, be bold about the "good news," or resurrection, that God is calling the congregation to live into with this situation. In this type of sermon, the preacher would be comfortable naming names, calling out specific harmful actions, and using stronger language in our moral vocabulary. But such a sermon can't just preach "law" about that which crucifies; it must also clearly and courageously proclaim the gospel, that which gives evidence of God's resurrection. Casting a vision of what is possible by telling stories of people and institutions that *have* changed allows theological imagination to take hold in

listeners so that they can actualize the gospel in their own lives and communities.
- *Collaborate before, during, after.* For this strategy, the preacher works collaboratively with members of a congregation on the sermon process. The preacher gathers a group of individuals who covenant with each other to listen deeply to lived experiences of those affected by the issue, think critically about the challenges of addressing the issue, and work creatively to craft a collaborative sermon that engages the congregation. In this process, they would explore different ways to activate moral and theological responses around a particular social issue. The group can host a feedback session with the congregation following the sermon to listen to what they heard, how they felt, what they learned, and what they might do in response to the issue moving forward. This process allows congregants to see that they have a stake in the endeavor and a say in the preaching process. In turn, they can put their faith into action for the good of their church and community.
- *Equip for justice.* This strategy is about equipping your congregation to be catalyzers for justice and "repairers of the breach" (Isaiah 58:12). This sermon makes it a point to cast a vision by calling for actions that catalyze the work of restoration and healing as well as advocating for changes in public policies and behaviors. In other words, the preacher encourages both "upstream" and "downstream" solutions to the social issue under consideration. Such a sermon urges listeners to bring about God's justice and mercy in relationships and society. This type of sermon can model what this looks like through narrative, role-play, scripted drama, and many other innovative ways for activating theological imagination. Using creativity can spark listeners to engage in the work of God's Realm in their families, schools, workplaces, and other secular circles.

Exercise: Robust Approach for Addressing Gun Violence Using Matthew 26:47-56

This is an exercise to give you a chance to try one of the strategies in the Robust approach. For this exercise, we'll look at the topic of gun

Gentle, Invitational, and Robust ~ 73

violence and bring it into conversation with Matthew 26:47-56 using each of the three strategies. Here is the passage:

> While he was still speaking, Judas, one of the twelve, arrived; with him was a large crowd with swords and clubs, from the chief priests and the elders of the people. Now the betrayer had given them a sign, saying, "The one I will kiss is the man; arrest him." At once he came up to Jesus and said, "Greetings, Rabbi!" and kissed him. Jesus said to him, "Friend, do what you are here to do." Then they came and laid hands on Jesus and arrested him. Suddenly, one of those with Jesus put his hand on his sword, drew it, and struck the slave of the high priest, cutting off his ear. Then Jesus said to him, "Put your sword back into its place; for all who take the sword will perish by the sword. Do you think that I cannot appeal to my Father, and he will at once send me more than twelve legions of angels? But how then would the scriptures be fulfilled, which say it must happen in this way?" At that hour Jesus said to the crowds, "Have you come out with swords and clubs to arrest me as though I were a bandit? Day after day I sat in the temple teaching, and you did not arrest me. But all this has taken place, so that the scriptures of the prophets may be fulfilled." Then all the disciples deserted him and fled. (Matthew 26:47-56)

- *Be blunt, be bold.* For this approach, you could begin by sharing statistics about the number of people who have died or been injured. Then, a move to the passage could show the way Jesus challenges the myth of power through violence, which tried to seduce the Christian community of Matthew's time and still tempts us today. Then, the preacher would proclaim the power of nonviolence as demonstrated by Jesus' restraint and refusal to continue the cycle of violence. The preacher would proclaim that the resurrection is the ultimate repudiation of the myth of power through violence. The sermon could end with a call to action, such as participating in a vigil for peace, community dialogues about addressing police brutality toward people of color, or meetings with state legislators asking for changes in state and federal gun laws.
- *Collaborate before, during, after.* In this strategy, the preacher could work with a team of people to discuss the meaning and application of Matthew 26:47-56. What is Jesus saying about who

he is and what he will do? What implications does this have for the church's conversations around gun violence? As you work with them to activate moral and theological imagination, listen deeply to the stories of those who have lost loved ones to gun violence or who have suffered from gunshot wounds. Then, work with your team to creatively craft a collaborative sermon. It could engage the congregation by telling these stories of gun violence along with what they discern as a gospel-centered response to this issue. The group can then host a feedback session over a meal after the service to listen to what they heard, how they felt, what they learned, and what they might do to respond to Jesus' command to put away our weapons.

- *Equip for justice.* This sermon could explore how other churches have taken seriously Jesus' teaching on nonviolence by becoming centers for peace and reconciliation. Using vibrant words and stories can activate the theological imagination of the congregation so that they can envision themselves engaging the work of God's Realm by participating in advocacy and activism for peace. The sermon could conclude with an invitation to a participate in training for nonviolence.

Tips and Advice for Preparing to Preach on Social Issues

In the chapters that follow, I'll provide ethical, biblical, theological, and homiletical guidance for sermons and social issues. But at this point, I want to give you some pointers to help you prepare for such a sermon spiritually, relationally, and pragmatically.

Spiritual and Relational Preparation

There are many qualities preachers can cultivate within themselves to enhance the effectiveness of their sermons that address social issues. Here, I'll focus on just four: humility, prayerful listening, trust, and integrity. *Humility* means inhabiting a posture of *kenosis* (Phil. 2:7), self-emptying one's ego to speak to the issue, even when you are firm in your convictions and bold in your proclamation. This humility allows us to engage in *prayerful listening* for the "pain points" surrounding an issue while also lifting up hope. Sermons that address social issues always come with some level of pain. Giving voice to that pain so that the invisible ones are seen, the voiceless are heard, and the immobile are given motion is necessary. Gardner encourages "listening and hearing people's fears then leading them into the redemptive truths from the Word of God."[11] This means proclaiming hope even in the midst of pain. Gardner suggests asking these questions during the sermon preparation: "What is the hope of Christ concerning this social crisis? How does the Word of God speak to this crisis by offering hope?"[12]

Thus, humility and prayerful listening are multidirectional, moving toward and from the congregation, our communities and the larger society, the Earth and our Earth kin, those who suffer, and God. All of this allows the preacher to establish *trust*. Having a high level of trust results from the pastor's living through crises with the congregation as well as the day-to-day, week-to-week, season-to-season experiences of people's lives. The baptisms, first communions, youth mission trips, committee meetings, Sunday school classes, Vacation Bible Schools, hospital bedsides, funeral gravesides—all of these comprise the incarnational aspect of ministry. Building trust is about putting flesh on the bones and getting calluses on the hands, blisters on the feet, sweat on the brow, and tears in the eyes with your people.

Integrity is about acting in alignment with one's beliefs and having those beliefs support one's actions. Integrity involves honesty, forthrightness, and sincerity. The opposites of those qualities are corruption, lying, being disingenuous, and exhibiting hypocrisy—all things that every preacher should avoid, especially those who address social issues. Gardner states that social crisis preaching requires that a minister approach Scripture with "exegetical, hermeneutical, and homiletical integrity."[13] He has found that "when preachers confront sensitive issues, even if people disagree, they return another Sunday to listen to another sermon, because they sense sincerity, honesty, and respect, even in messages that confront their long-held beliefs."[14] Throughout this book, we will be talking about how to ensure that your moral character and actions—as well as those of your congregation—come closer to the biblical witness of righteousness and justice, grace, community, reconciliation, and healing.

SPIRITUAL PRACTICES TO CULTIVATE HUMILITY AND INTEGRITY FOR PREACHERS ADDRESSING SOCIAL ISSUES

- Read books, attend talks, engage media, and watch television shows and movies about those outside of your demographic enclave and by creators who differ from you along the lines of race, culture, gender, and religion.
- To help rewire your discomfort around difference, seek out conversations with the people you are told to fear so that you can begin to build bridges of trust.
- Look for opportunities to meet with, listen to, and work alongside religious minorities, immigrants, and secular Americans.
- Put yourself in proximity to those who are different from your family of origin and, if your congregation is homogeneous, your church as well. You can do this through attending community events, volunteering, and availing yourself of service opportunities that expand your circle of social interactions.
- Learn what it is like to navigate spaces where you are in the minority, whether this is in terms of race, language, culture, sexual orientation, socioeconomic status, religion, or ability.
- If you are usually a person who asserts yourself in certain situations, become more comfortable with not having to be in control, take up space, claim your presence, or be the first (or loudest) to speak.
- If you usually occupy a place of privilege, practice habits that cultivate humility. Learn a new language. Let others call the shots. Listen and learn. Pay attention to the aha moments.
- When building relationships with others who are different from you, ask them, "What is it like to be you in this place?" And then listen without interrupting.[15]

Pragmatic Preparation

As you are reflecting on preaching about a topic of public concern, there are many practicalities to keep in mind. First, consider the degree and depth the congregation has been involved in the social issue. If the issue is new to them (at least in the context of formal teaching and preaching), then the Gentle and Invitational approaches are probably best. But if the congregation has a strong civic engagement, such as involvement in food justice, voter registration, interfaith dialogue, or policy advocacy, they are more likely ready for a Robust sermon strategy. Also, congregations that see social involvement as part of their discipleship and an expression of their spiritual development are often well suited for Robust sermons.

Another aspect to consider is that of *timing* and *proximity*. For example, Gardner encourages preachers to think about "how close the crisis is to the congregation, their loved ones, and the community where the church exists. How is the crisis affecting the congregation emotionally, mentally, and financially? How is it affecting their family structure? Is the congregation constantly dealing with or confronted with a social crisis daily, weekly, or monthly? Is it a recurring issue?"[16] If the situation is truly a crisis and one that has garnered national or international attention, he warns that "too long of a delay, or altogether avoiding the topic, will cause members to view the pastor as insensitive."[17]

Gardner points out that "[t]he time is always right to preach a word of hope when there is an immediate, well-known, and widespread crisis."[18] For example, catastrophic weather events, gun violence, or a local hate crime call for sermons that "focus on unity, hope, strength in Christ, the sovereignty of God, and faith [that] can accomplish much to galvanize congregations and strengthen individuals," says Gardner.[19]

To illustrate the importance of timing, a pastoral colleague of mine in Kentucky, Stephanie Moon, knew that she needed to address the opioid crisis in her community,[20] but she was hesitant at first because she knew that the stigma and shame of those affected by drug addiction might make her congregation reticent to talk about the issue. However, when she learned that three people in their community had died from overdoses in the first part of the year, she decided to use the sermon–dialogue–sermon strategy and preached a Lenten sermon series to accompany five weekly discussions. As it turned out, there was a drug roundup in their town during the series, so the timing of the sermons and dialogue enabled the congregation to process what was happening and how their church could respond.

Thus, as Thompson reminds us, "Preaching the headlines isn't about preaching the headlines at all. It's about determining what matters most and why it matters, and then, proclaiming out of that conviction for the sake of living according to those convictions. Hoping against hope, these convictions entail believing that something of a more just world is desperately needed and possible."[21]

If you are new to a congregation or to addressing social issues in a sermon or it's the first time you will be addressing a certain topic with the congregation, it's wise to take some preparatory steps before preaching about it. Following are some things you can do to "till the soil" to prepare your congregation for sermons that address a social topic.

1. *Have a preparatory conversation with your congregation's leadership group (e.g., board, council, and elders) before preaching the sermon.* To be clear, you would not be asking for their *permission* to address the topic but, instead, asking for their perspectives and input. Alerting key leadership that you'll be addressing a sensitive topic helps to prepare them so that they are not caught off guard if people come to them with pushback or complaints.
2. *Consider talking to folks in the congregation ahead of time whom you suspect may react negatively to a sermon you will preach.* This is being "wise as serpents and gentle as doves" (Matthew 10:16). Again, as with your governing board, you would not be asking for their *permission* to address the topic. Instead, you would be seeking their insights to help you better understand different perspectives. When people know they have been listened to ahead of time, they have a stake in the sermon and may be less likely to have a negative reaction.
3. *Talk with clergy colleagues or your mentor about your sermon.* Test-drive your ideas with them and ask them to make suggestions. Seeking advice from trusted colleagues can keep us honest, give us courage, and help us avoid unnecessary pitfalls.

Overall, having conversations with some key people, laying groundwork with teaching, and simply listening deeply to people's concerns about the issues that are affecting their lives can provide entry points for addressing contemporary issues. As Thompson reminds us, there are key questions we should be asking in these conversations: "What does it mean to be human? How do we live with integrity? How ought we interact with others, especially those who are different from us? And perhaps most importantly, how do we seek God's presence, guidance, and hopes in the midst of it all?"[22]

Conclusion: Speak the Truth in Love

Tisdale stresses how important it is to genuinely care about the people to whom you are preaching a prophetic message. "If prophetic preaching is born out of thinly disguised anger at a congregation, out of frustration with a congregation, or out of a desire to appear loving so that the message will be heard and accepted, people will know it. We cannot fake love in the pulpit."[23] However, she says, "if the message we bring is genuinely born out of love—a love regularly practiced even for the most recalcitrant of sinners—hearts may be opened to the prophetic message of the gospel in ways we cannot even begin to imagine or anticipate."[24]

To clarify, love is not always a warm, fuzzy feeling we have in our hearts toward our congregations. Rather, it is the spiritual discipline of actions and attitudes born out of compassion, empathy, and a genuine willingness to care—even when we don't feel like it. This love is sustained by the infinite nature of the divine love that we preach week in and week out in trust and hope that both we and our congregations will be continually shaped and transformed by this compassion, empathy, and care.

In whatever preaching context you find yourself—high, medium, or low stress—we must always preach in a way that proclaims who God is, what God has done and is doing now, and what this means for our lives in community today. Lift up the "big questions" that underlie the headlines or controversies. Acknowledge the complexities of individual human sin, as well as systemic evil, then frame these questions biblically and theologically. Be fair and avoid creating "straw men" or taking cheap shots against those whom you believe to be on the "wrong" side of an issue. Through empathy, authenticity, and rhetorical tactics that engage with different perspectives, preachers can help listeners encounter the gospel that will, through God's transformative power, be life giving, hope building, and world changing.

Figure 4.1 Three Approaches, Nine Strategies for a Sermon Addressing Social Issues, Leah Schade, 2024

Notes

1. Lisa L. Thompson, *Preaching the Headlines: Possibilities and Pitfalls* (Minneapolis, MN: Fortress Press, 2021),8.

2. Just one example of using exegesis to make connections between the biblical world and our own contemporary situation could include nearly the entire book of Acts, where the nascent Christian community was navigating how to share their resources (2:43-47, 4:32-37, 5:1-11), who should be fed and who should distribute the food (6:1-7), how they dealt with violence and persecution (the stories of Stephen and Saul in chapters 6–9), and who was permitted to be part of the church and what would be required of them (chapters 10–11). In chapter 6, we'll engage with several biblical scholars around more social issues.

3. Leonora Tubbs Tisdale, *Prophetic Preaching: A Pastoral Approach* (Louisville, KY: Westminster John Knox Press, 2010), 49, quoted in Walter Brueggemann, "The Preacher, the Text and the People," *Theology Today* 47 (October 1990): 237–47.

4. Tyshawn Gardner, *Social Crisis Preaching: Biblical Proclamation in Troubling Times* (Brentwood, TN: B&H Publishing, 2023), 111.

5. Deliberative dialogue was developed by the Kettering Foundation, founded in 1927 by Charles F. Kettering. The nonprofit, nonpartisan research foundation trades insights from its research with a broad network of institutions, organizations, and individuals from over eighty countries. The foundation focuses on basic political research, striving to understand how citizens and political systems can work together. Since the early 1990s, the foundation has researched how democracy can be strengthened. The foundation's primary research question is, what does it take to make democracy work as it should?

6. National Issues Forum Institute, "Climate Choices: How Should We Meet the Challenges of a Warming Planet?," accessed May 23, 2024, https://www.nifi.org/en/issue-guide/climate-choices.

7. Lisa Cressman, *The Gospel People Don't Want to Hear: Preaching Challenging Messages* (Minneapolis, MN: Fortress, 2020), 53.

8. Cressman, 53.

9. Gardner, *Social Crisis Preaching*, 111.

10. Gardner, 112.

11. Gardner, 19.

12. Gardner, 123.

13. Gardner, 21.

14. Gardner, 122.

15. This list is adapted and paraphrased from suggestions that Andrew L. Whitehead gives for addressing Christian nationalism in his book *American Idolatry: How Christian Nationalism Betrays the Gospel and Threatens the Church* (Grand Rapids, MI: Brazos Press, 2023),100–102, and includes suggestions of my own as well.

16. Gardner, 133.

17. Gardner, 135.

18. Gardner, 135.

19. Gardner, 135.

20. Moon's story is shared with her permission. See Leah D. Schade, "The Power of Preaching and Deliberative Dialogue to Catalyze Congregational Social Action: A Case Study from 'The Purple Zone,' *Religions*, forthcoming.

21. Thompson, *Preaching the Headlines*, 117.

22. Thompson, 6.

23. Tisdale, *Prophetic Preaching*, 43.

24. Tisdale, 43.

CHAPTER 5

Ethical Foundations for Preaching and Social Issues

In this chapter, I have in mind one particular biblical passage from Paul's Second Letter to the Corinthians that sets the tone for my approach to Christian preaching about social issues:

> All this is from God, who reconciled us to himself through Christ, and has given us the ministry of reconciliation; that is, in Christ God was reconciling the world to himself, not counting their trespasses against them, and entrusting the message of reconciliation to us. So we are ambassadors for Christ, since God is making his appeal through us; we entreat you on behalf of Christ, be reconciled to God (2 Corinthians 5:18-20).

In this letter, Paul was writing to the church in Corinth, which was struggling with internal discord exacerbated by leaders who were stirring up dissent and causing people to doubt Paul's leadership. In response, Paul gives a theological basis for reconciliation as he tries to repair his own relationship with the Corinthian church while also instructing them how to live as believers in Christ in a society that held very different values. For Paul, Christ's death and resurrection effected a healing in the brokenness of humanity that Christians must extend to each other and the world. Thus, being ambassadors of this reconciliation is a role entrusted to us as part of our Christian vocation.

To illustrate why this ministry of reconciliation is necessary today, I'll begin with a snapshot of what the current state of polarization and divisiveness looks like in the United States as described in an article by David Brooks. Then, we will move toward an ethic of reconciliation and ambassadorship by turning to homiletician Frank A. Thomas's work on how to preach—and survive—a "dangerous sermon." I will explain what Thomas means by a "dangerous sermon," outline what he identifies as the different "working gospels" in the United States, and summarize the two moral worldviews—conservative and progressive—which he sees as prevalent in this country. However, I will push us to look deeper beneath the two worldviews. Drawing on social psychologist Jonathan Haidt's work on moral foundations, we will see that there are, in fact, six matrices that can be combined in different ways to describe people's views on social issues. These matrices inform, shape, and are utilized by conservatives and progressives in various ways and to different degrees to determine what they see as right and wrong. By understanding these foundations, preachers wanting to address social issues can construct bridges of understanding to find common ground and shared values.

You may wonder why I'm starting with ethical frameworks rather than with the Bible and theology. The reason is because I believe moral worldviews and ethical foundations are independent of and undergird the ways in which Scripture is interpreted and conceptions of the divine are constructed. Naturally, there is an age-old chicken-and-egg debate over whether religion grew out of ethics or ethics was spawned by religion. While both Haidt and Thomas work with the assumption that they wrap around each other in complex ways, their consensus is that moral intuitions preceded religion. Thus, we will better understand how a preacher can approach social issues by first understanding some basic moral and ethical foundations.

The Loss of a Moral Center and the Need for Moral Formation

In a 2023 article for *The Atlantic*, David Brooks described the current state of America's "meanness" and what he believes has led to a culture that is morally deficient and devoid of the ethical foundations that enable a society to thrive. He observed the following:

> I was recently talking with a restaurant owner who said that he has to eject a customer from his restaurant for rude or cruel behavior once a week—something that never used to happen. A head nurse at a hospital

told me that many on her staff are leaving the profession because patients have become so abusive. At the far extreme of meanness, hate crimes rose in 2020 to their highest level in 12 years. Murder rates have been surging, at least until recently. Same with gun sales. Social trust is plummeting. In 2000, two-thirds of American households gave to charity; in 2018, fewer than half did.[1]

Other professions are also dealing with rude and cruel behavior that would have been unheard of even a generation ago. Some public school teachers have been vilified for teaching students to be compassionate and accepting of difference. Election workers are dishonestly accused of manipulating vote counts, which results in their being attacked or doxed (personal information revealed on the internet). Librarians are targeted with book banning campaigns. University professors in some states are prevented from teaching about the history of racism in the United States. And in the church, clergy are sometimes bullied, threatened, or fired simply for preaching that the love of God should extend to all people regardless of their skin color, sexual orientation, country of origin, gender, or any other markers of difference.

Brooks diagnosed this situation as a "sort of emotional, relational, and spiritual crisis" and asserts that this "undergirds our political dysfunction and the general crisis of our democracy."[2] He believes that "we inhabit a society in which people are no longer trained in how to treat others with kindness and consideration. Our society has become one in which people feel licensed to give their selfishness free rein."[3] As a result, virtues such as bravery, gratitude, and humility take a back seat to ambitions for wealth, material accumulation, power, and self-referential autonomy.

What Brooks wants to see is a revival of "moral formation"—a strengthening of the web of social institutions, such as families, schools, religious groups, community organizations, and workplaces—that can help "form people into kind and responsible citizens, the sort of people who show up for one another."[4] He suggests that moral formation should do three things: educate people on how to restrain their selfishness, teach people basic social and ethical skills, and guide people to find purpose in life and a meaningful existence. He also contends that one of the factors that contributes to people developing positive virtues and strong moral character is being part of a religious group. "Mere religious faith doesn't always make people morally good," he says, "but living in a community, orienting your heart toward some transcendent love, basing your value system on concern for the underserved—those things tend to."[5] Ultimately, what Brooks calls for is a return of moral formation across all sectors of society to cultivate "a community of common values, whose members aspire to earn one another's respect."[6]

However, as many pastors can attest, agreeing on what those "common values" are in a society or even in a congregation can be difficult. There are different and competing sets of values among those who align with certain political ideologies that determine how believers interpret the Bible, what aspects of God they believe in, and how they act in the world accordingly. As a result, it can seem like people are talking past each other when it comes to conversations about moral and ethical discernment. This can lead to feelings of being misheard, misunderstood, and disrespected. All of this can then escalate into actions such as shunning, sniping at, or silencing the very people with whom we are called to be in Christian communion.

To help us understand the sources of our competing values and resulting divisions, we'll sit at the feet of renowned African American homiletician Frank A. Thomas for guidance on how to bring moral imagination to the fractured state of America. Then, we'll turn to Jonathan Haidt, a social psychologist who developed a framework for understanding the complex ways in which people decide what is right and wrong. I believe that preachers can utilize both Thomas's and Haidt's frameworks in their engagement with social issues to better understand themselves and their congregants. In turn, they can more effectively communicate across political differences when preaching sermons about social issues.

Frank A. Thomas—Moral Worldviews and Working Gospels

Let's begin with what Thomas means by a "dangerous sermon." A dangerous sermon is one that "challenges unjust moral orders and dominance hierarchies and the resulting misallocation of freedom, resources, assets, and legitimacy."[7] Such a sermon "disrupts the legitimacy of the oppressive moral order that operates smoothly, efficiently, and often silently in the economic, political, cultural, and religious structures of a given society."[8] Thomas says that a dangerous sermon requires preachers to have "moral imagination," enabling them to empathize with those who are not seen as equal in a society, whether they are individuals or subgroups.[9] He would likely agree with Brooks that Americans on the whole have demonstrated a lack of empathy toward each other and that the church must step up its work of forming the moral imagination of believers.

Is every sermon that addresses social issues "dangerous"? That depends on whether it challenges the dominant social order and hierarchy by preaching the gospel. A sermon that speaks in support of the social order imposed by the ones in power might be addressing a social issue, but it would not be considered "dangerous"; rather, it would provide either implicit or explicit assent to the power structure. So how do we determine what the social order is? And what do we mean by the word *gospel*? Let's start with the first question.

The Two Moral Worldviews
Building on the work of distinguished professor of cognitive science and linguistics, George Lakoff, Thomas works with the premise that there are two "family-based" moralities that in broad terms, result in two moral worldviews.[10] There are, in essence, "two distinct moral imaginations operating in American culture: the 'Strict Father morality' of conservatives and the 'Nurturant Parent morality' of progressives."[11] Not only do these worldviews have different ideas about what the social order should be, but their tug-and-pull struggle shapes much of what our social order is. Granted, dividing the world into two camps is part of the very problem we have in our bifurcated body politic. However, what Lakoff, and thus Thomas, are attempting to do is *descriptive* rather than *prescriptive*. In other words, if we desire to restructure the social order according to a nonbinary paradigm, we must first try to describe and understand what that paradigm currently is and why it has such a hold on our political rhetoric.

Strict Father Worldview
Those who adhere to the Strict Father morality tend to be law-abiding, disciplined conservatives who support things such as a strong military

and a strict criminal justice system. They are usually opposed to government regulation of business as well as government-mandated social programs. At the core of this worldview is a negative anthropology, a belief that humans are basically bad (sinful) and must be kept in line with a strong-willed, strong-armed leader.

The Strict Father paradigm is hierarchical, with God at the top and humans just below ruling over nature. Also in this paradigm, Western culture rules over non-Western culture, and the United States rules over other countries. Within social relationships, men are over women, Whites are over people of color, straights are over gays, adults rule over children, the rich rule over the poor, and Christians rule over non-Christians.[12] Questioning the social order is frowned upon because authority must rest with the ones whom God has ordained to be on top.

For those who adhere to the Strict Father morality, social ills are blamed either on the individual for their lack of discipline and hard work or on government for enabling individual immorality. According to this worldview, "Blaming social and societal factors, such as background, upbringing, or neighborhood, is nothing but making excuses for moral failure."[13] Many in this worldview also hold that it is sometimes necessary to use force and even violence to maintain social order.

To those who do not adhere to the Strict Father paradigm, this position may sound harsh and lack compassion. However, adherents are usually nurturing and compassionate to people who they consider to be part of their community, whether that is their family, neighborhood, church, social club, or business. Yet they do not want their compassion and generosity to be mandated by the government. They want the freedom to choose those with whom they want to be compassionate and to determine how much they are willing to give or help.

Nurturant Parent Worldview

Those who are oriented toward the Nurturant Parent worldview are progressives who value empathy and compassion. They want to see military spending reduced and directed to social programming that benefits the whole of society. They support regulation of corporations and believe that the government exists to ensure fairness and protection of those most vulnerable. At the core of this worldview is a positive anthropology, a belief that humans are basically good and can flourish together with mutual care, respect, equity, and well-being.

The Nurturant Parent paradigm is more like an interconnected web where God works in and through mutual relationships of care while guarding against the exploitation of the weak and disadvantaged. Questions and curiosity are welcomed, and everyone is encouraged to participate in making important decisions. In this paradigm, nature is not seen as separate and below humans; rather, humans are part of the web of life and have the responsibility to ensure its health and vitality for all living beings.

For those who adhere to the Nurturant Parent morality, social ills are blamed on social and systemic factors that result in an unequal playing field and unfair advantages for some. Many in this worldview abhor violence and believe that loving, mutual interactions with children—not corporal punishment, dominance, or fear—produce responsible, productive adults. Their belief is that violence only results in more violence.

To those who do not adhere to the Nurturant Parent paradigm, this position may sound undisciplined and lack personal responsibility. However, adherents are generally hardworking and do not like to see people take advantage of the system or their own goodwill. They resent soulless companies and social systems that care only about power and wealth. Consequently, they want the government to ensure that guardrails are in place against corruption, pollution of the environment, exploitation of workers, and militarized police. They want all people to have equal freedoms, rights, and access to what is necessary to thrive, including health care, public education, and the arts.

GENTLE, INVITATIONAL, AND ROBUST SERMON APPROACHES INFORMED BY THE TWO MORAL WORLDVIEWS

Understanding the two moral worldviews can inform sermon strategies in the Gentle, Invitational, and Robust sermon approaches. Here are some examples.

- *The Gentle Approach – Share your own struggles with the issue.* A preacher could summarize the two worldviews and indicate where they locate themselves, but also say that they can relate to and agree with certain aspects of the other worldview. The preacher would convey with authenticity how they have wrestled with the different worldviews and where they see God at work in that wrestling. The theme of the sermon could be "Seeing Both Sides," rooted in the story in Acts 17:22-34 of Paul at the Areopagus. He was appealing to the common values of religiosity, love for poetry, and respect for divine mystery that he recognized in the Athenians, even as he sought to share his faith in the resurrection of Jesus Christ.
- *The Invitational Approach – Telling stories to create empathy.* The preacher could open the sermon with an example from the Braver Angels organization where people from two different worldviews engage in a discussion about a social issue and how they are able to respectfully listen to each other, find points of common agreement, and work together on a local issue across party lines.[14] The preacher could then suggest that their own congregation could be a site of this kind of "holy conversation" by offering training for dialogue moderators and hosting a community discussion on an issue.[15] The theme of the sermon could be "Under the Oak Tree," rooted in the Genesis 18:1-15 story of Abraham's hospitably welcoming strangers who turned out to be angels in disguise.
- *The Robust Approach – Equipping for justice.* A pastor preparing their church to become involved in a new project to help the community, such as Habitat for Humanity, a refugee resettlement effort, or a local women's shelter, would do well to explain the two moral worldviews so that parishioners understand the different perspectives they may encounter with the people they serve or with their fellow volunteers. The theme of the sermon could be "Ambassadors for Christ," rooted in 2 Cor. 5:16-21. It could include a role play between two people with different worldviews, pausing at key moments to highlight the values being articulated and suggest practical ways to live out Paul's "ministry of ambassadorship" in the situation.

Working Gospels

How do the moral worldviews relate to the gospel? That depends on what people mean when they use the term *gospel*. In his book, *Surviving a Dangerous Sermon*, Thomas draws on the work of homiletician André Resner to explain that there are several working gospels functioning within American religious discourse.[16] He lists seven in all:

- American sentimentalism—American civil religion often evoked during times of national crisis and tragedy or at large national events
- American exceptionalism—belief in the divine mission of America as God's chosen nation
- Prosperity Gospel—equates God's blessings with individual health, wealth, and success (while downplaying social critique)
- Denominational affiliation—the codified historical theological tenets and beliefs of individuals whose works, writing, and sermons founded a denomination
- Evangelicalism—characterized by a belief that the Bible has the highest authority, Jesus Christ's death on the cross is the only sacrifice that gives salvation, a Christian is compelled to encourage people to accept Jesus Christ as their Lord and personal Savior, and only those who trust in Jesus Christ as their Savior can receive God's free gift of eternal salvation
- Social justice—the application of Christian ethics to social concerns such as economic inequality, poverty, racism, environment, and equal rights for women and LGBTQIA+
- Identity politics—the use and application of ethnicity, gender, race, culture, ability, or social location as an interpretive lens for Scripture and theology[17]

Thomas advises that before addressing the challenges of social issues, preachers must understand what their working gospels are and which ones are in play in their congregation. "Every preacher has a constellation of culture, a family of origin, and ecclesiastical systems that influence, raise, and develop us from the earliest stages of life."[18]

This means that "preachers can read the same Bible and texts yet witness to different working gospels."[19] For example, Thomas notes that his working gospels are twofold: social justice and, as a Black man, identity politics. For my part, I also preach from the working gospel of social justice. And my working gospel of identity politics comes from my social location as a White female. But I was also formed in the working gospel of denominational affiliation as a Lutheran, and this has had a strong influence on my interpretation of Scripture as well as my theological template.

Once a preacher can see the moral worldview and working gospels from which they are preaching and can assess those in their congregation, they can develop "moral dexterity," which can speak in a nuanced way to issues of public concern. Such an approach increases the chances that the sermon can be heard by people of different moral persuasions and bring people together "by inspiring wonder, mystery, and hope."[20] However, this is a complicated process.

The Complicated Relationship between Working Gospels and Moral Worldviews

How do the working gospels relate to the two moral worldviews that Thomas sees as holding sway in America? "Family-based morality precedes morality based upon religion," Thomas explains.[21] "Conservative Christians have a metaphorical interpretation of the Bible, and it happens to be the Strict Father morality, and they apply that interpretation to their politics. Similarly, liberal Christians have a Nurturant Parent interpretation of the Bible, and they apply that interpretation to their politics as well."[22]

Thus, the Strict Father worldview meshes well with the working gospels of American sentimentalism and American exceptionalism because they both position America over and against other countries and against any citizens who may question the nation's divine appointment. The working gospel of prosperity also supports the Strict Father worldview in that individual success is a sign of one's discipline, moral rectitude, and hard work and is deserving of divine blessing. The working gospel of traditional Evangelicals also mirrors the Strict Father worldview with its insistence on the authority of the Bible, the supremacy of Jesus Christ, the mandate for conversion to Christianity, and the punishment of hell for all who do not follow the rules and support the divine order.

The working gospel of denominational affiliation can go either way when it comes to the moral worldviews. A denomination can align with the Strict Father worldview when the codified historical tenets and beliefs of the founder support a hierarchical paradigm. However, there are also progressive expressions of each of these denominations that organize their theology and ecclesiology around the Nurturant Parent worldview. They, too, point to the writings, teachings, and sermons of their founders to support a progressive paradigm.

Some may assume that the working gospel of social justice always aligns with the Nurturant Parent worldview. However, historically, the temperance movement utilized a Strict Father paradigm, emphasizing the need for individuals with strong morals while also pushing for the government to outlaw alcohol. Similarly, pro-slavery believers (who were certainly hierarchical in their worldview) were countered with a Strict Father ethic from the abolitionist movement, which pointed to God's authority in endowing all people with freedom and pushing for ending the slave laws that offended the very character of God. Thomas also notes that identity politics "does not have a negative connotation," even though it is a term used to criticize minorities "motivated by an irrational herd instinct to take political and religious positions based on the interests and perspectives of social groups with which they identify."[23] He points out that "white people have utilized identity politics since their arrival upon American soil," providing the rationale for conquest, slavery, and segregation.[24]

Thus, we can see that the relationship between the different working gospels and the two moral worldviews is complicated and not easily compartmentalized nor neatly aligned. Yet Thomas reminds us that if we're going to preach a dangerous sermon, we have to think about how to construct arguments that build a bridge to others with a different worldview.[25] His assertion is that "it is helpful in surviving dangerous sermons if the preacher has an understanding of and can communicate with both moral orders, based upon the likelihood that in most churches both moral orders are in the audience."[26] Thomas says that this kind of work requires nuance, which he defines as "the awareness of or ability to express delicate shadings of meaning, feeling, or value."[27]

Here, I want to pause on this concept of nuance in regard to the two moral orders. The bifurcation of Strict Father and Nurturing Parent, while descriptive and resonant with many people's experiences, invites us to look deeper to discover what might be undergirding the conservative and progressive worldviews. This can assist preachers in crafting sermons with the kind of nuance Thomas calls for. It is with this goal of nuance in mind that we move to Jonathan Haidt's research on moral foundations theory.

Jonathan Haidt: Understanding Morality, Politics, and Religion

Jonathan Haidt has conducted extensive research about moral psychology spanning cultures across the globe. He has come to the conclusion that there is no singular, universal moral code that people use for determining right and wrong. In his book *The Righteous Mind: Why Good People Are Divided by Politics and Religion*, he examined morality in different countries and contexts and found that Western, educated, and individualistic cultures have a narrow moral domain compared to other worldviews. In contrast, "Sociocentric cultures broaden the moral domain to encompass and regulate more aspects of life."[28] He also discovered that gut feelings, especially about disgust and disrespect, can have more to do with determining right and wrong than pure intellectual reasoning. Thus, ethics sometimes functions as a justification of these feelings. Complicating matters is that the things that constitute these feelings of disgust or disrespect are not always innate. Sometimes they are imbued by one's culture (i.e., the disgust Westerners have about the idea of eating certain animals is not shared by all cultures). Thus, he explained that "moral diversity" is the reality across the human social landscape.

Haidt's research demonstrates that people's *moral intuitions* have more sway than their *intellectual reasoning*, much like the rider of an elephant (reason) has only so much power over the elephant itself (emotions and gut reactions). Yet "intuitions can be shaped by reasoning, especially when reasons are embedded in friendly conversation or an emotionally compelling novel, movie, or news story."[29] And, as a homiletician, I would add that a sermon can be one of those vehicles that help shape moral intuitions, especially when they, too, are embedded in friendly conversation and contain emotionally compelling components, such as evocative imagery and storytelling.

Humans Are "Groupish"

Moral reasoning does not take place in a vacuum. Research shows that people are very concerned about what others think of them and desire to please and receive approval from their group, whether that is a family, school clique, congregation, or political faction. Humans are "groupish," which means that an individual's moral reasoning may be more of a rationalization to maintain one's place in the group. This explains, for example, why someone may justify lying, cheating, or using violence—as long as it serves the ends of the group. "We deploy our reasoning skills to support our team, and to demonstrate commitment to our team," Haidt explains.[30]

Here, we can see an overlap with the working gospels theory from Thomas. Each of the working gospels is both shaped by and contributes to the two moral orders. And people will defend themselves and their actions as they relate to the group to which they belong—whether that is determined by the conservative or progressive dichotomy, or by identity politics or denominational commitments, for example. Yet Haidt examined evolutionary theory and anthropological observations to determine that there is something deeper underlying the two moral orders. He found that there are six moral foundations that are innate within human beings and communities. Granted, how these moral foundations are expressed across different cultures through rules and virtues will vary. But these "taste buds of the righteous mind," as he describes them, are what inform the moral intuitions for determining right and wrong.[31]

The Six Moral Foundations

To categorize these moral intuitions, Haidt created a "map of moral space." We'll see how this map can assist preachers with identifying the values that drive people's choices in ethical dilemmas. The map can, in turn, be useful in framing sermons addressing social issues in a spirit of being an ambassador of God's reconciliation (Figure 5.1).

Haidt provides a concise summary of each of the moral foundations, which I quote in full here:

- The *Care/harm* foundation evolved in response to the adaptive challenge of caring for vulnerable children. It makes us sensitive

Figure 5.1   Haidt's 6 Moral Foundations. Jonathan Haidt, *The Righteous Mind: Why Good People are Divided by Politics and Religion* (New York: Vintage Books, 2012). Graphic created by Leah D. Schade.

to signs of suffering and need; it makes us despise cruelty and want to care for those who are suffering.

- The *Fairness/cheating* foundation evolved in response to the adaptive challenge of reaping the rewards of cooperation without getting exploited. It makes us sensitive to indications that another person is likely to be a good (or bad) partner for collaboration and reciprocal altruism. It makes us want to shun or punish cheaters.
- The *Loyalty/betrayal* foundation evolved in response to the adaptive challenge of forming and maintaining coalitions. It makes us sensitive to signs that another person is (or is not) a team player. It makes us trust and reward such people, and it makes us want to hurt, ostracize, or even kill those who betray us or our group.
- The *Authority/subversion* foundation evolved in response to the adaptive challenge of forging relationships that will benefit us within social hierarchies. It makes us sensitive to signs of rank or status, and to signs that other people are (or are not) behaving properly, given their position.
- The *Sanctity/degradation* foundation evolved initially in response to the adaptive challenge . . . of living in a world of pathogens and parasites. It includes the behavioral immune system, which can make us wary of a diverse array of symbolic objects and threats. It makes it possible for people to invest objects with irrational and

extreme values—both positive and negative—which are important for binding groups together.[32]
- The *Liberty/oppression* foundation . . . makes people notice and resent any sign of attempted domination. It triggers an urge to band together to resist or overthrow bullies and tyrants. This foundation supports egalitarianism and antiauthoritarianism of the left, as well as the don't-tread-on-me and give-me-liberty antigovernment anger of libertarians and some conservatives.[33]

How do conservatives and progressives utilize these moral foundations? Haidt theorizes that conservatives have an advantage over progressives when it comes to connecting with people because they "trigger every single taste receptor"; in other words, their moral arguments touch on all six of the moral foundations.[34] Progressives, in contrast, tend to appeal primarily to only three: care/harm, fairness/cheating, and liberty/oppression. Also, because humans are groupish, they tend to resonate more with conservative messages around loyalty, authority, and sanctity, all of which ensure group boundaries, cohesion, and survival. Yet neither group can claim a pure moral high ground. Haidt notes that liberals are often willing to "trade away fairness (as proportionality) when it conflicts with compassion or with their desire to fight oppression," while conservatives "are more willing than liberals to sacrifice care and let some people get hurt in order to achieve their many other moral objectives."[35]

The Role of Religion and Moral Foundations
Haidt notes that precisely because humans are groupish (he also uses the term "hive creatures"[36]), religion can help them transcend the profane world and enter into moments of great joy and awe, as well as a feeling of connection with the divine and their fellow humanity. Here, Haidt utilizes the theories of the French sociologist Emile Durkheim, who studied the way in which religion functions in society to unite people through shared beliefs, practices, and sacred items and rituals. In this way, religious rituals serve to create community.

Haidt cautions, however, that this feeling of unity is often limited to those with whom we share a moral matrix. "It would be nice to believe that we humans were designed to love everyone unconditionally. Nice, but rather unlikely, from an evolutionary perspective," says Haidt. "Parochial love—love within groups—amplified by similarity, a sense of shared fate, and the suppression of free riders, may be the most we can accomplish."[37]

Also, critics of religion point to the ways in which believers can justify war, genocide, terrorism, and the oppression of women by giving such evils a cloak of divine mandate. Nevertheless, researchers have found that on the whole, people who regularly attend religious services tend to be more generous, charitable, and helpful while also enjoying feelings of belonging, altruism, and connection to a higher purpose as well as with those who share their faith.[38] In other words, relationships within religious groups can bring out the best in people.

This being the case, preaching and worship can function as a community creator, especially when congregants are encouraged to expand the boundaries of their moral community to include those whom they might otherwise view as outsiders or enemies. Thus, a preacher wanting to address social issues can expand these boundaries by utilizing the map of moral space to help build bridges of understanding between people with different working gospels and moral foundations. Ministers can be a catalyst to inspire people to care about moral challenges and people beyond themselves. They can inspire listeners to come together around shared values with people who, on the surface, may not be part of their group. But because of their shared humanity, common values, and collective dreams, they can work together to help, share, build, and restore relationships and communities.

USING MORAL FOUNDATIONS TO BRIDGE WORLDVIEWS IN SERMONS: ENVIRONMENTAL ISSUES

It may surprise some to learn that there are conservative Christians who support a strong environmental ethic, which is typically (but not exclusively) considered the purview of progressives. Preachers in these conservative Christian churches have found that the way to draw in their congregants is to utilize more than just the Care/harm foundation typically employed by progressive Christian environmentalists. Instead, they appeal to the Authority foundation with a theological claim that God created the Earth and expects humans to fulfill their role as caretakers. In this way, the hierarchical worldview encourages a religious obligation to serve God by caring for the world God has made.

The other foundation sometimes used by conservative Christians concerned with Creation care is that of Sanctity. This moral value can be seen in messages that link the pro-life ethic with a call to have pure water, air, and food for the unborn and children. The logic is that if we truly value the child in the womb, we will do everything we can to ensure that the mother can host her baby as healthily as possible. While progressives may cringe at the idea of the mother as "host," I have seen preaching such a message in conservative churches move parishioners to take action on advocating for clean air and water, including lobbying lawmakers. In other words, when preachers expand their moral palette and find ways to address social issues that make sense to people along different points of the moral spectrum, they are more likely to be met with openness instead of suspicion.

The Necessity of Building Moral Capital

All of this work of connecting with people who resonate with different moral foundations enhances "social capital"—a term that emerged in the social sciences in the 1990s and became popularized by Robert Putnam's book *Bowling Alone*.[39] Social capital refers to "the social ties among individuals and the norms of reciprocity and trustworthiness that arise from those ties."[40] They are the bonds of trust that help people get things done, enjoy each other's company, work through tensions and conflicts, and feel a sense of shared purpose.

"Everyone loves social capital," says Haidt. "Whether you're left, right, or center, who could fail to see the value of being able to trust and rely upon others?"[41] However, he notes that structures and constraints are necessary for people to behave well, cooperate, and thrive—what he calls "moral capital." Haidt defines moral capital as "the resources that sustain a moral community."[42] Further, he explains that moral capital refers to:

the degree to which a community possesses interlocking sets of values, virtues, norms, practices, identities, institutions, and technologies that mesh well with evolved psychological mechanisms and thereby enable the community to suppress or regulate selfishness and make cooperation possible.[43]

This is applicable to ministers because belief in a God who sees and punishes wrongdoing, and adherence to a faith group that teaches civility and works for the liberation of oppressed people are aspects of religion that can function to shore up moral capital. Brooks, with whom we started this chapter, would probably agree with Haidt that it takes the wholistic and multilevel commitment of a society to develop the *moral* capital that is necessary for *social* capital. Further, those societies that have the support of healthy religious communities tend to survive and thrive more often and for a longer duration than societies that do not.

Like Brooks, Haidt notes that "moral communities are fragile things, hard to build and easy to destroy."[44] What makes the survival of a moral community—especially in a huge, diverse nation such as the United States—even more precarious is the fact that people have difficulty recognizing, much less appreciating, the moral matrix of those outside of their group. Thus, he advises that liberals, conservatives, and independents work to "connect with those who live in other matrices, which are often built on different configurations of the available moral foundations."[45] He also encourages those who wade into politically fraught waters not to bring up morality "until you've found a few points of commonality or in some other way established a bit of trust. And when you bring up issues of morality, try to start with some praise, or with sincere expression of interest."[46] This is sage advice for preachers wanting to address a social issue in a politically divided congregation.

In other words, approach a conversation about morality with nuance, just as Thomas advises preachers to do when preaching a "dangerous sermon." Thomas stated that "nuanced discussions start with equanimity, patience, deliberation, multiple conversations, and persistent dialogue."[47] In the same way, the goal of a morally nuanced sermon "is to broaden an issue to make it a human issue, and not just the issue of one deficient community."[48]

Preaching Social Issues Can Help Build an Ethical Community

Returning to Brooks's assessment about the current state of moral turpitude in the United States, he recognizes that "the emphasis on morality [doesn't] produce perfect people." Granted, the ethos of moral formation can calcify into self-righteousness, rigid hierarchies, and shaming those deemed morally unfit. Nevertheless, Brooks believes that "a culture invested in shaping character [helps] make people resilient by giving them ideals to cling to when times [get] hard."[49] Without moral frameworks, the result is social isolation, withdrawal, and separation from those around you as well as the larger community. An indication of this kind of alienation and disconnection is the increase of suicide rates in the United States by 30 percent since 2000.[50]

In contrast, moral formation urges people to ask "what is life for?" and offers "practical guidance on how to be a good neighbor, a good friend."[51] At the very least, providing people with a moral vocabulary along with frameworks and skills for determining what is good gives people the means by which to treat each other with decency and respect. He notes that healthy moral ecologies will not just magically appear. Rather, "they have to be seeded and tended by people who think and talk in moral terms, who try to model and inculcate moral behavior, who understand that we have to build moral communities because on our own, we are all selfish and flawed."[52] This is exactly what preachers can do in their sermons about social issues—they can talk in terms of morality and ethics, they can model ethical behavior, and they can build an ethical community within their congregation.

Conclusion

In this chapter, I have asserted that the church and Christian preaching have a vital role to play in moral formation. Our Sunday schools teach social skills to young people. Our service to those in need can cross the generation gap. Our leadership is expected to adhere to high moral standards and accountability. Our preachers can frame their sermons on social issues using ethical foundations. And the church can engage in the public square for the sake of advocating for fair and community-building policies.

The goal of this chapter has been to provide an ethical vocabulary and categories for making sense of the underlying impulses and motivations that drive people to take the positions that they do on social issues. Understanding what is important to people is essential to communicating with them in teaching, pastoral conversations, and sermons about the issues that are affecting our lives and communities. At a more basic level, however, this work is about learning how to listen deeply to people's concerns to articulate them fairly and honestly in a sermon. When people feel that they have been heard and taken seriously, they may be more willing to engage in that kind of deep listening themselves. This, in turn, can guide our self-understanding as moral agents within a community of other moral agents. And all of this is a way to live out Paul's vision for the church to be ambassadors of God's reconciliation.

As we will see in the next chapter, this work of building moral communities and ethical bridges is not only in alignment with the biblical witness but also integral to our Christian vocation in the world. I will show how this mapping of ethical matrices can be overlayed on the scriptural and theological foundations for preaching and social issues. After that, I'll give examples of how each of the three approaches—Gentle, Invitational, and Robust—can utilize these frameworks.

Notes

1. David Brooks, "How America Got Mean," *The Atlantic*, published August 14, 2023, accessed January 11, 2024, https://www.theatlantic.com/magazine/archive/2023/09/us-culture-moral-education-formation/674765/.
2. Brooks.
3. Brooks.
4. Brooks.
5. Brooks.
6. Brooks.
7. Frank A. Thomas, *Surviving a Dangerous Sermon* (Nashville, TN: Abingdon Press, 2020), xviii. Thomas first developed this concept in his book *How to Preach a Dangerous Sermon* (Nashville, TN: Abingdon Press, 2018).
8. Thomas, *Surviving a Dangerous Sermon*, xvii.

9. Thomas, xxiii–xxvi.

10. Granted, this bifurcated framework may appear to reify the divisiveness that we're trying to bridge in this book. However, Thomas's work is more nuanced than these two categories, as we shall see.

11. Thomas, *Surviving a Dangerous Sermon*, 39. See George Lakoff, *Moral Politics: How Liberals and Conservatives Think*, 3rd ed. (Chicago: University of Chicago Press, 2016).

12. Thomas, *Surviving a Dangerous Sermon*, 46, citing Lakoff, *Moral Politics*, 413.

13. Thomas, 47.

14. See: https://braverangels.org/

15. See: "Perspective: The Braver Angels plan to heal America," Jacob Hess, *Deseret News*, March 2, 2022, https://www.deseret.com/2022/3/9/22949616/perspective-the-braver-angels-miracle-polarization-democrats-republicans-dialogue-politics-election, accessed Jan. 27, 2024.

16. Thomas, 4–8. See also André Resner, "Reading the Bible for Preaching the Gospel," in *Collected Papers of the 2008 Annual Meeting of the Academy of Homiletics*, 223; "Do You See This Woman? A Little Exercise in Homiletical Theology," in *Theologies of the Gospel in Context: The Crux of Homiletical Theology*, ed. David Schnasa Jacobsen (Eugene, OR: Cascade, 2017), 19–24; *Living In-Between: Lament, Justice, and the Presence of the Gospel* (Eugene, OR: Wipf and Stock, 2015).

17. Thomas, *Surviving a Dangerous Sermon*, 8.

18. Thomas, 9.

19. Thomas, 10.

20. Thomas, xxix.

21. Thomas, 56.

22. Thomas, 56.

23. Thomas, 8.

24. Thomas, 8.

25. Thomas, 43.

26. Thomas, xxvii.

27. Thomas, 91.

28. Jonathan Haidt, *The Righteous Mind: Why Good People Are Divided by Politics and Religion* (New York: Vintage Books, 2012), 30.

29. Haidt, 83.

30. Haidt, 107.

31. Haidt, 131–49.

32. Haidt, 178–79.

33. Haidt, 215.

34. Haidt, 214.

35. Haidt, 214.
36. Haidt, 256–84.
37. Haidt, 284.
38. See Robert D. Putnam and D. E. Campbell, *American Grace: How Religion Divides and Unites Us* (New York: Simon and Schuster, 2010).
39. See Robert D. Putnam, *Bowling Alone: The Collapse and Revival of American Community* (New York: Simon & Schuster, 2000).
40. Haidt, *The Righteous Mind*, 339.
41. Haidt, 339.
42. Haidt, 341.
43. Haidt, 341.
44. Haidt, 342.
45. Haidt, 371.
46. Haidt, 371.
47. Thomas, *Surviving a Dangerous Sermon*, 91.
48. Thomas, 92.
49. Brooks, "How America Got Mean."
50. Matthew F. Garnett, Sally C. Curtin, and Deborah M. Stone, "Suicide Mortality in the United States, 2000–2020," Centers for Disease Control and Prevention, published March 2022, https://www.cdc.gov/nchs/data/databriefs/db433.pdf.
51. Brooks, "How America Got Mean."
52. Brooks.

CHAPTER 6

Why the Church Needs to Address Social Issues

Biblical and Theological Foundations

In a 2021 article, "The Evangelical Church Is Breaking Apart," Peter Wehner, a senior fellow at the Trinity Forum (a Christian think tank dedicated to the renewal of society), wrote about the ways in which politics and anti-intellectualism are tearing apart American evangelicalism. "The aggressive, disruptive, and unforgiving mindset that characterizes so much of our politics has found a home in many American churches," he said.[1] In the article, he describes campaigns of disinformation and falsehoods targeting clergy, coordinated efforts of bullying and mistreatment of fellow members, and an overall culture of divisiveness and toxicity throughout U.S. evangelical churches.

These phenomena are not limited to evangelical churches. Sometimes congregants in mainline Protestant churches twist or simply ignore the teachings of Jesus or use Christianity as a tool for culture wars and political grievances. And clergy themselves can be the ones doing the twisting or ignoring in those culture wars. But for those preachers who do attempt to teach and preach the love of Jesus, the twenty-four-hour, seven-day-a-week culture shaped by media outlets can feel overwhelming. Wehner observes that these media outlets "catechize" with doctrines of divisiveness, tribalism, and even violent hatred. "'What all those media want is engagement,' Wehner quotes a professor of humanities at Baylor University, 'and engagement is most reliably driven by anger and hatred. They make bank when we hate each other. And so that hatred migrates into the Church, which doesn't have the resources to resist it.'"[2] What the church needs to reclaim, says Wehner, is "the Jesus of the Gospels—the Jesus who won their hearts, and who long ago won mine."[3] This is the Jesus who urges Christians to live out their faith through acts of kindness, generosity, and love of neighbor.

In this chapter, I will make the case that this is where preaching about social issues can find purchase—by pointing the way back to Jesus and the love of God and neighbor. But I will argue against Wehner's assertion that the church "doesn't have the resources" to resist anger and hatred. In fact, I will demonstrate that the church has a plethora of resources right in our Scriptures and theological tenets if only we put them to use. By engaging the work of biblical scholars from three diverse standpoints, I'll show that the Bible can, in fact, provide the guidance we need because it addressed the social issues of its time and authorizes us to apply its teachings to our own contemporary issues.

I'll also assert that when addressing social issues in sermons, it is important to interrogate our theological foundations so that the claims we make about the nature of God are both reflecting and integrating perspectives of those who have been historically marginalized. While our theological claims are influenced by our working gospels, worldviews, and moral foundations, as we discussed in chapter 6, they must also include perspectives that challenge us to be expansive and inclusive of standpoints and experiences that widen the aperture through which we can experience and express God's grace, love, and justice.

In this chapter, we'll explore three biblical and theological interpretive lenses—historical critical, Latino/a, and womanist—and see how they track with different aspects of Jonathan Haidt's six moral foundations, which I discussed in chapter 5. I'll also suggest ways that a preacher can use the three approaches to social issues—Gentle, Invitational, and Robust—in concert with biblical and theological foundations.

Historical–Critical Exegesis: Jesus— and the Bible—Are Political

As we saw in chapter 2, most churchgoers are engaging in discussions about social issues when they are at church, even if they believe the preacher should "stay out of politics." The reality is that Christians already use the Bible to help them think about their positions on social issues, and there some who misinterpret, cherry-pick, or weaponize the Bible to justify harmful political positions and policies. This means that it's up to preachers to provide sound principles based on critical engagement with the Bible to guide parishioners as they think about how faith can inform and shape the relationship between the church and public policy. In other words, it's not a matter of *whether* the church and Christians should be involved in shaping laws and policy but *why* and to what *purpose*.

In his book *The Politics of Faith: The Bible, Government, and Public Policy*, biblical scholar Jerry Sumney asserts that the church should advocate for equitable social and economic policies because this is what the Bible both models and calls for.[4] In Sumney's view, informed by a historical–critical approach to biblical interpretation and a working gospel of social justice, Scripture demonstrates that God cares about the poor, the vulnerable, the outcast, and the marginalized. Consequently, God calls people to not only practice personal morality but to call for their legislators to enact laws that provide for the common good. Sumney insists, and I agree, that the Hebrew and Christian Scriptures are suffused with an ethic that, if enacted, would result in a more equitable and caring society.

WHAT IS THE HISTORICAL-CRITICAL METHOD OF INTERPRETING SCRIPTURE?

The historical-critical method is a process of interpreting the meaning of a biblical passage that investigates the origins of the text in order to understand what was happening at the time it was written so that readers can take the text on its own terms. Historical-critical biblical scholars research the history surrounding the text and use approaches such as textual criticism and theological analysis to determine what the biblical text meant to its original author and audience. This process is called *exegesis* and involves discerning the cultural, political, and religious matters that gave rise to the text. The opposite of exegesis is *eisegesis* wherein the reader imposes their own meaning on the text instead of drawing out the meaning from the text on its own terms.

Sumney points out that the Bible is a political document in the sense that it addressed the issues of public concern for its time. Everything from taxes to immigrants to capital punishment and many more controversial topics are included in the Bible. In the Hebrew Scriptures, we find an ethic that serves as "a blueprint for how to construct the kind of society God wants."[5] Especially noteworthy are the Levitical laws, which are intended to give very practical and detailed ways for the Israelites to live their lives in community. This is not just because God is pleased by this kind of holy living but because "God is these things"—justice, mercy, holiness, and compassion.[6]

The Israelites were charged with creating a society where immigrants are protected, widows and orphans are not left to fend for themselves, and economic predators are kept in check. And it's important to note that prophets, such as Nathan, Elisha, Micah, and Obadiah, were addressing the *leaders* about these issues. "Clearly, these prophets are not speaking primarily to the average person on the street. Their messages are spoken most directly to those in power, to the people who run the government," Sumney says.[7] Recognizing that the practice of speaking truth to power has its roots in ancient Israel helps us refute the argument that the church has no role in politics. In fact, the only logical conclusion we can reach from reading these ancient scriptures is that clergy and congregations *should* speak up about the need to shape social, economic, and judicial law so that it comes closer to reflecting God's justice, mercy, and equity for all people.

The writers of the Christian Scriptures continued and expanded on this tradition when it came to the social and economic powers of their time—the Roman Empire and the Jewish Temple system. The teachings of Christ and the expectations of the early church differed dramatically from the values of the Greek and Roman social orders. In Acts, for example, living and acting in such a way that reflects what God wants for the world meant redistributing wealth and rejecting economic systems that perpetuate exploitation and poverty.[8] The disturbing story of the death of Ananias and Sapphira in Acts 5, for instance is about rejecting "the accumulation of wealth that comes through the exploitation of others."[9]

> **A GENTLE APPROACH FOR A SERMON ON ACTS 5**
>
> Acts 5 is a story of dishonesty and death that may shock contemporary readers but contains important lessons that can be applied to a sermon about fairness in economic systems. A preacher could use the Gentle strategy of *Stand with the congregation and voice the feelings* for a sermon about the story of Ananias and Sapphira by explaining their own initial reaction to the story. What's wrong with holding back some of the proceeds from the sale of land? Wasn't the couple already being generous by giving any portion to the church? Don't they have a right to decide what they want to do with their own property?
>
> The preacher could then take listeners with them on their exegetical journey to discover what was really going on with this wealthy couple and why their actions resulted in their own deaths. The sermon could explore the way in which our own economy encourages deception and greed. The preacher could conclude by lifting up examples of churches that advocate for more ethical and equitable economic policies or challenge practices such as payday lending that targets and takes advantage of poor communities.

When it comes to the Gospels, all four show Jesus' public interactions on social issues. Jesus addressed the contemporary social issues of his day, including taxes (Matt. 22:15-22), resource distribution (the stories of feeding the crowds in Matt. 15:32-39 and Mark 8:1-13), poverty (Matt. 19:21, Matt. 25:31-46, Luke 4:18), and predatory economic systems (turning over the moneychangers' tables in Matt. 21:12-13). Even the Passion narratives are political. "Crucifixion was a political execution," Sumney reminds us. "In all four Gospels, Jesus is executed on a political charge."[10] This is because Jesus was a threat to the rulers of his day. Thus, the fact that he was resurrected is not just a story of God's power over death (which, of course, it is). It is also a theological repudiation of the entire economic, military, and religious system that demanded his death in the first place.

At this point, we can see that Sumney's interpretation of Scripture is buttressed by three of Haidt's moral foundations: care, liberation, and authority, the last serving as a theological mandate for the first two. Undoubtedly, however, the preacher may encounter those who have different working gospels and moral foundations. For example, some may insist that the Bible teaches that while the church's job is to follow Jesus' command to feed the hungry, care for the sick, clothe the naked, and visit those in prison (Matt. 25:31-46)—this does not entail questioning the policies that result in hunger, sickness, or unjust imprisonment in the first place. But Sumney refutes that limited view. "Since governments are the organized ways that people structure how they treat one another, the people in charge are expected to create systems that exhibit the values God demands of each person."[11]

But, some may counter, doesn't Romans 13:1-7 argue that God is the one who establishes governments and, as such, governments should be allowed to conduct their business without interference or critique from the church? Again, Sumney offers an important clarification: "Acknowledging that governments are set in place by God does not mean God's people should not oppose their unjust policies."[12] Paul's Letter to the Romans is clear that the government's role is not only to punish evil but to be "servants of God for your good" (Rom. 13:4). Thus, it is appropriate and necessary for Christians to "hold governments accountable to God for how they wield the power God has given them."[13]

But what about the principle of the separation of church and state? Many will invoke this concept to refute a preacher who addresses social issues. But Sumney corrects this view: "Separation of church and state does not mean that the church ignores the injustices that our laws allow or prescribe."[14] Rather, "we should want churches to speak out when candidates support policies that move further from God's will rather than toward it. We should clearly state that our cultural individualism has led us to give advantages to those who need it the least."[15]

Sumney's careful exegesis of the biblical texts make a compelling case that if preachers and their congregations take the Bible seriously and believe it should mean something for our lives and our society today, we need to discern the principles and values within its pages that can be applied to contemporary issues. With this in mind, we'll turn to Latino/a biblical scholars to help us understand the political dimensions of the Bible as an interpretive guide for making sense of social issues that particularly pertain to Latinos/as and the societies in which they live.

The Bible and Latino/a[16] Hermeneutics

Preachers using the historical–critical approach to the Bible know that this method of interpretation intends to center attention on the text and minimize the effect of the interpreter's identity on the interpretation. Yet, as Latino biblical scholar Fernando F. Segovia points out, "just as the world of antiquity is viewed as crisscrossed by the dynamics and mechanics of differential power along the lines of identity, so are the world of modernity and postmodernity. Consequently, any study of interpretation is perforce regarded as irretrievably contextual and perspectival."[17] In other words, ideological criticism, or perspective-explicit interpretations of Scripture, acknowledge, emphasize, and leverage the insights and responses that arise when readers engage with texts from their own social positions, identities, and ideologies. A Latino/a perspective is an example of the working gospel of identity politics in that it uses the intersections of ethnicity, gender, race, and culture as an interpretive lens for Scripture and theology.[18]

WHAT IS THE LATIN AMERICAN LIBERATION INTERPRETATION OF SCRIPTURE?

In many respects, the Latin American liberation reading of Scripture serves as the precursor to other perspective-explicit interpretations. Emerging in the 1960s with Gustavo Gutiérrez's A *Theology of Liberation*, Latin American liberation theologians and biblical scholars pioneered the consideration of context as a necessary dialogue partner for engaging with Scripture from the perspective of the poor and colonized. This approach reveals the ways in which the White, Western, colonialist dominance hierarchy contributes to the societal and economic subjugation of individuals. The aim is to perceive biblical texts through the lens of marginalized and oppressed communities with the goal of advocating for social change by accentuating biblical values that center God's concern for the poor and align with the liberation of the oppressed.

One of the most important features of the Latino/a hermeneutic is its emphasis on how we *respond* to what we find in our analysis so that the church can strategize about changes to the systemic structures and give space for liberation, equity, restoration, and flourishing to grow. In an essay for the book *Latina Evangélicas: A Theological Survey from the Margins*, Elizabeth Conde-Frazier focuses specifically on the ways in which Protestant Latinas (female Hispanics) in the United States read Scripture. She notes that "the Bible is not a neutral book. It was used to colonize peoples of Latin America . . . to control the colonized."[19] This means that *evangélicas* (female evangelicals) must pay particular attention to the role of authority in biblical interpretation. Conde-Frazier provides a list of Latina-informed questions that could easily be used by *all* interpreters of Scripture, including preachers:

> Who reads and/or interprets this text? Does the interpretation hold equal authority to other interpretations? With what purpose and in what context are the Scriptures read? Are there any checks and balances for the interpretive process? How has the text been a part of the meaning making of the community that reads it? How can this word from the past, read in contemporary times, bring understanding for one's life in the present and for the future? If the Bible is the word of God or divine communication with finite humans, how can human thought apprehend divine thought?[20]

To these questions, Conde-Frazier brings Christian theology to mediate between human subjectivity and biblical interpretation. "It is Christian theology that provides a framework within which human experience may be interpreted," she explains.[21] And she is quick to add that any theology that dismisses *experience* as an inferior interpretive lens runs the risk of shutting out women and the authority of their own voices, a practice that, historically, has marginalized women and other disenfranchised groups. Let's look at how Latino/a biblical scholarship and theology apply to a specific contemporary social issue: migration and immigration.

Latinxs,[22] *the Bible, and Migration*
Latinxs, the Bible, and Migration is a collection of ten essays written by Latino/a biblical scholars who explore not just how migrating peoples

have used the Bible to frame their experiences but also to make the case that the Bible itself is "a collection of texts of and about migration."[23] Their premise is that the Bible contains political theologies for peoples in exile, on the move, or seeking refuge. Sagas from the Hebrew texts, such as Joseph sold into slavery in a foreign land, the Lamentations written in exile, and Psalm 137 raging that the Israelites are made to sing their song in a foreign land, emerge from the pain and struggle of peoples forced from their homes and homelands. For immigrants then and now, the Bible can serve as a vehicle for expressing what it is like to endure violent subjugation under a conquering people.

New Testament scriptures, too, can be counted as migration texts. As Efraín Agosto points out, Paul was, in many ways, a migrant worker.[24] He crossed borders repeatedly in his journeys to spread the gospel of Jesus Christ and endured numerous hardships to fulfill his mission. His letters not only recount his experience as a person "on the move" but are also his way of making meaning as a border crosser. Agosto compares Paul's experiences with those of his native Puerto Rico, which has seen a mass exodus due to hurricanes, agricultural devastation, and economic deprivation. Whether forced or voluntary, those living as diaspora people, through assimilation, accommodation, or alienation, can find solidarity with Paul's migration experiences.

Granted, this may not be the way most people with documented citizenship understand the Bible. In fact, depending on where your church is located and who worships there, this claim may seem audacious, perhaps even preposterous. But the editors and authors take the position that the Bible is "a space of migrant urgency" and should be interpreted through "the lens of migration, exile, and diaspora with a focus on migrants and the children of migrants."[25] As such, they argue, the Bible should be read with those who are migrants whose lived experiences can inform those who have not lived through migration.

Of course, for congregations that serve communities of migrants and immigrants, this is not a new way to think about Scripture. For people forced to migrate, this is their reality every day. And, as the authors in this volume note, the Bible is a companion to migrants and frames their experiences. In other words, Scripture gives them a reference point as they are traveling and resettling and, with the aid of ancient stories, helps them to articulate their struggles.

What would such an understanding of the Bible, as a collection of texts about migration, mean for preachers addressing social issues? At the minimum, it should result in calling for U.S. policies and for Christian actions and attitudes to be reshaped so that migrants are seen as human beings rather than "problems," "animals," "illegals," "aliens," or "poisoning the blood of America," as they are often characterized in cultural and political parlance. Pastors whose parishioners have no reference point for the migration experience may rationalize that they do not need to speak about these issues since it is outside the realm of their congregation's experience. But especially for churches made up of the *descendants* of colonizers, there are important insights to gain from understanding the Bible as a collection of texts about migration.

First, we must show "how the Bible was not only produced by migrants but also affirms that settled communities are obligated to welcome, love, and affirm the humanity of migrants," says Agosto and Jacqueline M. Hidalgo.[26] Such a perspective gives us a window into the experiences of migrating peoples to which we might not otherwise have access. In turn, these insights can be integrated into sermons, Bible studies, and pastoral conversations to expand and deepen not only our understanding of the world of those who were migrants in the text but also the lives of those who can experience migration today.

For example, Hidalgo recounts her ethnographic research with Cuban immigrants at Calvary Chapel at Claremont University in California. She describes how the Bible is like a "homing device" for those who experience "unhomeliness." In this way, Scripture becomes "a basis from which to mediate and negotiate senses of home, especially for marginalized and migratory peoples."[27] As another example, Ahida Calderón Pilarski encourages us to read the story of Ruth and Boaz from the perspective of farmworker women of Hispanic origin in the United States, 80 percent of whom experience some form of sexual violence in the fields. How do they interpret Boaz's order to the men not to bother (i.e., sexually assault) Ruth, a foreign woman gleaning in the fields (Ruth 2:9)?[28]

What Latin American, and especially Latina, theology invites preachers to see is that when addressing social issues in sermons, we can turn to the "hermeneutics of experience" as an "intercultural, intertextual exchange between the ancient text and the modern experience.

Reflection on the exchange between Scriptures and experience produces an authority all its own."²⁹ Here, we can see how those from oppressed communities invert Haidt's moral foundation of authority so that it is no longer determined by a top-down hierarchy but, rather, emerges from the bottom up. Experience becomes its own authority, and it sometimes counters that of the dominant hierarchy. Regardless of whether or not the congregation can directly relate to that experience, listening to different interpretations of Scripture from those with a perspective that challenges oppressive systems is very much in keeping with the spirit of the Bible itself.

> **AN INVITATIONAL APPROACH FOR A SERMON ON RUTH 2**
>
> An Invitational sermon on the second chapter of Ruth can utilize the strategy of *Telling stories to create empathy.* The sermon could begin by describing what Ruth may have faced as a foreign woman scavenging for unpicked crops alone in the fields. The preacher could then share stories of what it is like for migrant women today to work in the fields picking crops in the heat of the day for countless hours trying to support their families while also facing discrimination, unhealthy working conditions, low wages, and the threat of violence and sexual abuse. The sermon could conclude by pointing to the efforts of churches and denominations who serve migrant communities through advocacy, education, and community organizing and invite the congregation to consider how they might support such efforts.

Womanists' Interpretations of Scripture

Another cultural perspective that supports the case for the church's addressing social issues is womanist theology and hermeneutics. Womanist biblical scholar Wilda Gafney notes that when it comes Scripture, "a womanist engagement looks to the experiences and articulations of black women throughout the diaspora . . . as an authoritative source and norm for biblical interpretation."³⁰ She clarifies and expands the meaning and ramifications of womanism this way:

Most simply, womanism is black women's feminism. It distinguishes itself from the dominant-culture feminism, which is all too often distorted by racism and classism and marginalizes womanism, womanists, and women of color. Womanism emerged as black women's intellectual and interpretive response to racism and classism in feminism and its articulation and in response to sexism in black liberationist thought.[31]

In this section, we'll explore the work of three Black feminist theologians and biblical scholars—Jacquelyn Grant, Delores Williams, and Wilda Gafney. Each of them takes seriously Black women's experience as a source of theological reflection and biblical interpretation to remedy the historical and contemporary injustice of excluding their stories, participation, and reflections on the authority of Scripture. Here, we will see the working gospel of identity politics intersecting with both race and gender as well as the working gospel of social justice seeking liberation for Black women. The primary moral foundations for womanism would be care, fairness, and liberation, with an inverted authority matrix that arises from Black women's experiences.

WHAT IS THE ORIGIN OF THE TERM WOMANISM?

Alice Walker coined the term "womanist" in 1984 to delineate "a black feminist or feminist of color." She drew the word from the term "womanish" meaning a black woman who, in the parlance of Black folk, exhibits "outrageous, audacious, courageous, or willful behavior."[32] She went on to explain that a womanist is "committed to survival and wholeness of entire people, male and female," and that such a person "Loves Music. Loves dance. Loves the moon. Loves the Spirit. Loves love and rood and roundness. Loves struggle. Loves the Folk. Loves herself. Regardless."[33] Walker's definition has been the bedrock for many Black feminist theologians, biblical scholars, and homileticians.

Jacquelyn Grant

In her book, *White Women's Christ, Black Women's Jesus*, Jacquelyn Grant explains that slave masters would quote certain passages of Scripture to justify the institution of slavery. To counter this flawed and harmful interpretive lens, the Bible must be read using an "internal critique . . . in the light of Black women's own experience of oppression and God's revelation within that context."[34] Echoing the Latino/a liberationist approach, womanists must "read and hear the Bible and engage it within the context of (their) own experience. This is the only way that it can make sense to people who are oppressed."[35]

What Grant wanted to show is that there is an interstructuring of oppression that involves sexism, economics, and racism. According to Grant, Black feminist theology "holds that full human liberation cannot be achieved simply by the elimination of any one form of oppression. Consequently, real liberation must be 'broad in the concrete'; it must be based upon a multi-dimensional analysis."[36] As Grant astutely points out, while liberation for White women is *fulfillment* of their potential, their hopes, their dreams, their voice, their agency, and their power, liberation for Black women is *survival*. "A womanist is one who has developed survival strategies in spite of the oppression of her race and sex in order to save her family and her people."[37]

Therefore, each theologian—and each preacher—must be cognizant of these interwoven complexities and recognize their location within the web of oppression. This applies not just to White communities but to the Black church as well. This is because, as Grant points out, the Black church, as an androcentric institution, has historically overlooked and sometimes perpetuated Black women's oppression.

Delores Williams

In tracing the development of womanist thought, it becomes clear that biblical interpreters—as well as preachers—have complex identities that preclude categorizing them in monolithic ways. Delores Williams's book, *Sisters in the Wilderness*, deals with the complexities of Black women's identities and struggles by lifting up the figure of Hagar in Genesis as a kind of patron saint of womanism. Hagar was the Egyptian slave girl of Abraham and Sarah. She was raped and forced to bear Abraham's son while suffering Sarah's abuse. She ran away to the wilderness yet returned to her enslavers at God's command and endured humiliation and suffering to ensure her son Ishmael's survival. Later, she and her son were forced out of their home without resources or assistance and faced certain death in the wilderness.

Yet her encounter with God revealed provisions for their survival and ensured that her descendants would become a great nation, though at odds with their kin.

Williams interrogated the passages of Genesis 16:1-16 and 21:9-21 and found that "Hagar's predicament involved slavery, poverty, ethnicity, sexual and economic exploitation, surrogacy, rape, domestic violence, homelessness, motherhood, single-parenting, and radical encounters with God."[38] Likewise, many African American women have faced congruent predicaments and, like their "sister in the wilderness," have testified that "God helped them make a way out of no way."[39]

The experiences and actions of Hagar provided Williams with a critical lens through which to view Black women as oppressed yet resourceful, powerless yet mobilized for survival, and in desperate circumstances yet sustained by God. Her premise was that Black women have shared threads of common history and experiences that differentiate them from women of other races and cultures and enable them to find solidarity with each other. She asserted that Black women, like their sister Hagar, "had their wilderness experience of courage, fear, aloneness, meeting God and obeying God's will for transformation in their lives. Finally, all the women and Hagar could testify, 'Me and God stood up.'"[40]

What can preachers learn about addressing social issues from Williams's work? First, Williams shows us what it looks like to hold the tension between the strands of liberation and oppression that are intertwined within the biblical text. On the one hand, for example, God liberates the Israelites from Egypt. But God does not liberate Hagar, nor does God restructure the system of oppression that led to her and her child's suffering. This means that preachers need to ask questions about how they or their congregation interpret the text:

> Have they, in the use of the Bible, identified so thoroughly with the theme of Israel's election that they have not seen the oppressed of the oppressed in scripture? Have they identified so completely with Israel's liberation that they have been blind to the awful reality of victims making victims in the Bible? Does this kind of blindness with regard to non-Hebrew victims in the scripture also make it easy for [theologians] and biblical scholars to ignore the figures in the Bible whose experience is analogous to that of black women?[41]

It follows that because the biblical text is clearly written from the perspective of the Israelites, it is easy to overlook the person of Hagar and "invisibilize" her experience. So, when preachers are approaching a text, "they must assume an additional hermeneutical posture—one that allows them to become conscious of what has been made invisible in the text and to see that their work is in collusion with this 'invisibilization' of black women's experience."[42] Thus, pointing to the resilience in Hagar and in Black women and others who have struggled to survive oppression is an imperative for preachers addressing social issues. In chapter 7, we'll look at a sermon on Hagar by Lisa L. Thompson, which will demonstrate how the womanist perspective can inform our preaching.

A ROBUST APPROACH FOR A SERMON ON GENESIS 16:7-16

A Robust sermon on the enslavement, rape, and mistreatment of Hagar can use the *Be blunt, be bold* strategy. Such a sermon would be for a congregation that does not need to be convinced to take the struggles of women of color seriously. But the angle for the sermon would depend on whether there are women in the congregation who can relate to Hagar's experience or, if they have not personally experienced the struggle, desire to assist and support such women.

For example, a sermon at a women's shelter can describe Hagar's ordeal and the theological complexity of being told by God to return to those who are doing her harm. In this case, the preacher would assure listeners that this was not the end of Hagar's story and that when God finds her and Ishmael later on, God gives her freedom, sustenance for the journey, and the promise of a future.[43] In contrast, a sermon for a congregation that supports the ministry of a women's shelter would still recount Hagar's story and connect it to the situation faced by women in the shelter today, but the preacher would invite the congregation to consider how it can extend God's presence in the wilderness of these women's lives. Perhaps the shelter needs volunteers who can help with legal issues and advocacy. The preacher could cast a vision of what is possible for these women and urge the church to be active in this ministry as a sign of their faith in the same God that ensured Hagar's survival.

Wilda C. Gafney

Wilda C. Gafney is a womanist biblical scholar who created a four-volume series called *The Women's Lectionary for the Whole Church* that centers the visibility of women and girls in Revised Common Lectionary texts while being attentive to issues such as antisemitism, patriarchy, and violence against women.[44] Her work is informed by what she calls a "womanist midrash," *midrash* being the Jewish term for exegesis. She explains that the four primary womanist principles that undergird her midrash are "(1) the *legitimacy of black women's biblical interpretation* as normative and authoritative, (2) the *inherent value of each member of a community* in the text and interpreting the text, (3) *talking back* to the text, and (4) *making it plain*, the work of exegesis from translation to interpretation."[45]

These are principles that a preacher can adapt for their own interpretive work when preparing and writing sermons that address social issues. For example, talking back to the text gives the preacher and the listeners permission to question, push back, and bracket texts that assert divine approval for domination, oppression, or harm. And "making it plain" means that preachers will clearly and creatively convey the message of the biblical text in their sermon so that listeners can receive and be transformed by the Word of God.

Like Delores Williams, Gafney has developed her own set of interpretive questions informed by the experiences and perspectives of Black women. I include the list of questions here for several reasons. First, preachers can apply these questions to their own interpretive work when preparing sermons that address social issues. Second, while emerging from a womanist interpretation, her questions can be useful for thinking about the perspectives of other marginalized groups. For example, a preacher could substitute "black women" with "Asian women," "queer folks," or "those with disabilities" to shift the interpretive lens. Third, these questions invite a deeper engagement of the biblical text that promises insights for application to one's contemporary context. And, finally, question 12 is essential for thinking about our theology—our "God talk"—in sermons. Just as the biblical text constructs an understanding of God, so, too, do our sermons. Questioning whether that theological construction is helpful or harmful for marginalized persons is essential for sermons to be consistent with the God of righteousness and justice.

Interpretive Questions for Reading Biblical Texts

1. Who is speaking and/or active?
2. Where are the women and girls, what are they doing, and what are their names?
3. When women or other marginalized characters speak and act, whose interests are they serving?
4. Who (and where) are the characters without which the story could not have unfolded as articulated?
5. What are the power dynamics in the narrative?
6. What are the ethical implications of the text when read from the perspective of the dominant character(s)?
7. What are the ethical implications of previous (especially traditional) readings of the text for black women?
8. How have black women historically related to the text?
9. In what ways do the contemporary circumstances of black women readers shape new and renewed interpretations?
10. How do the values articulated in the text and its interpretation affect the well-being of the communities that black women inhabit?
11. How does (can) this text function as Scripture for black women?
12. Who is (what is the construction of) God in the text? Is s/he/it invested in the flourishing of black women, our families, and our worlds?[46]

For preachers and congregants who happen to occupy places where Whiteness, maleness, and heterosexuality are normative, these kinds of interpretive questions may feel uncomfortable at first. It can be jarring and even upsetting to consider perspectives outside of one's own experiences. But Gafney clarifies that "[w]omanist interpretation does not privilege the embodiment and experiences of black women at the expense of other members of the interpretive community."[47] In other words, this is the work of expansion—not of replacement. In solidarity with womanist scholars, a preacher addressing social issues must be committed to the thriving of the entire community, especially those whose wholeness and flourishing have been heretofore sacrificed, diminished, or ignored.

Conclusion

There are many other perspective-explicit interpretations of Scripture that a preacher can consult in their sermon preparation, such as queer, Asian, ecological, and disabilities.[48] These perspectives help preachers to be attentive to the narratives, characters, teachings, and voices within the text that might otherwise go unnoticed and unheard, thus depriving us of the fullness of God's revelation in Scripture. This, in turn, helps us to be attentive to the narratives, people, wisdom, and voices within our own communities today who can show us the fullness of God's revelation, which we can then proclaim in our preaching.

Another reason to attend to marginalized voices when addressing contemporary topics in sermons is because their perspectives correct the tendency to overgeneralize and universalize people's experiences. They compel us to contextualize and particularize our message so that we are not erasing, ignoring, overlooking, or diminishing the experiences of those who have a stake in what we preach, whether they are within or beyond our congregation. Our words matter because they help form the assumptions, beliefs, and actions of those who listen to us. As Lisa L. Thompson reminds us, "The most effective preaching recognizes that we are best able to tell the story of biblical texts anew when we listen deeply to them as the stories of a world that is different from ours yet familiar in that the people long ago lived with enigmas, power struggles, vulnerabilities, pursuits of life, failures, and successes similar to our own."[49] In other words, being attentive to an explicit perspective can help preachers to be better informed, more grounded, and even more creative and engaging in their sermons.

As we end this chapter, my hope is that you've realized how important it is to keep expanding the sources of your biblical and theological reflections when preaching about the issues that affect people's lives. When we encounter scholars and communities from different standpoints, our sermons can more fully participate in God's purpose of expanding inclusiveness in ever-widening circles. Granted, this expansiveness must be balanced with the need to speak to a congregation "where they are" to build bridges of understanding across chasms of difference. But on the whole, most preachers will find that many in their congregations are eager for perspectives that challenge them and open them up for encounters with the Word that speak to them in new and vigorous ways.

In the next chapter, we will delve into the work of homileticians who have contemplated ethics, morality, Scripture, and theology from diverse standpoints for sermons on social issues. We will analyze how they employ moral foundations, working gospels, and various strategies within the Gentle, Invitational, and Robust approaches. All of this will help us consider how our sermons can inspire believers to enact God's vision for dismantling systems of oppression and generating communities of equity, peace, and flourishing.

Notes

1. Peter Wehner, "The Evangelical Church Is Breaking Apart," *The Atlantic*, published October 24, 2021, accessed August 10, 2023, https://www.theatlantic.com/ideas/archive/2021/10/evangelical-trump-christians-politics/620469/.

2. Wehner, quoting a conversation with Alan Jacobs, a distinguished professor of humanities in the honors program at Baylor University.

3. Wehner, "The Evangelical Church Is Breaking Apart."

4. Jerry L. Sumney, *The Politics of Faith: The Bible, Government, and Public Policy* (Minneapolis, MN: Fortress Press, 2020).

5. Sumney, 15.
6. Sumney, 19.
7. Sumney, 27.
8. Sumney, 41.
9. Sumney, 39.
10. Sumney, 70.
11. Sumney, 61.
12. Sumney, 89.
13. Sumney, 91.
14. Sumney, 120.
15. Sumney, 121.

16. There is debate in the Latino/a community about the term that should be used to refer to them. Some use the term *Hispanic*, while others use *Latinx* or *Latio/a*. In this chapter, I use the terms interchangeably, depending on the book from which I am quoting.

17. Fernando F. Segovia, "Approaching the Bible in Latino/a Theology: Doing Theological Construction and Biblical Criticism in an Ethnic-Racial

Key," in *Latino/a Theology and the Bible: Ethnic-Racial Reflections on Interpretation*, ed. Francisco Lozada Jr. and Fernando F. Segovia (Lanham, MD: Lexington Books/Fortress Academic, 2021), 7.

18. Frank A. Thomas, *Surviving a Dangerous Sermon* (Nashville, TN: Abingdon Press, 2020), 8.

19. Elizabeth Conde-Frazier, "Evangélicas Reading Scriptures: Readings from within and Beyond the Tradition," in *Latina Evangélicas: A Theological Survey from the Margins*, ed. Loida I. Martell-Otero, Zaida Maldonado Pérez, and Elizabeth Conde-Frazier (Eugene, OR: Cascade Books, 2013), 74.

20. Conde-Frazier, 75.

21. Conde-Frazier, 77.

22. As mentioned in note 16, I'm using the term *Latinx* to match the book I am quoting.

23. Efraín Agosto and Jacqueline M. Hidalgo, eds., "Introduction," in *Latinxs, the Bible, and Migration* (Cham, Switzerland: Palgrave Macmillan, 2018), 7.

24. Efrain Agosto, "Islands, Borders, and Migration: Reading Paul in Light of the Crisis in Puerto Rico," *Latinxs, the Bible, and Migration*, ed. Efraín Agosto and Jacqueline M. Hidalgo (Cham, Switzerland: Palgrave Macmillan, 2018), 149–70.

25. Agosto and Hidalgo, "Introduction," 2.

26. Agosto and Hidalgo, 13.

27. Jacqueline M. Hidalgo, "The Bible as Homing Device among Cubans at Claremont's Calvary Chapel," *Latinxs, the Bible, and Migration*, ed. Efraín Agosto and Jacqueline M. Hidalgo (Cham, Switzerland: Palgrave Macmillan, 2018), 22.

28. Ahida Calderón Pilarski, "Gendering (Im)migration in the Pentateuch's Legal Codes: A Reading from a Latina Perspective," in *Latinxs, the Bible, and Migration*, ed. Efraín Agosto and Jacqueline M. Hidalgo (Cham, Switzerland: Palgrave Macmillan, 2018), 43–66.

29. Calderón Pilarski, 85.

30. Wilda C. Gafney, *Womanist Midrash: A Reintroduction to the Women of the Torah and the Throne* (Louisville, KY: Westminster John Knox Press, 2017), 4.

31. Gafney, 6.

32. Alice Walker, *In Search of Our Mothers' Gardens: Womanist Prose* (San Diego: Harcourt Brace Jovanovich, 1984), xi.

33. Walker, xi.

34. Jacqueline Grant, *White Women's Christ and Black Women's Jesus: Feminist Christology and Womanist Response* (Chişinău, Moldova: Scholars Press, 1989), 212.

35. Grant, 212.
36. Grant, 202.
37. Grant, 205.
38. Delores S. Williams, *Sisters in the Wilderness: The Challenge of Womanist God-Talk* (Maryknoll, NY: Orbis Books, 1993), 4.
39. Williams, 6.
40. Williams, 139.
41. Williams, 149.
42. Williams, 149.
43. For an excellent sermon on the complexities of Hagar's story, see Lisa L. Thompson's sermon excerpt, "Struggles for Belonging," in *Preaching the Headlines: Possibilities and Pitfalls* (Minneapolis, MN: Fortress Press, 2021), 107–115.
44. See Wilda C. Gafney, *A Women's Lectionary for the Whole Church: Year W* (2021), *Year A* (2021), *Year B* (2023), *Year C* (2024) (New York, NY: Church Publishing).
45. Gafney, *Womanist Midrash*, 8.
46. Gafney, 8.
47. Gafney, 7.
48. For example, Yung Suk Kim's *How to Read the Gospels* (Lanham, MD: Rowman & Littlefield, 2024) offers close readings of the gospels from various perspectives, such as feminist, postcolonial, womanist, and ecological.
49. Lisa L. Thompson, *Preaching the Headlines: Possibilities and Pitfalls* (Minneapolis, MN: Fortress Press, 2021), 22.

CHAPTER 7

Homiletical Conversation Partners for Addressing Social Issues

The challenge of addressing social issues in sermons is something that many homileticians have thought about a great deal in the last several decades. Broadly speaking, a sermon addressing social issues would fall under the genre of *topical preaching*. In this type of preaching, a "topic, issue, or concern within the contemporary world of the listener" is the sermon's central focus, Ronald J. Allen explains.[1] For example, in times of crisis or when there is a need for understanding a contemporary issue or situation, topical preaching not only addresses the concerns of listeners; it also brings the Bible and theology into conversation with the topic. Even when the Bible does not directly address a contemporary situation, it still provides an interpretive approach to the underlying theological concerns of the topic.[2] When used in this way, "the preacher can search for a thematic substratum within the Bible that sheds light on the topic."[3]

In this chapter, we'll engage with several homiletical conversation partners to help us think about preaching and social issues. We'll begin with John S. McClure's four ethical approaches to preaching and note how Jonathan Haidt's moral foundations map onto those approaches. Then, we'll look at three homiletical traditions that offer important framing, insights, and accountability practices for sermons that address social issues: conversational and collaborative, African American, and postcolonial homiletics. We'll discuss ethical approaches in these traditions and how various Gentle, Invitational, and Robust strategies can be used.

Four Ethical Approaches to Preaching

In his book *Ethical Approaches to Preaching: Choosing the Best Way to Preach About Difficult Issues*, John McClure suggests four categories for addressing challenging topics in sermons: communicative ethic, witness ethic, liberation ethic, and hospitality ethic. He explains that there are four basic aspects for each category: (1) the way preachers theologically frame the problem; (2) what enables their listeners to connect with, understand, and engage with the problem; (3) "signposts" the preacher should follow to organize the content and flow of their sermon about the issue; and (4) what the end result of such a sermon should be as well as how to get there. Understanding the four categories will assist preachers in thinking about the purpose of their own sermons when addressing a social issue.

Communicative Ethic

The communicative ethic establishes a moral consensus. McClure calls this an *intersubjective* ethic because "it relies on determining and understanding the best arguments put forward by groups of people who occupy clear subject positions within the social order."[4] The goal of this approach is to build communal consensus about the moral norms that should guide the community's stance and engagement on issues. He points to the Rev. Dr. Martin Luther King Jr.'s preaching during the civil rights movement as a good example of the communicative ethic.[5] King appealed to the moral goodness of people across racial lines and drew on shared values, such as human dignity and freedom, to further the cause of justice and freedom.

Haidt's moral foundations work well with a communicative ethic sermon. A preacher could identify one or two of the values (care, fairness, loyalty, authority, sanctity, or liberty) and use theological and biblical examples to make the case for why and how listeners can come together around that issue. As an example, McClure provides a sermon where he paints a picture of both the conservative and progressive worldviews and then moves the congregation toward the universal yearning for "belonging" that transcends politics and is God's desire for all people.[6]

The Gentle strategy of *name the issue and frame it biblically* can be used with the communicative ethic to help a congregation understand the background and biblical grounding of an issue. Also, the Invitational strategy of *history, mission, future* would work well for identifying the ethical orientation of the congregation's past and current mission to rally around an issue going forward. The communicative ethic is useful "when the preacher decides that what is needed is clarity, good judgment, moderation, mediation, and pursuit of the binding/bonding moral high ground between all persons. This will include any situation where divisiveness is destroying the fabric of the civility, decency, honesty, truthfulness, and shared hopes and dreams that motivate and inspire all persons," McClure explains.[7] This is the kind of sermon that David Brooks, whose essay on the "meanness" of America is featured in chapter 5, would appreciate.

Witness Ethic
The witness ethic asserts an alternative and countercultural moral vision against meta-narratives that "forcefully and sometimes violently" try to have their own way.[8] Unlike the communicative ethic, which tries to find the universal moral high ground, the witness ethic calls for listeners to be moral agents against hegemonic powers by exposing the domination system. This includes confessing one's capitulation to that system, testifying about what is necessary to take a stand, and pointing to exemplars who practice resistance while embodying God's disruptive and liberative power against oppression.

The three primary foundations from Haidt's list that would be found in the witness ethic are care/harm, fairness/cheating, and liberty/oppression. The Robust approaches of *be blunt, be bold*; *collaborate before, during, after*; and *equip for justice* would work well for sermons in the witness ethic category. Such sermons cultivate a virtue ethic, "helping listeners claim unique forms of Christian moral agency in the public arena."[9] However, the Gentle strategy of *share your own struggles with the issue* could also work with a witness ethic sermon to create a posture of humility and allow the preacher to *stand with the congregation, voice the feelings* around the issue. As well, the Invitational strategies of *tell stories to create empathy* and *history, mission, future* can be effective ways to both unveil the systemic problems and envision the congregation's part in confronting systemic evil and providing healing.

McClure advises that the witness ethic sermon works best when the congregation is responsive and aligned with the preacher's position. These sermons are useful in times when people are actively protesting, engaging in civil disobedience, or preparing for actions to stand against opposing powers. In these sermons, the Bible "defines and motivates the alternative life of moral agency withing the new nonviolent community."[10] The bottom line for witness ethic sermons is that they require "a creative desire to accentuate the uniqueness of the Christian faith and Christian moral agency in the midst of the larger culture, and an unwillingness to dumb down this uniqueness within one's congregation and community."[11]

Liberation Ethic

Sermons in the liberation ethic category are about educating and enrolling people in revolutionary change. These preachers are "motivated by an unsettling awareness of systemic inequities of power and resources for selfhood that exist in the world."[12] While this approach shares some of the same values with the witness ethic, such as care and fairness, the primary moral foundation is liberty and is directed toward "the unmasking, critique, and change of current social systems (economic, political, religious, educational, health care, etc.)."[13] This is not just about cultivating moral agency; it's about organizing for justice. And rather than finding universal moral values, as in the communicative ethic, the liberation ethic identifies intersections where marginalized groups can come together in solidarity to effect change.

What's important to note about the liberation ethic is that it's not just about liberating the poor and oppressed. It's also for the middle and upper classes, which are held by the same social systems that placate them with certain privileges and commodities while utilizing them to keep the structures of oppression in place. For example, I once preached a sermon on the systemic sin of the criminal justice system in a congregation where many of the members worked for a federal prison. I preached on the story of Paul and Silas imprisoned for exorcising the demon from a slave girl (Acts 16:16-40). I illustrated the way that the system chains everyone involved by having members of the congregation stand in as the characters of the story, with each holding onto a chain that stretched from the girl, to Paul and Silas, to the prison guard, and to the magistrates. My "ask" in the sermon was for congregants to take part in studying and giving feedback on a proposed social statement from our denomination about reforming the criminal justice system. The sermon not only raised awareness about systemic injustice but gave congregants an opportunity to give their input on the denomination's statement.

One of the Invitational strategies that can be very effective for a liberation ethic sermon is *tell stories to create empathy* and to do so in a way that enables hearers of privilege to recall times or circumstances where they experienced a loss of agency, resources, or selfhood and to ask, "What was that like for you?" The next step is to activate their moral imagination to understand what it's like for people who are different from them to suffer things that they may not have experienced directly but with whom they can empathize about loss, fear, uncertainty, pain, and longing for change.

McClure emphasizes that whether the preacher is addressing a congregation of the oppressed or those complicit in oppressive systems, *hope* is a necessity for such a sermon. "Hope is built on the burnt ground on which we stand, and involves struggle, imagination, and bold experimentation," says McClure.[14] Robust strategies of *be blunt, be bold,* and *equip for justice* are also useful for liberation ethic sermons because they can motivate a congregation to organize or take part in actions for justice.

Hospitality Ethic

The fourth category, hospitality ethic, aims to create face-to-face relationships through collaboration and conversation that will welcome unheard voices into the process of moral renewal, understanding, and solidarity. This ethic shares with the communicative ethic the desire to understand the different positions people take on social issues and the values that inform those positions. In this way, the preacher would draw on Haidt's moral foundations to articulate what is important to people when it comes to a social issue. However, the goal is not to then proclaim a universally acceptable moral norm, as in the communicative ethic, but to honor the vulnerabilities and gifts that people bring with them to the dialogue to affirm their humanity and treasure their fragile yet beautiful otherness.

The hospitality ethic asserts that "moral truth is always in process and moral relationships are constantly developing."[15] Therefore, the preacher seeks to meet with others, ask what they experience, listen deeply to their responses, and give expression to all of this in the sermon. The Invitational strategies all come into play here, especially with the *sermon–dialogue–sermon process*. Also, the Gentle strategy of *stand with the congregation, voice the feelings* allows the preacher to come alongside their listeners and honor their emotional responses to the issue. And the Robust strategy of *collaborate before, during, after* the sermon is an ideal way to put the hospitality ethic to use because it enables the preacher and a small group of parishioners to meet before the sermon to learn about the issue and make a proposal about how to respond. These individuals can even be invited into the sermon event itself, perhaps through a collaborative art project, such as making a real-time collage of images as the sermon is preached, or forming a kind of Greek chorus to echo key words and phrases at certain points to punctuate the sermon.

"A homiletic ethic of hospitality is oriented toward a future that is always emergent from within the organic and aesthetic rhythms of interhuman dialogue," McClure explains.[16] It's best used when the minister sees the need to cultivate relationships within the community of believers so that they can sustain and improve their ethical reflections over time. The hospitality ethic also works well in situations where a community is struggling with protracted moral distress about a problem, such as environmental pollution, opioid addiction, or immigration. Sermons in this category enable the preacher to communicate their respect and value of people's experiences, perspectives, and moral discernment while also building community as they consider possible solutions. In this type of preaching, the Bible can be shown to both mirror and model the kind of hospitality that God desires for God's people.

Four Ethical Approaches in Homiletics

Communicative Ethics
* Understand different positions to build moral consensus
* Unity around common ethical value(s)
* Seeks the moral high ground
* Emphasizes shared hopes and dreams

Witness Ethics
* Countercultural moral vision against harmful metanarratives
* Exposes hegemonic power, domination systems
* Cultivates virtue ethic, calls for moral agency

Liberation Ethics
* Educates for systemic change
* Organizes the church for justice
* Emphasizes hope in the face of inequity, injustice, disempowerment

Hospitality Ethics
* Builds relationships through collaboration, conversation
* Orients toward emerging future responsive to different perspectives
* Community-building

Figure 7.1 Four Ethical Approaches to Homiletics. *Source: Approaches to Preaching: Choosing the Best Way to Preach About Difficult Issues*, John S. McClure (Eugene, OR: Cascade Books, 2021). Graphic created by Leah D. Schade.

With these four ethical approaches to preaching in mind, we can examine specific traditions within the discipline of homiletics that can inform a preacher's approach to social issues. Keep in mind that there is overlap between and among the different ethical approaches and that what I'm featuring here is only a slice of what you will find within these strands of homiletics.

Conversational and Collaborative Preaching: Communicative and Hospitality Ethics

Conversational homiletics emphasizes "the embeddedness of preaching within a range of conversations taking place within the academy, congregation, community, nation, and across the globe."[17] Homileticians in the collaborative vein see the process of preaching as an opportunity for reciprocity between the preacher and the listeners. To be clear, this is not the same as a sermon that takes the *form* of a conversation (i.e., a dialogue happening during the sermon), although conversational preaching can do that. Rather, this approach is more about the desire of the preacher to listen to their parishioners, those outside of the church, and those who have been historically marginalized in order to expand their conversation partners.

A commitment to collaborative preaching is an ideal place from which to address social issues with a congregation that is just beginning to engage with a social issue because it views the listeners as co-conspirators in the church's work of confronting injustice and working toward communal flourishing. This approach can work with either the communicative ethic (with an end to proclaim a universal moral truth) or the hospitality ethic (with an end of building relationships of understanding). Haidt's moral foundations theory is a useful tool for conversational and collaborative preaching because it can give a common vocabulary for the preacher and congregation to understand people's different ethical matrices regarding social issues.

Collaborative preaching was first introduced by John McClure in 1995. His approach to the weekly preaching task got pastors out of their studies and into conversation with their parishioners. McClure's book *The Roundtable Pulpit: Where Leadership and Preaching Meet* integrated principles of participative dialogue with exegesis by putting preachers with listeners *before* the sermon to explore the biblical text from their perspectives and experiences.[18] The roundtable pulpit method entails regular meetings between the preacher and a group of parishioners to discuss the upcoming biblical text for the sermon. Insights derived from these discussions are then adeptly woven into the sermon rhetoric. Ideally, parishioners are not only more invested in the preaching process, but they also come to see themselves as collaborators in the sermon. This both broadens and deepens the sermon experience for both the preacher and congregation.

Lucy Atkinson Rose built on McClure's model and expanded the roundtable pulpit to specifically include marginalized voices. Her nonhierarchical approach to preaching in *Sharing the Word* insisted that the preacher's voice is just one among many within the congregation and should not be assumed to have a privileged position with an authoritative and final word on the Bible or social issues.[19] She envisioned a partnership and cooperation between the preacher; listeners; and those whose voices have been ignored, shunned, silenced, or excluded. She saw preaching as an ongoing process of provisional "wagers" inviting the "household of God" into dialogue.

O. Wesley Allen Jr. expanded on the work of McClure and Rose with *The Homiletic of All Believers*, in which he offered a variation on the theme of conversation. Like McClure and Rose, he agreed that hierarchical approaches to preaching are not appropriate, especially since postmodernism has demonstrated that authority from a single privileged source imposed upon the people can do real damage. Yet he does see the preacher's voice as having *limited* authority. Using the Wesleyan Quadrilateral categories of Scripture, tradition, reason, and experience as sources of divine revelation, Allen notes that preachers are tasked with gaining expertise in biblical and ecclesiological critical reflection for the sake of the congregation's discernment. But when it comes to reason and experience, the congregation has as much authority to assert truth claims as the preacher. Thus, he proposes that ministers see preaching as part of a matrix of personal, sociohistorical, theological, congregational, and liturgical conversations that are continually making meaning for the church.[20] Allen's approach could work with either the communicative ethic, by naming different perspectives on an issue and offering a provisional truth claim, or the hospitality ethic, by cultivating a spirit of ongoing dialogue about a topic.

O. Wesley Allen Jr. built on his work by joining with Ronald J. Allen in 2005 to write a book called *The Sermon without End: A Conversational Approach to Preaching*, in which they urged preachers to engage the plurality of cultures in society.[21] A conversational homiletic sees cultures as dialogue partners with which to "make meaning of God's presence and purposes."[22] But they are clear that these conversations must include biblical material and that exegesis is necessary to hear the Bible in its own voice.

Preaching in the Red–Blue Divide

My own approach to conversational and collaborative preaching in *Preaching in the Purple Zone* is to suggest a method for preachers to address controversial topics with their congregations in the midst of a divisive culture.[23] In this book, I suggest five paths of prophetic preaching: "rooting" (grounding the sermon in biblical principles and theological frameworks), "flowering" (raising awareness about a social issue and bringing it into conversation with the Bible and theology), "pollinating" (showing how the Bible models dialogue and authorizes dialogue among believers today), "leafing" (suggesting ways that a congregation may put their faith into action), and "fruiting" (committing to sustained conversation over time that transforms the culture of the congregation to healthy engagement with social issues).[24]

To support these five paths, I offer a "dialogical lens" for interpreting Scripture: (1) point out the dialogical aspects of the passage in terms of its internal, external, and interbiblical conversations; (2) determine what's at stake for the original author and audience; (3) identify the values that underlie the actions of the author or characters in a biblical narrative; (4) explain how God, Jesus, and/or the Holy Spirit is active in the text; (5) recognize what the dialogue within the text is teaching us about how to "be church" in the midst of contentious public issues; and (6) suggest possible next steps for responding to God's invitation to engage with the issue.[25]

These preparatory steps open the door to the sermon–dialogue–sermon process. This method of engaging in social issues begins with a "prophetic invitation to dialogue" sermon that makes the biblical and theological case for the church to address a social issue and encourages the congregation to engage in a deliberative dialogue. This sermon utilizes the hospitality ethic because it would not make a moral claim beyond the need and biblical authorization for dialogue. Then, the dialogue takes place with diverse participants agreeing to ground rules, sharing their personal stake in the issue, discussing pros and cons to three approaches to the topic, identifying common ground and shared values, and proposing next steps for how the congregation might respond and move forward.

The minister then preaches a follow-up sermon, called the "communal prophetic proclamation," which summarizes the dialogue using biblical and theological framing and encourages the congregation to continue in their process of ongoing engagement and reflection.[26] This sermon moves toward the communicative ethic in making its claim but with the understanding that it was arrived at through community discernment. In summary, the sermon–dialogue–sermon process is a way for preachers to "tap into the social context of their congregations and, together with their parishioners, develop a prophetic voice."[27]

The Prophetic Aspect of Conversational and Collaborative Preaching

Just because conversational and collaborative preaching utilizes more strategies in the Gentle and Invitational approaches does not mean that it's not prophetic. Since prophetic preaching focuses on flourishing for all, a sermon in this vein can move toward the communicative ethic that appeals to a universal value of well-being. However, if the sermon is initiating a conversation that the congregation has not yet engaged in, the preacher will want to utilize the hospitality ethic to help the congregation articulate different perspectives, interpretations, actions, and responses to the issue. For these sermons, the Gentle strategy of *name the issue, frame it biblically* and the Invitational strategy of *tell stories to create empathy* are especially useful to recognize different moral foundations and values within and outside of the congregation. As Allen and Allen note, one of the most important tools in the homiletical toolbox is a powerful narrative or illustration to help people "hear the other from the perspective from which the other seeks to be understood."[28]

Alternatively, if the sermon is being offered amid an ongoing conversation that the congregation has been having for some time and they are already aware of how a social issue is affecting people, a more Robust approach, through *be blunt, be bold* or *equip for justice* strategies, might be better suited. Allen and Allen note that "at its heart, the aim of prophetic preaching is to help the community name God's covenantal purposes, reflect on points at which the community is fulfilling those purposes, and to encourage the congregation (and perhaps the world) to take action (often repentance) that would bring God's purposes and the faith and behavior of the community into closer alignment."[29] Thus, the preacher serves as a kind of "theological and ethical ombudsperson who leads the community to think about its own life from the perspective of its own core values in dialogue with the core values of others."[30]

Ultimately, the conversational approach to preaching is "not an end [or] a destination," nor does it expect that the preacher must "say everything." Neither does the sermon have to be "right" about everything. Instead, "[t]he preacher continues to be open to others, and, hence, to the possibility of coming to better (if still provisional) understanding."[31]

African American Preaching Perspectives

Cleophus J. LaRue has noted that African American preaching has concerned itself with social issues since the first slaves began to read and interpret the Bible. This is because they perceived a profound theological truth that "scripture revealed a God of infinite power who could be trusted to act on their behalf."[32] For Black Christians, "God acts in very concrete and practical ways in matters pertaining to their survival, deliverance, advancement, prosperity, and overall well-being," and this belief guides a preacher's interpretation of Scripture.[33]

This means that Black preachers speak to their congregations knowing that they expect to hear a word about how God reveals God's self and acts in the particularities of their lived experiences, especially regarding issues that affect their lives and communities. Black preachers "sharpen their powers of observation by constantly seeking to name God's presence in every aspect of human existence," keeping in mind "their social, political, educational, and economic surroundings," LaRue says.[34] But the ways in which Black preachers approach social issues varies, depending on their congregational context, their "working gospels," the moral foundations they choose, and the homiletical ethics they employ for their sermons. In this section, we'll contrast two homileticians: Tyshawn Gardner and Lisa L. Thompson.

Tyshawn Gardner's Social Crisis Preaching: Communicative and Liberation Ethics

Tyshawn Gardner is an African American Baptist preacher and professor of ministerial studies who has concentrated on developing a sacred anthropology of preaching to enable ministers to engage social crises in their sermons. He devised the concept of sacred anthropology as the process of "exegeting" (i.e., carefully studying and interpreting the specific context, needs, characteristics, and dynamics of one's congregation to understand deeply who they are, what concerns them, and how to respond to their community most effectively). By social crisis, Gardner means "a disordered condition within a community that disrupts people's *shalom* (peace) and flourishing."[35] And he defines *social crisis preaching* as "biblically rooted, Spirit-enabled proclamation that develops and drives congregations to compassionately care for and radically confront social crises in the communities where their neighbors live, work, worship, and play."³⁶ Social crisis preaching uses expository, thematic, and narrative preaching to raise awareness and "prompt a congregation to consider how they might leverage their influence and power in advocacy" about the issue.³⁷ This approach demonstrates the communicative ethic because of its insistence on finding and living out biblically centered moral values.

Recall from chapter 5 that Frank Thomas named seven possible working gospels operating within American religious discourse: American sentimentalism, American exceptionalism, prosperity, denominational affiliation, evangelical, identity politics, and social justice. Using Thomas's categories, we can see that Gardner's homiletic is informed by three: social justice, identity politics, and evangelical. Regarding the latter, Gardner is careful to connect certain theological tenets of evangelical belief with his social crisis homiletic. For example, he locates the impetus for responding to social crises in an individual's process of conversion, salvation, and sanctification, which should, he argues, give rise to a public engagement with social realities. Ultimately, however, the goal of social crisis preaching is bringing people to Christ and the transformation he brings through the crucifixion and resurrection. Gardner also holds to substitutionary atonement theory as a theological basis for social crisis preaching, the logic being that because all people deserve God's wrath and yet are justified through Christ's death, it follows that everyone deserves to be liberated from economic inequity, racism, and other social ills.

Gardner's primary moral matrix within the Haidt foundations is liberation. "The totality of the gospel means liberation," he states. "Social crisis preaching recaptures and reclaims what it means to be liberated. Liberation, as both a word and a concept, has deep biblical roots and is a major aspect in the ethics of Christian theology and ministry."³⁸ He identifies this liberation as a key mark of the African American church, which he sees as an exemplar of developing sound and orthodox biblical interpretation in the face of social crises.³⁹ Yet he is quick to point out that a Black homiletic is not limited to the Black community. In fact, Gardner believes that "Christians of every ethnicity and race can embrace the same fervor to fight against forms of injustice that threaten the life, freedom, and humanity of God's people."⁴⁰

Because of his evangelical working gospel, Gardner's theology uses strong theological language to name the cause of social crises: sin, which he defines as "separation from God."[41] And, while he encourages a more understanding position on abortion to account for its "root social causes," he omits reasons for the social crisis of abortion that are gender focused, such as rape and medical necessity. Nor does he address the role of men in the occurrence of an unwanted pregnancy.[42] From my perspective as a progressive feminist, these tend to be blind spots (or indications of patriarchy and sexism) of evangelical theology. Nevertheless, Gardner does have a more nuanced approach informed by the care/harm moral foundation than many other evangelicals.

Sermons for social crisis preaching would use the Robust approach, more than the Gentle or Invitational approaches. This is because Gardner wants preachers to do more than preach "about" social crisis; he wants them to preach "to" social crisis. "Social crisis preaching is not an eloquent diatribe that simply identifies problems and introduces solutions [as does a hospitality ethic and conversational and collaborative homiletic]; rather, it demands that the hearer break from any and all political, racial, economic, or theological loyalties that are complicit in social crises."[43]

In Gardner's approach, there is a keen awareness that "the people of God are often the headlines," so they need to "hear a word from the Lord concerning the headlines that affect their lives and the people they love."[44] Here, the Robust strategy of *be blunt, be bold* would be appropriate for two responses he suggests for a social crisis sermon: *lament* and *interruption*. The former gives voice to the pain, while the latter speaks up and defies the status quo, which causes the pain. Gardner points to the story of Esther as a biblical example of both: Mordecai's lament to Esther about the impending genocide, and Esther's interruption of King Ahasuerus and the immoral laws that would result in the death of her people.[45]

Lisa L. Thompson's Womanist Homiletic: Liberation and Witness Ethics

As we learned in chapter 6, womanist biblical and theological scholars carve out a space for the experiences of African American women to bring their unique intersection of race, sex, and class to bear on how we read and interpret the Bible. As Raquel A. St. Clair explains, a womanist homiletic holds us accountable to ask whether our "exegetical conclusions or sermon points promote the wholeness of African American women [and enable them to] embrace their full humanity as persons created in the image of God *and* whether non-African American female persons would be encouraged to acknowledge and treat them as the same."[46]

In her book *Ingenuity: Preaching as an Outsider*, Thompson reminds us that while there is no universal experience of Black women, they do share the blessings, burdens, and challenges placed upon them from the legacy of having built this country with their forced and unpaid labor. This history, "while not the beginning of black womanhood, shaped and continues to shape the lived realities of black women's economic, physical, mental, and relational well-being," she says.[47] What womanist preachers show us, then, is the necessity of putting flesh on the bones of these lived realities. In other words, *embodiment* is critical when it comes to those whose bodies have been stolen, abused, raped, demonized, equated with animals, or otherwise harmed. In this way, womanist preaching moves us from an abstract and distant exegesis of the text to using sensory and active engagement both in sermon preparation and performance.[48]

When this commitment to bodies and embodiment happens in preaching, "The hope is not only to recover ignored and dispossessed voices but also to make space for their full inclusion."[49] How this space is made depends on the preacher and the listeners, and whether a witness or liberation ethic is used. For example, "When one preaches as an outsider or for the sake of the outsider, we have to determine ways to name the practical demands that call for one to be both self-reliant and God-reliant in the everyday stuff of life," says Thompson.[50] This would require the witness ethic that claims one's moral space amid immoral systems. At the same time, however, "we also have to determine ways to help a community and individuals envision an alternative path forward that makes space for tangible helpers in the here and now."[51] This would require the liberation ethic that motivates a community to organize around creating that alternative path.

In *Preaching the Headlines*, Thomspon notes that attending to embodiment in preaching means that "we cannot skip over matters of money, politics, and religion in preaching—because they are places that expose our faithlessness and cry out for a more just future."[52] Thus, preaching about social issues "connects to our bodies and how we make determinations about our personal autonomy, collective fate, and ability to live."[53] Here, we see Thompson invoke the care ethic in Haidt's moral foundations. And this ethic is firmly rooted in an incarnational theology that finds meaning in Jesus' earthly, fleshly life, death, and resurrection. "An incarnational faith does not leave room to ignore sufferings that are carnal at their core. Instead, it reclaims what happens to our physical bodies as being connected to our vitality and flourishing," she says.[54]

The care ethic is evident in a sermon Thompson preached on Hagar in which contemporary survivors of sexual and domestic violence were on her mind. She begins the sermon by describing Hagar's predicament as a slave whose body and sexual agency are not her own: "For the rest of her life, Hagar has to live with the marks of someone else making plans for her."[55] For Hagar, this takes the form of bondage, trauma, forced pregnancy, and even a forced return to her captors at the behest of God after she managed to escape. While God sends her back with "a promise of life, not death," Hagar will continue to suffer at the hands of Abraham and Sarah. Here, Thompson forthrightly names her discomfort with the theological ramifications of this situation. In other words, she is "talking back to the text," as Wilda C. Gafney puts it (see chapter 6). This is a bold, witness ethic move—pushing back against the theodicy question and preaching *against* the text itself.

In the second half of the sermon, Thompson sits with Hagar, now a mother to Ishmael and no longer a runaway but, rather, a refugee, forced from her home and into the wilderness. This is the place where Hagar will get temporary provisions to sustain her before she moves into God's plans for her and her son. One can imagine preaching about "getting a plan" to listeners who find themselves in Hagar's temporary liminal place—perhaps women in a shelter, girls running from abuse, or mothers living with family members to escape a violent partner. Her words both comfort and empower: "We do not have to make a choice between surviving, our sanity, our safety, our health, our joy, and the promises of God. Promise goes along with you wherever you go. It zigzags around you in innocent joy and grows, just like Ishmael. And as a matter of fact, you have to survive in order for the promise to survive."[56] She concludes by proclaiming that "God's desires are for us to live, to thrive—our whole self, flesh, spirit, and mind—here in this place. . . . Let's make life anew. Amen."[57] This sermon clearly demonstrates the witness ethic to empower listeners who identify with Hagar's plight and uses both storytelling and a Robust *be blunt, be bold* strategy.

Postcolonial Homiletics: Liberation and Witness Ethics

Postcolonial homiletics is a vibrant, emerging discipline of the field of preaching that examines the cultural, social, and political effects of colonialism and imperialism, especially in terms of power dynamics, identity, and representation. Postcolonial homileticians interrogate the ways in which the history of colonized peoples shapes their interpretation of biblical texts, their relationship to power structures, and the cultural dynamics that affect styles of preaching. Their goal is to resist hegemonic systems of power and liberate preaching from the shackles of White, Western patriarchy. These homileticians tend to use either the liberation or witness ethic, depending on their audience and goals for a particular sermon.

For postcolonial preachers, there is no option *not* to address social issues. This is because their very lives and communities are affected by social issues at every turn. Whether it's the dangers of migration, the suffocation of racism and xenophobia, the dehumanization of extractive labor and poverty, or the intersections of gender and sexuality within colonial issues, postcolonial preachers and congregations face multiple levels of trauma that require a pastorally prophetic word. But *how* postcolonial preachers craft their sermons is as rich and varied as the many diverse cultural, geographic, and historical contexts from which they emerge.[58] Here, we'll encounter two postcolonial preachers: HyeRan Kim-Cragg and Lis Valle-Ruiz.

HyeRan Kim-Cragg's Linguistic Homiletic

HyeRan Kim-Cragg holds a unique vantage point to present a postcolonial preaching methodology. Her working gospels are social justice and identity politics as a Korean woman teaching homiletics in a Canadian city situated on unceded Indigenous land. She brings firsthand insights into the intersections of culture, immigration, language, misogyny, and racial and ethnic stereotyping. In her book *Postcolonial Preaching: Creating a Ripple Effect*, Kim-Cragg skillfully weaves these perspectives into a postcolonial homiletic approach, offering valuable tools for preaching about social issues.[59] Her method facilitates the deconstruction of oppressive colonialist hegemony while enabling the creation of multilayered sermons that convey a liberative and hope-filled truth. Her moral foundations are grounded in care and liberation.

The central theme of Kim-Cragg's book revolves around the ripple effect, creating waves that disrupt the prevailing narratives of the White, Western, patriarchal Christian paradigm. This paradigm has historically justified actions such as invasion, extraction, domination, enslavement, and erasure of those labeled as "other." The term "RIPPLE" serves as an acronym for "rehearsal, imagination, place, pattern, language, and exegesis," all of which form the concentric circles of a postcolonial approach to preaching.

For preachers addressing social issues, a postcolonial perspective is necessary for the deconstruction and reconstruction process. "The church has too often been complicit with colonialism and its more recent manifestation, neoliberal transnational capitalism," Kim-Cragg says. Thus, "postcolonial preachers have a distinctive role to play in terms of faithfully interrogating and scrutinizing the [biblical] text as a way of challenging the status quo."[60] By incorporating postcolonial perspectives into their preaching, ministers can create a more inclusive, culturally aware, and socially just approach to their sermons.[61]

Preachers who attend to postcolonial perspectives learn to actively listen to the voices that have been silenced; appreciate cultural and linguistic distinctions among colonized communities; unveil power imbalances between the colonized and colonizers; and, ideally, compose imaginative sermons that declare liberating good news for both the oppressed and oppressor. Her approach modulates between the liberation and witness ethics, depending on the context and purpose for her sermon.

For example, one of her sermons highlights the intricacies of the term *family*, examining its portrayal in Chinese characters ("all will be well when family is well") as well as its significance in the Cree language ("all my relations," encompassing Earth-kin).[62] She then intertwines these linguistic nuances with Jesus' assurance in John 14:15-21 that he will not abandon his followers but, rather, will send the Spirit, fostering connections among them, with himself, and with God. The social issue she addresses is the plight of essential workers in Canada during the height of the COVID-19 pandemic, many of whom were Asian. Kim-Cragg urges her listeners to see the people whose sacrifice is enabling their own survival as part of their own family. Thus, the sermon effectively uses the liberation ethic by placing emphasis on and acknowledging the culture and language of colonized people while offering insights into Jesus' concern for individual and communal well-being.

In a sermon about Zaccheus's repentance in Luke 19:1-10, however, Kim-Cragg demonstrates the witness ethic. She preached at the 2018 Annual Meeting of the Saskatchewan Conference of the United Church of Canada in the city where a jury acquitted a White man of murdering a young Indigenous Cree man whom he had shot dead. Pointing to Jesus as a "trickster" who upends the expectations of his community, along with Zaccheus's ensuing repentance and reparations, she notes that the tree he climbed symbolizes the presence of God's forgiveness and generosity. Thus, she uses the Gentle strategy of *name the issue and frame it biblically*. Her sermon was meant to encourage those in need of hope while they awaited repentance, justice, and reparations on the part of the White community. "Waiting alone without knowing the future is hard work. Waiting together can build expectations," she says.[63] She encourages them to draw their strength from the tree: "Stand for a new history, imagine a new future, and greet the realm of God in the grace of the Holy, who calls us to be 'humble like the Earth and stand tall like a tree.'"[64] In this way, she invokes the Invitational strategy of *history, mission, future*.

Lis Valle-Ruiz's "Burlesque-esque" Homiletic

One postcolonial preacher who pushes the boundaries of both embodiment and language is Lis Valle-Ruiz. She emerges from a Puerto Rican Amerindian ancestral heritage to present a "burlesque-esque" proclamation through an alter ego by the name of Sophia Divinatrix. In what she calls preaching through "negation," Valle-Ruiz reveals the underlying assumptions that White, Western Christians bring to both the worship space and the very act of preaching. Valle-Ruiz traces her homiletical approach back to the lineage of street preaching in the tradition of Israel's prophets and Jesus, who saw public spaces as open for prophetic proclamation. In the same way, Sophia Divinatrix claims her space in the public square to bend and break the rules of preaching in order to bend and break the Whiteness that constrains her.

In her ethical matrix, she effectively upends three of Haidt's moral foundations: authority, sanctity, and loyalty. Her witness ethic homiletic demonstrates that in the face of White colonial supremacy, the real moral good is not authority (a tool of White hegemony) but, rather, subversion. What becomes the source of authority for postcolonial bodies is not the White hierarchy but, rather, the experience of those whom the hierarchy has sought to dominate. And, when it comes to sanctity, her embodiment as a brown, colonized female body, which Whiteness considers degraded, is, in fact, holy. In the same way, loyalty is exited in Valle-Ruiz's homiletical ethic, and betrayal of the hegemonic systems becomes a moral virtue. Thus, liberty and care are the primary moral foundations for postcolonial preachers, and all the other matrices are deconstructed and reconfigured in the service of liberation and flourishing.

Valle-Ruiz's homiletical approach is best characterized by the witness ethic in that it claims and encourages the moral agency of listeners to stand against an unjust and inhumane world order. What makes her preaching as Sophia Dominatrix unique is that it uses no speech, thus exiting even the colonial constructs of language. Without words but with provocative gestures, props, and music, her sermon "An Exorcism of White Supremacy" vividly reveals, confronts, ties up, and ultimately gives over the "cloak" of Whiteness to the cross. "She ties whiteness in a bundle so that it takes less space and stops being the invisible force that covers and measures it all," Valle-Ruiz explains.[65] Part theater, part dance, and part pantomime, this sermon "showed through symbolic action, rather than by public speech, a utopian vision of a possible future: white supremacy bound and away, under the power of the Christian cross."[66] This is a strong witness ethic and utilizes a Robust strategy of *be blunt, be bold*—even without words.

This kind of preaching through negation using the theatricality of burlesque-esque may not be a style that most preachers can use on a regular basis. However, Valle-Ruiz explains that "what all preachers can most certainly do is to step into their tradition's definition of preaching, deploy their best skills at the service of the preaching task, and honor their own community's ways of preaching and communicating for the sake of testifying about their own experience of the Divine."[67]

Conclusion

In this chapter, we learned about four ethical categories for preaching—communicative, witness, liberation, and hospitality—to give us a way to organize different approaches to sermons about social issues (see Figure 7.1). We then looked at three traditions within homiletics—conversation and collaborative, African American, and postcolonial. We traced the development of conversational and collaborative preaching and noted how this tradition usually employs either the communicative or hospitality ethic. We then turned to two African American homileticians—Tyshawn Gardner and Lisa Thompson—who provided perspectives and tools for activating moral imagination; preaching into social crises and news headlines; and drawing on the deep wisdom of Black preaching forged in the furnace of slavery, Jim Crow, White patriarchal supremacy, and modern-day racism. Their approaches used three of the ethical approaches, communicative, liberation, and witness.

Finally, we looked at a postcolonial perspective for preaching and social issues, first with Korean-Canadian homiletician HyeRan Kim-Cragg and then with Puerto Rican homiletician Lis Valle-Ruiz. Kim-Cragg's postcolonial homiletic dismantles oppressive colonialist dominance while expressing a liberating and hopeful message of the gospel. Valle-Ruiz's approach from a postcolonial Puerto Rican perspective upends traditional White, Western assumptions about preaching and sermons through her use of theater, music, dance, and a wordless but fully embodied proclamation. In this section, we saw that postcolonial preaching typically uses the liberation and witness ethics and inverts three of Haidt's moral foundations with stirring and evocative results.

Together, these homiletic approaches offer transformative possibilities for reimagining and revitalizing a preacher's approach to social issues by challenging established norms and fostering inclusivity in the proclamation of the gospel. In the next chapter, we'll apply what we've learned so far about ethics, biblical interpretation, theological framing, and homiletical approaches to three social issues: immigration, systemic racism, and Christian nationalism.

Notes

1. John S. McClure, *Preaching Words: 144 Key Terms in Homiletics* (Louisville, KY: Westminster John Knox Press, 2007), 142.

2. See Ronald J. Allen, *Preaching the Topical Sermon* (Louisville, KY: Westminster John Knox Press, 1992).

3. McClure, *Preaching Words*, 143.

4. John S. McClure, *Ethical Approaches to Preaching: Choosing the Best Way to Preach About Difficult Issues* (Eugene, OR: Cascade Books, 2021), 1.

5. McClure, *Ethical Approaches*, 3.

6. McClure, 16–25.

7. McClure, 26.

8. McClure, 37.

9. McClure, 37.

10. McClure, 53.

11. McClure, 54.

12. McClure, 60.

13. McClure, 61.

14. McClure, *Preaching Words*, 72.

15. McClure, *Ethical Approaches*,92.

16. McClure, 105.

17. McClure, *Preaching Words*,18.

18. John McClure, *The Roundtable Pulpit: Where Leadership and Preaching Meet* (Nashville, TN: Abingdon, 1995).

19. Lucy Atkinson Rose, *Sharing the Word: Preaching in the Roundtable Church* (Louisville, KY: Westminster John Knox Press, 1997).

20. O. Wesley Allen Jr., *The Homiletic of All Believers: A Conversational Approach* (Louisville, KY: Westminster John Knox Press, 2005), 49.

21. Ronald J. Allen and O. Wesley Allen Jr., *The Sermon without End: A Conversational Approach to Preaching* (Nashville, TN: Abingdon, 2015).

22. Allen and Allen, 119.

23. Leah D. Schade, *Preaching in the Purple Zone: Ministry in the Red-Blue Divide* (Lanham, MD: Rowman & Littlefield, 2019).

24. Schade, 59–65.

25. Schade, 65–71.

26. Schade, chapters 6, 7, and 8.

27. Schade, 139–40.

28. Allen and Allen, *The Sermon without End*, 136.

29. Allen and Allen, 127.

30. Allen and Allen, 127.

31. Allen and Allen, 139.

32. Cleophus J. LaRue, "African American Preaching Perspectives," in *The New Interpreters Handbook of Preaching*,ed. Paul Scott Wilson (Nashville, TN: Abingdon Press, 2008), 294.

33. LaRue, 294.

34. LaRue, 295.

35. Tyshawn Gardner, *Social Crisis Preaching: Biblical Proclamation in Troubling Times* (Brentwood, TN: B&H Publishing, 2023), 3.
36. Gardner, 2.
37. Gardner, 7.
38. Gardner, 10.
39. Gardner, 66.
40. Gardner, 70.
41. Gardner, 13.
42. Gardner, 116–117.
43. Gardner, 18.
44. Gardner, 23.
45. Gardner, 91–93.
46. Raquel St. Clair, "Womanist Criticism," in *The New Interpreters Handbook of Preaching*, ed. Paul Scott Wilson (Nashville, TN: Abingdon Press, 2008), 170.
47. Lisa L. Thompson, *Ingenuity: Preaching as an Outsider* (Nashville, TN: Abingdon Press, 2018), xi–xii.
48. Thompson, 91–94.
49. Thompson, 140.
50. Thompson, 155.
51. Thompson, 155–56.
52. Thompson, *Preaching the Headlines: Possibilities and Pitfalls* (Minneapolis, MN: Fortress Press, 2021), 59.
53. Thompson, 33.
54. Thompson, 40.
55. Thompson, 111.
56. Thompson, 114.
57. Thompson, 115.
58. Christine Marie Smith's edited volume, *Preaching Justice: Ethnic and Cultural Perspectives* (Cleveland, OH: United Church Press, 1998, reissued by Wipf and Stock in 2008), gives a sampling of diverse marginalized voices, illustrating the complexity and profound influence of identity on a preacher's approach to their role. Chapters include perspectives of the disabled, Native Americans, African Americans, Filipinos, Hispanics, Korean Americans, Jews, and lesbians.
59. HyeRan Kim-Cragg, *Postcolonial Preaching: Creating a Ripple Effect* (Lanham, MD: Lexington Books, 2021).
60. Kim-Cragg, 118.
61. See Eunjoo Mary Kim, *Preaching Jesus: Postcolonial Approaches* (Lanham, MD: Rowman & Littlefield, 2024).

62. Kim-Cragg, *Postcolonial Preaching*, 99–102.
63. Kim-Cragg, 62.
64. Kim-Cragg, 63.
65. Lis Valle-Ruiz, "Non-Preaching? Unmasking (White) Preaching through Negation," in *Unmasking White Preaching: Racial Hegemony, Resistance, and Possibilities in Homiletics*, ed. Lis Valle-Ruiz and Andrew Wymer (Lanham, MD: Lexington Books, 2022), 207.
66. Valle-Ruiz, 210.
67. Valle-Ruiz, 214.

CHAPTER 8

Three Social Issues for Applying Ethics, Scripture, and Theology for Preaching

Immigration, Systemic Racism, and Christian Nationalism

So far in this book on preaching and social issues, we've looked at the ethical and moral foundations for addressing social issues in sermons, interwove them with biblical and theological frameworks from scholars with diverse hermeneutical standpoints, and connected all of this with homiletical theory and traditions that have taken different approaches to sermons about difficult topics. Along the way, I demonstrated how different strategies within the Gentle, Invitational, and Robust approaches to preaching on social issues can shape effective responses to societal challenges through preaching.

Now, it's time to utilize our ethical foundations, biblical and theological frameworks, and homiletical strategies to engage with three social issues that, at the time I'm writing this, are urgent and prevalent, affecting churches as well as the larger society. First, we'll focus on immigration, followed by an examination of systemic racism, and ending with Christian nationalism. This exploration aims to provide practical insights and offer workable ideas for addressing these complex societal challenges through nuanced and effective preaching.

Using Moral Foundations and Sermon Approaches for Preaching about Immigration

Recall from chapter 5 the six moral foundations outlined by Jonathan Haidt: care/harm, fairness/cheating, loyalty/betrayal, authority/subversion, sanctity/degradation, and liberty/oppression. The Latino/a biblical scholars we heard from in chapter 6 primarily work from the moral foundations of care and liberty, based on their reading of the Bible as a collection of stories about people on the move who face hardship, violence, vulnerability, oppression, and exploitation. They especially call for immigrants to be liberated from policies that exploit their labor, demonize their personhood, and deny their human rights solely on the basis of citizenship.

However, those who oppose welcoming migrants into their country also invoke two moral foundations: fairness/cheating and sanctity/degradation. For instance, some will argue that it's not fair for certain migrants to be allowed entrance into the country ahead of others who have waited patiently for their turn to gain citizenship. Even when it can be shown that these migrants are escaping a perilous situation in their own country, opponents argue that they are "cheating the system."

With the sanctity/degradation foundation, the harmful rhetoric used to describe migrants invokes imagery of parasites who drain our country's resources and whose language and culture pollute America. Even when data shows that migrants contribute a great deal to the country's economy,[1] as well as its culinary, cultural, and linguistic richness, opponents remain suspicious and hostile. To a lesser degree, the loyalty/betrayal foundation also comes into play in that expressing openness to people from a different nation could be interpreted as disloyalty to one's country.

But there is another layer complicating the issue of immigration—that of the two moral worldviews (Nurturing Parent and Strict Father) that we learned about from Frank Thomas in chapter 5. When it comes to immigrants themselves, many would identify with the Strict Father conservative worldview. Seventy-five percent of U.S. Latinos are either Catholic (50 percent) or Evangelical (25 percent),[2] so it's not surprising that as of 2021, Gallup calculated that half of Hispanics are Republican (however, nearly 60 percent of Hispanic Catholics lean toward Democratic candidates[3]). Republican Latinos were more supportive of border security and stricter policing of visa overstays than their Democratic counterparts who were more in favor of policies such as finding paths to citizenship for "Dreamers" (residents who came to the United States as undocumented children).[4]

It's also worth noting that views on immigration policy appear to be shaped by one's citizenship status. For example, a 2021 Pew Research Center study showed that Latinos/as who were natural born or had attained citizenship were less supportive of allowing children of undocumented parents to stay in the United States than those who were not yet citizens.[5] They were also less in favor of finding pathways to citizenship for undocumented citizens. All of this is to say that there is no monolithic Hispanic worldview because their politics are complicated and their views on policy issues are shaped by their lived experiences. This means that the way a preacher approaches immigration in a sermon will depend on whether their congregation is made up of Latinos/as or non-Hispanic Whites, and what citizenship status, political affiliations, worldviews, moral matrices, and working gospels are in play.

How might a preacher use the map of moral foundations for the Gentle, Invitational, and Robust approaches in a sermon on the issue of immigration? And how might they connect with the four ethical approaches in homiletics (communicative, witness, liberation, and hospitality)? Here are some suggestions.

Gentle Strategies for Immigration

At the basic level, the preacher can point out that there are, in fact, multiple ways to look at the issue of immigration. When a preacher acknowledges that different moral matrices exist on the issue of immigration, it communicates to listeners that what's important to them is also being considered by the one in the pulpit. This would work well with the hospitality ethic.

The matrices can also be shown to coexist within the biblical text itself. For example, a text in Leviticus has God calling on the Israelites to welcome the stranger ("When a stranger sojourns with you in your land, you shall not do him wrong. You shall treat the stranger who sojourns with you as the native among you, and you shall love him as yourself, for you were strangers in the land of Egypt: I am the Lord your God" [Leviticus 19:33-34]). This is clearly based on a care/harm foundation. Yet, in other texts, there are qualifiers on that welcomeness. For instance, Ezra and Nehemiah assert that foreigners cannot be allowed to intermarry with the Israelites (Ezra 9:1-2; Nehemiah chapter 13). And Deuteronomy states that the children of such unions are forbidden from entering the holy place of worship (7:3-6, 23:2). Here, we can see the loyalty/betrayal, authority/subversion, and sanctity/degradation foundations invoked. These texts also show us that differences in attitudes about how to treat those outside of one's group are as old as the Bible itself.

So, if the Bible doesn't even have clear instructions about how to receive and integrate foreigners, what can a preacher say about this kind of moral deadlock? Here, identifying the underlying ethical impulses to clearly, fairly, and accurately articulate them in the sermon is important. For example, a sermon addressing immigration in a politically divided congregation can name these moral foundations and be clear that the people holding them are doing so with the desire to do the right thing based on their moral matrix. In other words, it's not wrong to want to care about vulnerable migrants. At the same time, it's not wrong to value fairness and not want people to cheat the system. It's also not wrong to feel loyal to one's country. Nor is it wrong to want liberation for people who are being exploited and dehumanized.

For some, this may sound like being wishy-washy or capitulating to a "good people on both sides" position. So I want to clarify that such a sermon should be only a *starting point* for moving to deeper biblical and theological reflection about how people of faith can and should respond to their neighbors from other countries. This kind of sermon would be in the Gentle category, utilizing the strategy of *name the issue and frame it biblically* for a congregation that is caught in a fight-or-flight mode. The naming and framing approach is ideal for the hospitality ethic in homiletics to communicate that people are heard, their values are taken seriously, and their moral reasoning is respected. This allows the congregation to build and maintain relationships through ongoing collaboration and conversation. Once trust, respect, and openness have been established, a preacher can consider Invitational strategies for a deeper level of engagement on immigration.

Invitational Strategies for Immigration

After a preacher has given a sermon that accurately and fairly articulates the concerns of people about the many aspects of immigration, they could use the *sermon–dialogue–sermon* strategy within the Invitational approach to initiate a discussion about immigration in the congregation. In this scenario, the preacher's first sermon could explain the different perspectives and ethical values as discussed above and then invite people to a dialogue either that day or later in the week. For this discussion, the congregation could use resources from Living Room Conversations (LRC), a nonprofit organization founded in 2010 that focuses on bridging divides through conversation.

LRC offers "a simple, sociable and structured way to practice communicating across differences while building understanding and relationships." Typically, four to six people meet in person or by video call for about ninety minutes to listen to and be heard by others on one of their nearly one hundred topics. Rather than debating or convincing others, participants take turns talking to share, learn, and be curious. Because no preparation is required, these conversations can be led by the pastor or anyone else who's willing to host the conversation (although it is helpful if the person has had training in how to moderate public dialogue). The LRC website has resources with balanced views for those who want to be better informed before beginning the conversation.

For the dialogue, try to invite participants who have different perspectives and life experiences. The more diversity within the conversation, the more enriching it will be. But be sure to begin with the Conversation Agreement, which sets the respectful tone for the conversation with points such as *Be curious and listen to understand. Show respect and suspend judgment. Note any common ground as well as any differences. Be authentic and welcome that from others.*[6]

Following introductions, the group engages in two rounds of discussion. In one round, participants take approximately two minutes to answer one of the provided questions without interruption or cross talk. After everyone has answered, the group takes a few minutes for clarifying or follow-up questions and responses. Here are the questions for discussing immigration:

- What is at the heart of the immigration issue for you?
- What personal experiences inform your beliefs about immigration? It may be experiences of your family and friends.
- How does considering legal versus illegal immigration impact your feelings or positions?
- What about refugees? How welcoming should America be of people fleeing hardship and/or violence?[7]

Additional faith-based questions could also be included such as the following:

- How does your faith inform your views about immigration?
- In what ways do you think the Bible can inform our discussion about immigration?
- What do you think the church's role should be when it comes to people seeking a new life in this country?

In the next round of the conversation, the group discusses the following questions:

- In one sentence, share what was most meaningful or valuable to you in the experience of this Living Room Conversation?
- What new understanding or common ground did you find within this topic?
- Has this conversation changed your perception of anyone in this group, including yourself?
- Name one important thing that was accomplished here.
- Is there a next step you would like to take based on the conversation you just had?[8]

This last stage is especially helpful for the preacher when crafting the follow-up sermon after the dialogue. For example, people may have discovered that they share a mutual concern for the safety and well-being of children coming across the U.S. border. This would fall within the care/harm matrix, so the story of Mary and Joseph bringing their child Jesus to Egypt (Matt. 2:13-23) could find resonance. There may also be shared concern about the hurdles for seeking asylum or becoming a legal citizen in the United States. For this, both the fairness/

cheating and care/harm matrices can be utilized while invoking the story of Boaz easing the transition of Ruth into her new country (Ruth, chapters 2–4).

At the end of each Living Room Conversation, there is a question about next steps, which can point the way forward for a preacher who wants to go beyond the Gentle and Invitational approaches and toward a more Robust strategy.

Robust Strategies for Immigration
The *collaborate before, during, after* strategy would work well for a preacher whose congregation has a high level of trust and is ready to hear a message that is more direct. In this case, the preacher works collaboratively with members of a congregation on the sermon process so that there is an integration of the different viewpoints of those who would like to see the congregation put their faith into action. In preparing for a sermon about the issue of immigration, the preacher could gather a group of individuals who covenant with each other to listen deeply to lived experiences of those in their community who have migrated from other countries. This could be done in cooperation with a local refugee resettlement program or a neighboring church that ministers for and with a migrant community.

Then, the preacher would work with this group of parishioners in crafting the sermon. They would think critically about the challenges of addressing immigration and work creatively to craft a collaborative sermon that engages the congregation. They might consider a reader's theater type of sermon where members of the team each share their perspective and what they learned. Or each might share about one of the people they met who has endured the process of migration. (Be sure to obtain the person's permission first, or change significant details to ensure their anonymity.) The pastor could bookend the sermon with one of the many stories of migration in Scripture, such as Joseph's being sent into slavery in a strange land (Genesis 37-46), or the biblical summary of Israel's ancestral migration to Egypt, the exodus from Egypt, and the entry into the promised land (Deut. 26:5-9). The sermon could emphasize one of the moral foundations that undergirds this work, such as care or liberty.

The goal in this sermon would be to move toward a call to action for the congregation that reflects one of their core ethical values.

The group can then host a session with the congregation to receive feedback about what they heard, how they felt, and what they learned about their own ethical values as well as what they intend to do to live out their faith with regard to those who are migrants in their community. This type of sermon could be in the communicative ethic if it proclaims a strong moral value that has emerged from the congregation's mutual discernment process. Or it could be in the liberation ethic if it calls for a specific action in which the congregation can participate.

Using Moral Foundations and Sermon Approaches to Preach about Systemic Racism

In chapter 6, we engaged with three Black feminist theologians and biblical scholars—Jacqueline Grant, Dolores Williams, and Wilda Gafney—who showed us how the experiences of Black women are integral sources for theological reflection and biblical interpretation. Their work helps to rectify the historical and ongoing injustice of neglecting Black women's narratives, experiences, and insights regarding the authority of Scripture. Then, in chapter 7, we explored African American preaching perspectives of two Black homileticians. Tyshawn Gardner's social crisis preaching grew out of his formation in the Black church and made the case that addressing social issues is a necessary response to the salvation of Jesus Christ, the liberating work of the Holy Spirit, and the sovereignty of God's justice. Lisa Thompson's womanist homiletic brings the layers of gender, race, and economics to the pulpit through a liberationist theology of embodiment that centers the struggles, joys, and hopes of Black women.

If you are a White preacher and/or serving a primarily White congregation, you may be wondering how best to apply these vital insights into sermons that address the issue of systemic racism. Carolyn Helsel, a White preacher and professor of preaching, has been asking this question for nearly two decades, and her work on preaching about racism in White congregations offers important guidance. She points out three reasons why White Christians need to address systemic racism: (1) White people were the ones to construct racist ideologies to justify enslaving African peoples, (2) they did so using racist interpretations of the Bible, and (3) they continue to benefit from a racist system.[9]

In *Preaching about Racism*, she provides a comprehensive approach for pastors to dismantle racism in their congregations through preaching that is biblical, theological, attentive to context, and prophetic. A preacher could utilize strategies in the Gentle, Invitational, and Robust approaches using Helsel's work.

Gentle Strategies for Addressing Racism

Helsel acknowledges that preachers who are hesitant about addressing racism often worry about sounding "political." So she offers advice that is very much in line with what we have learned in this book about focusing on shared values: "Key for religious leaders who live in 'purple areas,' where there are numbers of people on both sides of the political spectrum, is to focus on values shared in common."[10] She encourages preachers to provide opportunities for people to take part in conversations and "listen to perspectives that share different values."[11] These conversations should engage biblical texts that convey the struggles of oppressed peoples in the past. And it should include the history of slavery, Jim Crow laws, segregation, and the civil rights movement as well as the ongoing legacy of systemic racism that manifests in voter suppression, health care inequities, redlining neighborhoods, and police brutality.

Helsel recommends starting from a place of *gratitude*—expressing gratefulness for the presence and gifts of the congregation and their willingness to listen to God's call to live differently and respond to the invitation to address such a challenging subject. This would fit well with the *name the issue and frame it biblically* strategy within the Gentle approach. Then, the preacher would move into the role of teacher.[12] At a basic level, this involves educating the congregation about what the term *racism* means—including debunking common myths and "wishful thinking" that racism will just go away on its own. Such a sermon can help them understand the ramifications of living in a racialized society and articulate the complicated feelings that emerge when people learn about all of this. For this, the *stand with the congregation, voice the feelings* strategy would work well.

Key to this work is the preacher's willingness to tell their own story about their journey of learning about racism and what emotions they felt along the way. Here, the *share your own struggles with the issue* strategy can work in a sermon located within the hospitality ethic because it helps the congregation build trust to go to a deeper level of confronting racism.

Invitational Strategies for Addressing Racism

As the preacher and congregation move into the more intense work of anti-racism, Helsel encourages strategies that fit well with the Invitational approach. One would utilize *tell stories to create empathy* but with a twist, because the story is about what *Whites* lose in a racist economy and society. The preacher would explain that it's not enough to feel empathy toward racialized *others*; White people must see that systemic racism actually harms their own well-being. "If our white congregations are going to challenge racism, they need to see it as impacting their own lives, not just the lives of other people," Helsel says.[13]

One book that is helpful for this is Heather McGhee's *The Sum of Us: What Racism Costs Everyone and How We Can Prosper Together*.[14] McGhee is a public policy expert who uses both data and compelling stories to illustrate the harmful fallacy of the zero-sum mentality that pits different racialized groups against each other. Her ethic of fostering interconnectedness and economic parity for the well-being of all is an approach that preachers can utilize in their sermons addressing social issues, particularly around race. For example, in recounting the demise of public swimming pools in America after desegregation, she shows how White people lost this public treasure. The same goes for health care, education, the environment, homeownership, and wages—all of which have been affected by racist policies that actually harm White people alongside their neighbors of color. Thus, a sermon series on racism could be accompanied by a book discussion group on *The Sum of Us* so that the stories of empathy would be about *ourselves*, what we have lost through racist policies, and what we can do to restore the common good—and common wealth—for everyone.

Robust Strategies for Addressing Racism

Addressing racism is more than just a societal issue. For White Christians, it's about understanding that confronting racism "also meets a deep need for their own spiritual growth and development."[15] In other words, this work is about our faith identity as both individuals and congregations. Helsel believes that by casting a prophetic vision for what it means to work toward greater justice for everyone, it will speak to a deep need within White congregants to both "recognize the painful legacy of racism *and* connect . . . to a promised redemption that includes all of God's people."[16] Here, an anti-racist sermon would turn toward a communicative ethic in that it would appeal to a moral high ground by inspiring listeners to follow God's call toward racial justice.

Helsel also suggests giving space for members who are engaging in this work to "share their experiences and invite others to join them . . . as part of our identity as people of faith."[17] This would be moving toward a more Robust approach where a preacher could use *collaborate before, during, and after*. For example, if a group of parishioners joins the preacher in undertaking anti-racism training or joins in community efforts of racial and cultural bridge-building, the preacher could work with them before the sermon to develop short testimonials to share during the sermon about what it's like, what they are learning, and why it's important to their faith. As more people join the work, the process of "preflection" (reflecting before a planned encounter or service event), action, and reflection can be expanded to include others from different perspectives and with varied experiences.

As you've seen from this exploration of preaching on immigration and systemic racism, a preacher wanting to address a social issue can utilize Haidt's moral foundations within any of the Gentle, Invitational, or Robust strategies. And while these are just two examples, you can apply these strategies to any topic, be it transgender rights, women's access to reproductive health care, gun violence, or any issue that may require a process of moving from Gentle to Invitational to Robust.

But we must also consider the ways in which the dialogue on a social issue may become blocked or derailed due to people who have opinions about a topic that are shaped by propaganda, misinformation, and intentional fearmongering. These are the tactics of Christian nationalism, a movement that has hijacked civil discourse in the United States to the point where dialogue is sidelined and preaching is muzzled. So our third section will focus on Christian nationalism—what it is; how ministers can try to build bridges of understanding; and how ethical, biblical, and theological framing can counter this divisive and dangerous ideology.

Using Moral Foundations and Sermon Approaches for Preaching about Christian Nationalism

To help us make sense of Christian nationalism and how to respond to it in preaching, we turn to two scholars—Pamela Cooper-White and Andrew L. Whitehead—who have thought deeply about approaches to this movement and how congregations and clergy can counter this belief system in order to steer the church back to the teachings of Jesus.

WHAT IS CHRISTIAN NATIONALISM?

Andrew L. Whitehead and Samuel L. Perry define Christian nationalism as "a cultural framework—a collection of myths, traditions, symbols, narratives and value systems—that idealizes and advocates a fusion of Christianity with American civic life."[18] They note that in Christian nationalism, "Christianity represents something more than religion. . . . It includes assumptions of nativism, white supremacy, patriarchy, and heteronormativity, along with divine sanction for authoritarian control and militarism."[19] The term Christian nationalism itself came into usage in the early 2000s, but the phenomenon it names—fusing national identity with Christianity—has been in existence since the 1800s. In the U.S., Christian nationalism finds its roots in the fusion of conservative Christianity, White supremacy, and right-wing politics.[20]

Carter Heyward identifies seven key features of Christian nationalism: lust for omnipotence, entitlement, White supremacy, misogyny, capitalist spirituality, domination of the Earth and its creatures, and violence.[21] She uses the term *christofascism* to describe the Christian nationalist agenda, "a seductive form of authoritarianism taking shape among us in the guise of Christian faith and all-American values, especially the value of liberty, or freedom, even at the expense of the common good."[22] A term first coined by the German theologian Dorothee Soelle, christofascism is the unholy trinity of Christianity, capitalism, and conservative political power. As early as the 1980s, Soelle recognized the beginnings of American theocracy made in the image of rich, White Christian men—exactly as she saw in fascist Germany in the 1930s.

How is nationalism different from patriotism? Pamela Cooper-White explains that "Patriotism, simply stated, is love for one's country, while nationalism is the identification of that country with a historically dominant ethnic, cultural, and/or religious group and a fierce loyalty to protecting that national identity."[23] In other words, one can be patriotic and not be a Christian nationalist. However, Christian nationalists often use the term "patriotism" to rationalize their harmful stances and actions.

According to a study by Public Religion Research Institute and Brookings, approximately 30% of Americans are either "adherents" or "sympathizers" with Christian nationalist beliefs.[24] Cooper-White's terminology is "true believers" (hardcore) and "soft Christian nationalist" (nationalist-leaning). There are different degrees of Christian nationalism (CN), and scholars use different terminology to describe them. Below is a chart that explains the terms that scholars use.

An excellent book for understanding an historical perspective of preaching against christofascism is Dean G. Stroud's edited volume, *Preaching in Hitler's Shadow: Sermons of Resistance in the Third Reich*. Stroud describes how Hitler used Christianity to give a patina of religious legitimacy to his Nazi ideology, a process eerily paralleled by today's Christian nationalists. The book includes thirteen sermons by German pastors who saw what was happening and courageously spoke out against the Third Reich. These sermons can serve as inspiration and models for those wanting to preach against Christian nationalism today.[25]

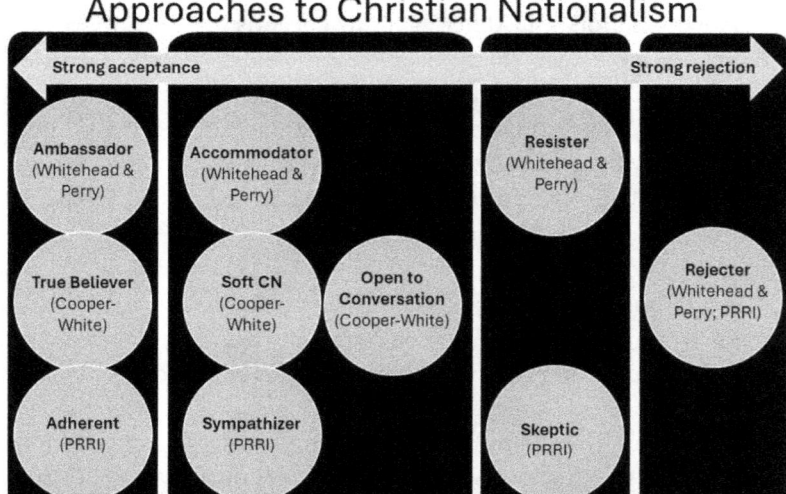

Figure 8.1 **Approaches to Christian Nationalism.** Graphic created by Leah D. Schade. Referencing the following works: "A Christian Nation? Understanding the threat of white Christian nationalism to American democracy and culture," Public Religion Research Institute [PRRI], Feb. 28, 2023; Andrew L. Whitehead and Scott L. Perry [Whitehead & Perry], *Taking America Back for God: Christian Nationalism in the United State*s (Oxford University Press, 2020); Pamela Cooper-White, *The Psychology of Christian Nationalism: Why People Are Drawn In and How to Talk Across the Divide* (Minneapolis, MN: Fortress Press, 2022).

Gentle and Invitational Strategies for Christian Nationalism—Pamela Cooper-White

Pamela Cooper-White has dedicated her research to the study of psychology and religion with an emphasis on pastoral theology, care, and counseling. She has written extensively on social issues from a Christian perspective, spanning the topics of gender; violence; racism, antisemitism; and, most recently, Christian nationalism. In her 2022 book, *The Psychology of Christian Nationalism: Why People Are Drawn In and How to Talk across the Divide*, Cooper-White not only explains the values that undergird Christian nationalism (and how they are manipulated and exploited by politicians and those intent on undermining democracy) but also suggests an approach for finding at least some points of common ground to start rebuilding relationships within congregations and the larger society.

In her quest to understand why people are drawn in by extremist beliefs, Cooper-White identifies the conscious motivations that are manipulated and weaponized by leaders with a Christian nationalist agenda. She names the most prominent conscious motivations as "evangelism and the need for belonging and a sense of purpose; fear of loss of white social status, resentment, and a desire for power; fear of loss of patriarchal authority; and the irrational allure of conspiracy theories."[26]

Here, we can overlay Haidt's moral foundations and recognize the values that motivate people who are attracted to Christian nationalism. Loyalty is a core value undergirding the need for belonging and a sense of purpose, which they find with fellow Christian nationalists. The desire for liberty morphs into exercising personal agency and power over others without constraints on one's own behaviors. The foundation of authority is a pillar of the male-dominated hierarchy within Christian nationalism. And, when it comes to conspiracy theories, we can see that one of the reasons fabricated stories activate the outrage impulse is because they manipulate one or more of the moral foundations. For example, fear about liberal elite child abuse rings activates the care/harm ethic.[27] Fear about stolen elections triggers the fairness/cheating matrix. And anti-vaccination campaigns invoke both the sanctity/degradation foundation, by calling for a purity untainted by the ingredients of inoculations, and the liberty/oppression foundation, by demanding freedom from government-mandated vaccines.

So how can Christians talk across the divide and extend compassion and understanding across the chasm of extreme difference? Cooper-White acknowledges that the task is not easy because many White Christians live "for all intents and purposes, in an alternate reality where nationalistic rhetoric, lies, and disinformation look like a last best hope. Splitting between good and evil abounds in the thought world of Christian nationalists."[28] The echo chamber of conservative news shows, right-wing social media, and conservative religious preaching and evangelism can make it seem like honest, open conversation is not even possible.

Yet she believes that this kind of conversation is the best way to bridge the divide, and she offers a triage process to determine if fruitful conversation is possible. First, you have to ask, "Am I the right person to have this conversation with this person?" And "is this the right time, the right place, [and] the right social context in which to have such a discussion?"[29] Then, she offers three possibilities for engagement using the metaphor of a traffic light: "(1) red light: STOP—talking will do no good—at least not here, not now, not by me; (2) yellow light: try but tread lightly; and (3) green light: go deeper, gently and wisely."[30] This traffic light metaphor is helpful for thinking through who, when, where, and why to preach a sermon addressing Christian nationalism (or any volatile public issue, for that matter)

Red Light—STOP!
If a preacher has Christian nationalist true believers, adherents, or ambassadors in the congregation, Cooper-White's instruction about ensuring one's own integrity and safety is apt. This is a red-light situation which requires us to stop because direct confrontation has been shown not only to be ineffective but actually results in further entrenchment. So, if you preach a sermon that takes on Christian nationalism and you are confronted about it in a way that makes you feel that you or others are unsafe or that your sense of integrity is being violated by hate speech or psychological manipulation, it is usually best to change the subject or walk away calmly and respectfully. Cooper-White clarifies that this is not being acquiescent. "In fact, part of our self-care in such a situation is precisely the opposite of retreat—it is simply moving our ethical work and our energy for what we believe to be right where it will fall on more receptive ears, and working actively for justice and for social change in the long run."[31]

Yellow Light—Tread Lightly
A yellow-light situation involves a person who is an accommodator, sympathizer, or soft Christian nationalist—someone who is nationalist leaning but might be open to meaningful, honest conversation. In this

case, Cooper-White advises, "the first step is probably not to talk much at all—at least not right away—but to listen and show respect."[32] Preachers can find this kind of opening with parishioners with whom they already have some level of trust through pastoral care; healthy fellowship; and positive interactions during service events, church meetings, or volunteering.

A yellow-light conversation is best served by asking questions that help unearth the moral foundations underlying the person's position. From my own training in deliberative dialogue, I have found the following questions helpful for cultivating genuine curiosity and empathy:

- What is it like for you in this place or this situation?
- Can you tell me more about how you came to think or feel this way?
- Is there a story you can tell me about an experience you've had that can help me understand where you're coming from?
- (*If you detect one of the underlying moral foundations*): It sounds like [fairness, loyalty, freedom, etc.] is very important to you in this situation. Is there someone from your life or your childhood who instilled that value in you? Can you tell me about them?

Questions like these can open a path to genuine dialogue and relationship-building. However, Cooper-White cautions that the conversation could veer into a red-light situation if it starts to feel unsafe or "feels too much like signaling agreement and betraying one's own values." If this happens, she says, "it's time to calmly say, 'I'm afraid I just can't agree with that.'"[33] And, I would add, be sure to thank the person for being honest with you and sharing their thoughts and feelings. Saying "You've given me a lot to think about" or "I've learned a lot from this conversation" are honest and respectful ways to end the discussion.

Green Light—Go Deeper, Gently, and Wisely
A green-light situation is for a person who is open to conversation—they may hold some Christian nationalist views but are not completely drawn in. In this case, the conversation partners demonstrate authentic openness and willingness to reexamine their

own convictions—not just attack and tear down the other person's position. In these situations, Cooper-White emphasizes that "building and maintaining relationship always comes first."[34] Thus, the hospitality ethic for preaching would be appropriate in that the sermon would seek to establish trust and openness between people with diverging viewpoints. This means finding common ground and practicing kindness and compassion, even while speaking truth in love. She also advises that we must recognize that these kinds of conversations can stir up old family dynamics both within ourselves and within our conversation partner. So we need to be cognizant of our own habitual responses to anxiety and have a plan for getting ourselves "unhooked," or disengaged.[35] This requires breathing, pausing, and checking ourselves before reacting out of a conditioned response. Noticing our own feelings (especially defensiveness) can help disengage reactivity. (See chapter 11 for more detailed steps about how to handle negative pushback to a sermon.)

Also helpful in a green-light conversation is listening with intentionality so that you can truly understand and be able to paraphrase what you've heard the other say. For example, a response could be "What I hear you saying is . . . Do I have that right? Am I understanding you correctly?" This allows us to avoid making assumptions and to adjust our thinking about the other's position if we've misunderstood. Then, when we want to make our own point, we use *I* language to avoid overgeneralizing or universalizing our own experiences or conclusions. Here, Cooper-White shares a summary of Jonathan Haidt's advice that I believe can be helpful:

> To get along better, we should all be less self-righteous. We should recognize that nearly all of us are good people, and that our conflicts arise from our belonging to different cultural groups with different moral intuitions. We're very good at seeing through our opponents' moral rationalizations, but we need to get better at seeing our own. More specifically, liberals and conservatives should try to understand one another, be less hypocritical, and be more open to compromise.[36]

Figure 8.2 contains a graphic with the "traffic light" for a summary of the three approaches for talking to someone about Christian nationalism.

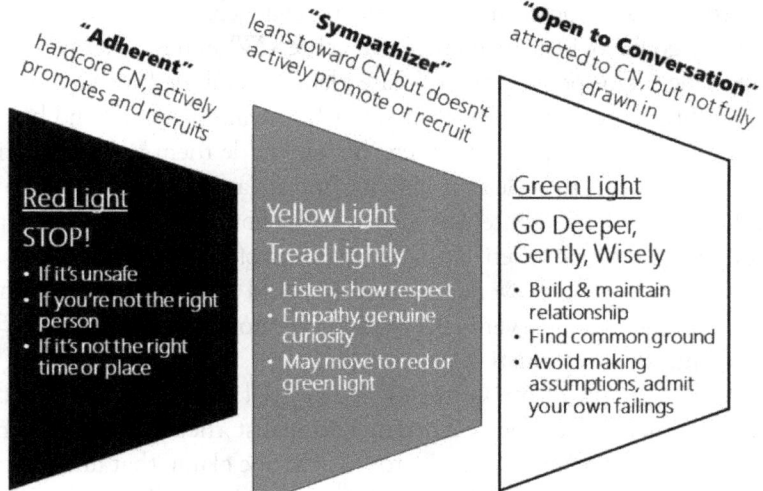

Figure 8.2 How to Talk Across the Divide with Christian Nationalists. Graphic created by Leah D. Schade based on the work of Pamela Cooper-White in *The Psychology of Christian Nationalism: Why People are Drawn In and How to Talk Across the Divide* (Minneapolis, MN: Fortress Press, 2022).

Strategies for Sermons on Christian Nationalism

Andrew L. Whitehead is a social scientist specializing in religion and American culture. While he uses data and scholarly research to verify the danger and harm of Christian nationalism, he also counters the beliefs of this movement with Christian teachings based on the Bible and, specifically, the life of Jesus. He brings a unique perspective to the study of Christian nationalism because he was raised in the evangelical church. With an insider's insight into the fusion of this branch of Christianity with the conservative political agenda in the United States, Whitehead issues a compelling and undeniable warning about the threat of Christian nationalism in his book, *American Idolatry: How Christian Nationalism Betrays the Gospel and Threatens the Church*. He points out that not only does this movement hurt those affected by its violent and fascistic agenda; it is the exact opposite of what the church is called to be.

Christian nationalists adhere to the Strict Father conservative worldview and utilize the working gospels of American sentimentalism,

American exceptionalism, prosperity, and evangelism. They also have a working gospel of identity politics that centers Whiteness and the White experience. This privileging of White identity combined with conservative political ideology leads to citizens who "demand and defend [their] own rights at the expense of others, not alongside them."[37] Taken to its extreme, such attitudes lead to bullying, intimidation, stripping of rights, and violence. This, Whitehead argues, is the consequence of American idolatry, and it is antithetical to the teachings of Christ.

With Whitehead's work, a preacher could start with Invitational strategies that would eventually lead into a more Robust approach for preaching against Christian nationalism.

As an example of Invitational strategies, *tell stories to create empathy* can work to deconstruct Christian nationalist rhetoric about immigrants. Whitehead encourages us to "look at one claim, that immigrants or religious minorities coming into our communities will raise the crime rate. Who isn't afraid of increasing levels of crime?"[38] Here, we can see the moral foundation of care/harm in that people are concerned about safety. But, Whitehead advises, "when we sense fear, we should commit to examining whether the fear is warranted."[39] Further, he poses questions that can be helpful for releasing our fears and seeing things from another's perspective, thus cultivating empathy: "What would we hope to receive from those in power if we were immigrants and refugees? If we found ourselves in a country that was not our own, at the mercy of those who could claim the benefits of citizenship all to themselves, how would we hope to be received?"[40] These are questions that can be asked in a sermon to cultivate ethical imagination and empathy.

Such a sermon would move toward the communicative ethic because it would build consensus about the moral norms that should guide the community's stance and engagement on immigration. The preacher would do so by echoing Whitehead's conclusion that ultimately, "focusing on fear and threat makes us bad neighbors. Our fear keeps us from living out the call of Christ. We cannot embrace a nationalist vision of Christianity that desires control and dominion over others when Jesus came to liberate all so we could freely love all."[41] In summary, the preacher would interrogate Christian nationalist assumptions and stake a claim based on the care and liberation moral matrices.

In my own work of creating homiletical resources for countering Christian nationalism, I developed a Lenten sermon series for the

Wisconsin Council of Churches' study-action guide, *Jesus and Justice in Public*, with sermon themes and prompts for readings in Year A of the Revised Common Lectionary.[42] The Robust strategy for each entry was *be blunt, be bold* in that I urged preachers to explicitly critique aspects of Christian nationalism using biblical stories. For example, for the First Sunday of Lent, based on Matt. 4:1-11 (Satan tempting Jesus), I focused on countering the temptations of Christian nationalism and urged preachers to draw parallels between the three temptations Satan offers Jesus (bread, jumping from the pinnacle, all the kingdoms of the world) and the allures of Christian nationalist ideology (status and agency, sacrifice for a leader, and political power). The preacher would urge listeners to "resist those demonic temptations and stay true to our faith in God."[43] This type of sermon would adhere to the witness ethic because it would provide a countercultural moral vision against the Christian nationalist meta-narrative.

Other sermon starters in the series countered anti-Semitism, misogyny and toxic masculinity, and disability discrimination. And, for the entry on White supremacy, based on Ezekiel 37:1-14 (the valley of dry bones), I recommended a Robust strategy of *equip for justice* by encouraging congregations to advocate for voting rights and call for the end of gerrymandering, "which literally disconnects Black neighborhoods from the body politic."[44] Similarly, in the entry for Palm Sunday, countering the violence of Christian nationalism, based on Matthew 27:15-31, I urged preachers to have their congregations join grassroots movements of nonviolent civil disobedience, such as the Poor People's Campaign. These types of sermons could be categorized either as the witness ethic (if the sermon's goal is cultivating a virtue ethic of moral agency against Christian nationalism) or liberation ethic (if the preacher wants the congregation to organize or join with other groups working for social change that counters Christian nationalism).

Conclusion

Now that we've seen how to apply ethical, biblical, theological, and homiletical foundations to sermonic approaches to three social issues—immigration, systemic racism, and Christian nationalism—it's time to look at examples from preachers who can give us further insights and models for this work. In the next chapter, we will examine two sermons by preachers who used the same biblical text but tackled different topics in two different settings. After that, I'll share case studies in chapter 9 from students who have experimented with the tools and tactics in this book. These exemplars will illustrate that when a preacher engages in profound and strategic contemplation about ethics, Scripture, and theology for shaping our perspective on contemporary issues, they can boldly articulate God's Word. In doing so, they can increase their capacity to confront injustice, champion the cause of the vulnerable, foster the unity of the church, and inspire the determination of a congregation to translate their faith into meaningful action. This approach to preaching and social issues can go a long way toward bridging political divides, drawing together people from different ideological poles, and living out the "ministry of reconciliation" for which Paul advocates (2 Cor 5:18-19).

Notes

1. An article by the World Economic Forum notes that as the debate rages over "whether immigrants 'steal' jobs and lower national wages or expand the economy through hard work and innovation," a study finds that while immigrants make up roughly 15 percent of U.S. workers, they are 80 percent more likely to become entrepreneurs. This means that they start companies and hire new workers, which creates a positive overall effect on the economy. See World Economic Forum, "Here's How Immigrants Have Boosted the U.S. Economy," published September 17, 2020, accessed January 13, 2024, https://www.weforum.org/agenda/2020/09/immigrants-expand-the-us-economy/.

2. Pew Research Center Religious Landscape Study, "Latinos Who Are Conservative," published 2014, accessed February 1, 2024, https://www.pewresearch.org/religion/religious-landscape-study/political-ideology/conservative/racial-and-ethnic-composition/latino/.

3. Jens Manuel Krogstad, Khadijah Edwards, and Mark Hugo Lopez, "Latinos and the 2022 Midterm Elections," Pew Research Center, accessed February 1, 2024, https://www.pewresearch.org/race-ethnicity/2022/09/29/latinos-and-the-2022-midterm-elections/.

4. Jens Manuel Krogstad and Mark Hugo Lopez, "Most Latinos Say U.S. Immigration System Needs Big Changes," Pew Research Center, published April 20, 2021, accessed February 1, 2024, https://www.pewresearch.org/short-reads/2021/04/20/most-latinos-say-u-s-immigration-system-needs-big-changes/.

5. Krogstad and Lopez.

6. Living Room Conversations, "Conversation Agreements," accessed January 16, 2024, https://livingroomconversations.org/conversation_agreements/.

7. Living Room Conversations, "Immigration Conversation Guide," accessed January 16, 2024, https://livingroomconversations.org/topics/immigration/.

8. Living Room Conversations, "Immigration Conversation Guide."

9. Carolyn B. Helsel, *Preaching about Racism: A Guide for Faith Leaders* (St. Louis, MO: Chalice Press, 2018), 4.

10. Helsel, 6.

11. Helsel, 6.

12. For an excellent book on how preachers can claim their identity as teachers to help their congregations critically engage in social issues, see Richard W. Voelz, *Preaching to Teach: Inspire People to Think and Act* (Nashville, TN: Abingdon Press, 2019).

13. Helsel, *Preaching about Racism*, 44.

14. Heather McGhee, *The Sum of Us: What Racism Costs Everyone and How We Can Prosper Together* (New York, NY: One World, 2022).

15. Helsel, *Preaching about Racism*, 44.

16. Helsel, 44–45.

17. Helsel, 53.

18. Andrew L. Whitehead and Scott L. Perry, *Taking America Back for God: Christian Nationalism in the United States* (Oxford University Press, 2020), 10.

19. Whitehead and Perry, 10.

20. See: Tim Alberta, *The Kingdom, the Power, and the Glory: American Evangelicals in an Age of Extremism* (New York: Harper, 2023); Kristen Kobes Du Mez, *Jesus and John Wayne: How White Evangelicals Corrupted a Faith and Fractured a Nation* (New York: Liveright Publishing Corp, a division of W.W. Norton & Co., 2020); Philip S. Gorski and Samuel L. Perry, *The Flag and the Cross: White Christian Nationalism and the Threat to American Democracy* (New York: Oxford University Press, 2022).

21. Carter Heyward, *The 7 Deadly Sins of Christian Nationalism: A Call to Action* (Lanham, MD: Rowman & Littlefield, 2022).

22. Heyward, xii.

23. Pamela Cooper-White, *The Psychology of Christian Nationalism: Why People Are Drawn In and How to Talk Across the Divide* (Minneapolis, MN: Fortress Press, 2022), 25.

24. "A Christian Nation? Understanding the threat of white Christian nationalism to American democracy and culture," Public Religion Research Institute, Feb. 28, 2023. https://www.prri.org/research/a-christian-nation-understanding-the-threat-of-christian-nationalism-to-american-democracy-and-culture/. Accessed June 1, 2023.

25. Dean G. Stroud, *Preaching in Hitler's Shadow: Sermons of Resistance in the Third Reich* (Grand Rapids, MI: Wm. B. Eerdmans Publishing Co., 2013).

26. Pamela Cooper-White, *The Psychology of Christian Nationalism: Why People Are Drawn In and How to Talk across the Divide* (Minneapolis, MN: Fortress Press, 2022), 41. She also notes that there are unconscious motivations that provide an undercurrent of emotional power for Christian nationalism. Some of those unconscious allures are the magnetism of groupthink, the identification and idealization of narcissistic leaders, and the effects of trauma and its resultant psychological splitting (see 82–99).

27. Fabricated stories about "a secret cabal of pedophiles rules the Democratic Party" get people's attention by "by evoking vulnerable children. They engage one of humankind's most primitive and powerful emotions—disgust. And they place members of this evil cabal in a class beyond redemption." Melissa Healy, "Why Do Conspiracy Theories about Pedophilia Hold Such Sway with Some Conservatives?" *Los Angeles Times*, published October 16, 2020, accessed February 3, 2024, https://www.latimes.com/science/story/2020-10-16/why-do-conspiracy-theories-about-pedophilia-hold-such-sway-with-some-conservatives.

28. Cooper-White, *The Psychology of Christian Nationalism*, 103.

29. Cooper-White, 104.

30. Cooper-White, 104.

31. Cooper-White, 106.

32. Cooper-White, 107.

33. Cooper-White, 107.

34. Cooper-White, 108.

35. Cooper-White, 110–111.

36. This is Joshua Greene's concise summary of Haidt's central message in his book *Moral Tribes: Emotion, Reason, and the Gap between Us and Them* (New York, NY: Penguin, 2013), 335.

37. Andrew Whitehead, *American Idolatry: How Christian Nationalism Betrays the Gospel and Threatens the Church* (Grand Rapids, MI: Brazos Press, 2023), 48.

38. Whitehead, 99.

39. Whitehead, 99.

40. Whitehead, 102.

41. Whitehead, 103.

42. Leah D. Schade, "Countering White Christian Nationalism: Reflections for a Lenten Sermon Series Based on Readings from the Revised Common Lectionary, Year A, 2023," in *Jesus and Justice in Public: A Study-Action Guide* (Wisconsin Council of Churches, 2023), https://www.wichurches.org/2023/02/jesusjustice/.

43. Schade, 45.

44. Schade, 49.

CHAPTER 9

Two Sermons on Social Issues Based on Philippians 2:1-13

In chapter 6, we learned that the Bible is "political" because the authors within both the Hebrew and Christian Scriptures were writing to audiences who were embedded in the nexus of political forces of their day and, thus, addressed the social issues of their time. In fact, there would have been little need to write books such as Esther, Ruth, Acts, or Revelation if the community hadn't been wrestling with how to deal with the contemporary issues that were affecting their lives, such as military occupation, migration, distribution of goods and services, and caring for the most vulnerable in the community. This being the case, it is not only appropriate to address social issues in our own time but even morally and ethically incumbent on preachers and congregations to bring Scripture and theology into conversation with the complexities of today's social issues, such as health care, food insecurity, or mental illness.

Yet chapters 2 and 3 show us how challenging it can be to preach a sermon about topics of public concern. Much depends on your own vulnerability, the stressors impinging on the congregation, their history with conflict, and everyone's feelings of safety and trust. So, in chapter 4, I offer suggestions for three approaches—Gentle, Invitational, and Robust—with different strategies to experiment with in your own preaching context. These can be used in conjunction with ethical foundations, exegesis, theological reflection, and homiletical techniques to craft effective sermons about social issues.

In this chapter, we will look at one passage, Philippians 2:1-13, to consider how Paul's letter can inform a sermon on a contemporary topic. After a brief exegesis, we will look at two sermons, both of which are based on the Philippians passage but have different subject matters and approaches. This will allow you to see how context, working gospels, moral foundations, and homiletical ethical approaches can shape such a sermon.

PHILIPPIANS 2:1-13

If then there is any encouragement in Christ, any consolation from love, any sharing in the Spirit, any compassion and sympathy, [2] make my joy complete: be of the same mind, having the same love, being in full accord and of one mind. [3] Do nothing from selfish ambition or conceit, but in humility regard others as better than yourselves. [4] Let each of you look not to your own interests, but to the interests of others. [5] Let the same mind be in you that was in Christ Jesus, [6] who, though he was in the form of God, did not regard equality with God as something to be exploited, [7] but emptied himself, taking the form of a slave, being born in human likeness. And being found in human form, [8] he humbled himself and became obedient to the point of death— even death on a cross. [9] Therefore God also highly exalted him and gave him the name that is above every name, [10] so that at the name of Jesus every knee should bend, in heaven and on earth and under the earth, [11] and every tongue should confess that Jesus Christ is Lord, to the glory of God the Father. [12]

Therefore, my beloved, just as you have always obeyed me, not only in my presence, but much more now in my absence, work out your own salvation with fear and trembling; [13] for it is God who is at work in you, enabling you both to will and to work for his good pleasure.

Exegesis of Philippians 2:1-13

Philippians is an epistle that Paul wrote to the first Christian church in the city of Philippi in Macedonia (modern-day Greece). Scholars believe the letter was written in the latter years of Paul's missionary career, sometime in the mid- to late 50s CE. Paul spent a great deal of time and effort founding and establishing this church, returning several times during his ministry. For this letter, Paul was writing from prison in a different city and was appreciative of the generous gifts from the congregation that sustained him during a difficult time.

An initial read of this passage raises some questions. Why does Paul think it necessary to encourage the Philippians to be "of the same mind" (Phil 2:2) and assume a position of humility? What was happening in the congregation at that time that would necessitate Paul's imploring them to put the interests of others first? What was going on in the Philippian church that required Paul to remind them to empty themselves just as Christ had done?

Scholars believe the church at Philippi was experiencing strife from both external sources and internal conflict. So Paul looked for a way to get the Philippians back to a place where they could be the people of God together. He said that one of the reasons they were divided was because they were not thinking about their relationships the way they should. This passage tells them that they should "be of the same mind," "having the same love," and "being in full accord and of one mind" (Phil 2:2). He encouraged them to look to the person of Christ as the model of humility and self-emptying for the sake of love.

To understand the larger context of our passage, it's helpful to read the whole letter to get a sense of how it's situated in the overall flow. Our passage comes after Philippians 1 in which Paul expresses his sincere gratitude for their support of his ministry, even as he is in prison. He commends them for being prayerful, generous, steadfast, and courageous in the face of opponents. Chapter 2 contains what some scholars believe is the fragment of a liturgy or an early hymn (Phil 2:6-11). Thus, he is using what they already know and sing or recite together to remind them of who Christ is, what Christ does, and what this means for them as they are struggling to live in community together, especially when facing opposition from the outside and fights from within.

Later in the letter, he calls on two leaders of the church to stop arguing with each other and to "be of one mind" (Phil 4:2), recapitulating the exhortation from chapter 2. Two women, Euodia and Syntyche, are having a dispute that is threatening to divide the church. It is serious enough that Paul calls on them by name and asks others to help them resolve the issue. Now, we see what all of this has been leading up to—urging these church leaders to empty themselves of ego, selfishness, malice, and rancor for the sake of the church and for the ministry of Christ. The letter ends with an acknowledgment of the financial support and gifts given to him by the congregation while he is in prison and unable to support himself. In this way, he is further reinforcing their qualities of generosity, care, and compassion as a congregation. He is also reminding them that no matter what strife they are dealing with, God will provide for them, as God has done for all of them since the beginning.

A primary theological emphasis of this letter is ecclesiology, calling believers into right relationship with God and each other through Christ, especially when they are experiencing disputes. This passage answers the questions, how will we regard each other and how will we treat those with whom we have disagreements so that our disputes do not split the church and undermine the very ministry of Christ? The answer Paul gives in chapter 2 is to tell them how much Christ loves them and how far he is willing to go to demonstrate that love. That willingness to self-empty, even to the point of giving up one's life for the sake of love, is the "one mind," which Philippians are urged to adopt.

Two Sermons Addressing a Social Issue Based on Philippians 2:1-13

In this section, you'll see one sermon that tackles the contemporary issue of political divisiveness and another that takes on the complex problem of economic and social inequality. Prior to each sermon, I explain each preacher's context and the Central Question, Central Claim, and Central Purpose for the sermon.[1] Following each sermon, I will analyze the ways in which they used ethical foundations, working gospels, exegesis, theological claims, and homiletical ethical approaches as well as point out how they used either Gentle, Invitational, or Robust strategies.

CENTRAL QUESTION, CENTRAL CLAIM, AND CENTRAL PURPOSE STATEMENTS

Central Question, Central Claim, and Central Purpose statements are part of a process that I developed for *Introduction to Preaching: Scripture, Theology, and Sermon Preparation* to help preachers determine the drive, direction, and destination for the sermon. Here's a brief explanation:

- *The Central Question* is the compelling inquiry for the sermon. In one sentence, it asks the question that is at the heart of one's biblical exegesis of a passage as well as one's preaching context. Informing the Central Question is the basic inquiry, "Why does this matter?" The Central Question is like the "engine" of the sermon, providing its intellectual, emotional, and spiritual energy.
- *The Central Claim* is the main point of the sermon, which should mean something for the congregation, the community, and/or God's Creation. It is the primary assertion and message of the sermon stated in one sentence. The Central Claim must mention God, Jesus Christ, and/or the Holy Spirit and say something substantive about their nature, character, or actions. The Central Claim also needs to make an explicit connection between the content of the biblical text and the preaching context.
- *The Central Purpose* is a statement that articulates where you want the sermon and the congregation to arrive *and* why you want them to be there. The Central Purpose is the primary goal of the sermon, stated in one sentence, and explains what you want the sermon to do or accomplish in and for the listeners as well as the reason for or outcome of this intention (the "so what").

"One Mind in a Divided Church: Giving Ourselves for the Good of Others"
—Jerry L. Sumney's Sermon and Analysis

Background and Questions for Analysis

Jerry Sumney, professor of biblical studies at Lexington Theological Seminary, preached this sermon at a chapel service for students, faculty, and staff in January 2021 just after the contentious 2020 election and the events of January 6, 2021, which many agree was an attempted coup. With that context in mind, he focused on Philippians 2:6-8 and developed the following Central Question, Central Claim, and Central Purpose:

> Central Question: How did Paul encourage his divided congregation to become "of one mind," and what can we learn from his teaching that can apply to our postelection church and society divided by partisan politics?
>
> Central Claim: Because Christ was willing to put the good of others ahead of his own to give us the gift of salvation, we are to adopt this same selfless attitude in our churches and toward our political enemies.
>
> Central Purpose: This sermon challenges the seminary community to see their vocation of ministry and teaching in terms of putting others ahead of their own good to show what it means to be the church in a divided society.

As you read this sermon, here are the things to look for and think about:

1. In what way does Sumney's awareness of his context shape the sermon and connect with his listeners?
2. What is his hermeneutical lens (e.g., historical critical, liberation, African American, womanist, Latino/a, Asian, ecological, queer, postcolonial, disability, etc.), and how does he integrate his exegesis into the sermon?
3. Identify the following:
   a. His working gospels (e.g., American sentimentalism, American exceptionalism, prosperity, denominational affiliation, evangelical, social justice, identity politics)
   b. The sermon's moral foundations (i.e., care/harm, fairness/cheating, liberty/oppression, loyalty/betrayal, authority/subversion, sanctity/degradation)
   c. The homiletical ethic (i.e., communicative, witness, liberation, hospitality)
   d. The strategies used from the Gentle, Invitational, and Robust approaches (see Figure 9.1)

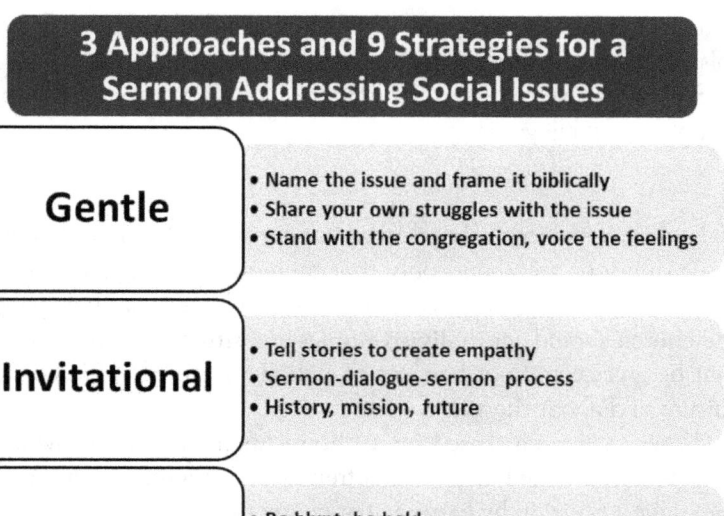

Figure 9.1 Three Approaches, Nine Strategies for a Sermon Addressing Social Issues

Sermon: "One Mind in a Divided Church: Giving Ourselves for the Good of Others"

I.

It is hard to believe that it's been less than a week since some elected representatives put the advance of their political party before the Constitution and before what they know is the truth. Less than a week from people trying to take over the Capitol building.

It's also less than a week after the great news from Georgia that an African American, the Rev. Raphael Warnock, has been elected to the Senate in that Southern state.

So we ask you to come to your classes, sit in front of your computers, and calmly think about how to do theology and preach sermons and interpret the Bible. But it's hard to keep ourselves from doom scrolling, especially since we know that the divisions have spilled into our churches. Whatever happens in Washington, DC, and our state capitols, we have to live with as the church.

So how *are* we to live as the church? Paul's letter to the Philippians can offer us some guidance.

II.

Paul is addressing a church that has divisions. We don't know what those divisions are about, only that there are church leaders on both sides. The passage we read is some of Paul's advice about how people in the church should act in divisive times and situations. And the advice that he gives could not be more of a challenge to what Greco-Roman culture said about the way to live.

Their society was based on an honor/shame culture in which you work to accumulate honor. That often means shaming others. You seek the highest position by besting your competitors. You might do that by being a more powerful speaker or getting a business deal over someone else. Gaining that kind of advantage might get you invited to a banquet where other powerful people would be. Maintaining your honor was seen as one of the most important things a person could do. Wealthy people constantly demonstrated their honor by denigrating and shaming those who had less. Those with political power often used it to socially embarrass rivals and enemies.

Against that social order, Paul says, "Do nothing from selfish ambition or conceit, but in humility regard others as better than yourselves. Let each of you look not to your own interests but to the interests of others" (Phil 2:3). When that part of this letter was read at the church in Philippi, I expect someone in the congregation piped up and said, "What? I think I misheard that; read that again. Put the good of others above our own good? Consider others better than yourselves? He can't mean that literally, can he? How could Paul expect that?"

Paul did indeed expect that response from the Philippians and tells them why. He gives them the example of Christ's self-giving incarnation and death as the example they are to follow. He tells them they need to have the mind of Christ as seen in his willingness to leave glory, take a lowly place on earth, and be completely humiliated with a crucifixion. He says that is what Christ was willing to do to bring them the amazing gifts of salvation—relationship with God, the presence of the Spirit, the promise of fulness of life with God. All those blessings come from Christ's willingness to put the good of others ahead of his own good.

This is a countercultural value, to be sure. But Paul tells the Philippians that that kind of humility and generosity of Christ is the pattern of life that church members are to adopt.

III.

So what about this divided church in our time? We know what we are divided about, at least in part. We know how deep political differences go and how those differences have been expressed in more and more vicious rhetoric. Both sides probably think that the other is somehow opposing the will of God. People on both sides certainly invoke God's name.

So how does Paul's advice to consider others better than yourselves and do what is in the interest of others, not yourself, sound in our culture and our churches?

These expectations violate all kinds of things we believe. We don't think of others as better than ourselves—we are told we are to love ourselves because we can't love others unless we love ourselves first. In our world, everyone seeks what is good for themselves first, and while it's also good if that helps others, that is a secondary concern to helping those in our own circle. After all, if we did things like considering others better than ourselves or putting the good of others above our own, people would take advantage of us, right? We'd be seen as doormats. Paul doesn't seem to understand how the world works.

So, yes, these expectations are as radical today as they were when Paul wrote Philippians.

But the same example of Christ makes the same demand that we take up this way of living.

Now, to be clear, this is not a call for people who are vulnerable to allow themselves to be abused. It is a call to use the power we do have for the good of others. Also, this is not a call for communities to allow prejudice and discrimination to continue. Rather, it is a call for all Christians, especially those with power, to adopt this way of viewing fellow Christians and fellow human beings. Remember, Christ was the most powerful being in the cosmos when he gave himself in this way.

The most powerful one gave up that power to help those who needed assistance, those who needed salvation.

IV.

I have to tell you that I am not quite ready to think of a Trump voter as better than myself. This is a difficult demand, especially in times like these when divisions are so extreme and rudeness and hateful speech are now seen as permissible, even celebrated. I am convinced that the way I voted is what pleased God and am sure I can show that with Scripture. *But* I am still to value the person who acted otherwise.

This is not some glossing over of the issues to avoid talking about them. Really valuing the other person, really putting their interests above my own will mean that I show love by teaching about what the gospel really does demand of our social and economic policies. I show this love and concern by carefully thinking about—and helping others think about—how God wants Christians to live as church members and as citizens.

Having these conversations can create problems for ourselves; they will make some people unhappy, even angry with us. It could well get us into trouble with some people in our churches. But it is the way we show love, it is the way we consider their good, their fuller understanding of the gospel, as more important than our good.

Our way of privileging the interests of others by talking about the social and political implications of the gospel cannot be about getting people to vote for a particular party. And I'm not telling you to go get yourself fired. This work must be done in ways that it can be heard—that is how we privilege the interest of the other person.

I am saying it is the work of ministers to help the church think about the implications of the gospel for the church's life, including in relation to the world around us. We, as the church, need to begin discussing all aspects of our participation in our social and political world through the lens of the gospel. Helping each other think about all of life through that lens is important to what it means to be the church.

That can only happen when we begin to follow the example of the One who gave himself for the good of others and when we teach others to do the same.

Through Christ, we can live toward following that example. Amen.

Two Sermons on Social Issues Based on Philippians 2:1-13 ~ 185

Analysis of the Sermon

Sumney's working gospel in this sermon is that of social justice as seen from his Central Claim, "Because Christ was willing to put the good of others ahead of his own in order to give us the gift of salvation, we are to adopt this same selfless attitude in our churches and toward our political enemies." Starting in part II, we see that he utilized a historical–critical hermeneutic to help listeners understand the context of the text (the honor/shame dynamic in Greco-Roman society) and showed that even today, Paul's instruction is countercultural. The moral foundation of care shapes Sumney's interpretation of the passage in part II.

In terms of his sermonic approach, the opening paragraph hints at the fact that although there is a high level of trust between him and the seminary community, stress was high for his listeners in light of the aftermath of the attempted coup. So this sermon used more of the Gentle approach while also using one Robust strategy. The sermon used the Gentle strategy of *Name the issue and frame it biblically* through his exegesis and application to today's context of divisiveness. He also used *Stand with the congregation, voice the feelings* in part III when he articulated the consternation we feel upon hearing Paul's expectation that we should consider others better than ourselves and do what is in the interest of others. In addition, he stood with his congregation by putting the text over them all and wrestling with what it means for how they will be in relationship with the people who are their political opponents. And in part IV, he used the strategy of *Share your own struggles with the issue* of divisiveness to express how he personally was wrestling with the demands of the text.

At the same time, you could see the Robust strategy of *Be blunt, be bold*. This was evident both in his forthright naming of the contemporary issue of divisiveness and in the sermon form he used, beginning with the bad news in the world (the election and attempted coup), followed by bad news in the text (Paul's divided church), then good news in the text (Christ using his power to save the world), and good news in the world (what it looks like for a seminary community to apply Paul's teaching in their contexts).

Thus, we can see a communicative ethic in that the sermon is trying to build unity around the common value of selflessness in the face of society's competitive and ruthless modus operandi. We can see in parts

III and IV that Sumney used a conversational homiletic to encourage "discussing all aspects of our participation in our social and political world through the lens of the gospel." It's worth noting that after the sermon, there were follow-up conversations during the community lunch and in the classroom. These conversations helped students and others in the seminary community process the message so that they could take tentative steps toward those who are in opposition to them and be agents of Christ's *kenosis* (self-emptying) to bring healing and reconciliation to their congregations and communities.

"Cleaning Up and Clearing Out"— Emily Askew's Sermon and Analysis

Background and Questions for Analysis

Emily Askew, professor emeritus of theology at Lexington Theological Seminary, preached this sermon at the invitation of one of her African American students who was being ordained for ministry. The original version of this sermon was preached on Juneteenth 2010, a holiday that marks the emancipation of slaves in the United States. The following version is one that has been updated for this book.

In her preamble to the sermon, Askew gave these remarks: "I am honored to be standing before you this afternoon. And I feel blessed because I got to witness this courageous woman find her strong, faithful, prophetic voice in the face of sometimes conflicting influences. She has walked with the Black church through the White academy; she has listened to the concerns of her local community, keeping in mind the largest needs of our fragile planet. She strengthens her faith through the stories and heartaches of undocumented Latino/a migrants and the hopes and challenges of being an African American woman. Her walk with God has been an inspiration to me. Let me do justice today to both of them."

With that context in mind, Askew focused on Philippians 2:13 for the sermon: "for it is God who is at work in you, enabling you both to will and to work for God's good pleasure." Here are her Central Statements:

> Central Question: Paul's letter to the church at Philippi calls for humility, obedience, and servanthood, but how does this apply to people who

have suffered from justice delayed and denied by people who use this passage to exercise unfair advantage?

Central Claim: God alone shows each of us what "cleaning up and clearing out looks like" so we are freed from the dictates and manipulations of those who misuse this text to further oppression.

Central Purpose: The purpose of this sermon is to liberate listeners from an oppressive interpretation of the text to experience a "cleaning-up God," who clears the way for a justice-oriented love.

As you read this sermon, here are the things to look for and think about as you're analyzing the form and content:

1. In what way does Askew's awareness of her context shape the sermon and connect with her listeners?
2. What is her hermeneutical lens (e.g., historical critical, liberation, African American, womanist, Latino/a, Asian, ecological, queer, postcolonial, disability, etc.), and how does she integrate her scriptural exegesis into the sermon?
3. Identify the following:
   a. Her working gospels (e.g., American sentimentalism, American exceptionalism, prosperity, denominational affiliation, evangelical, social justice, identity politics)
   b. The sermon's moral foundations (i.e., care/harm, fairness/cheating, liberty/oppression, loyalty/betrayal, authority/subversion, sanctity/degradation)
   c. The homiletical ethic (i.e., communicative, witness, liberation, hospitality)
   d. The strategies used from the Gentle, Invitational, and Robust approaches (see Figure 9.1)

Sermon: "Cleaning Up and Clearing Out"

I.

On a warm Sunday afternoon about ten years ago in Nashville, Tennessee, my friend Julie watched everything she owned submerged in five feet of river water. When the water receded, the river mud stayed. It coated everything the river had touched with sticky, smelly clay. In the days after the flood, friends and strangers helped her carry most of her material possessions out of her house and toss them onto a huge pile on her lawn. The final step in the unloading was to watch the contents be scooped into an enormous dumpster and hauled off to a landfill along with hundreds of other anonymous piles of people's lives.

Thrown together with sheets of rotting drywall and sopping wet insulation, we pulled out her ruined sofa and television and her now broken washer and dryer. But we also had to carry out photo albums with baby pictures of her brothers and sisters and the newspaper clippings from her parents wedding in Tuscaloosa, Alabama. We pulled out warped drawers filled with her undergarments; her grandmother's desk; the recipes on note cards left to her by her mom who had passed away three years before; and the family Bible with her grandmother's rosary. All of this, the sacred and the profane, sat baking together (or maybe boiling together) in the hot Tennessee sun. And in the middle of her shock and confusion and sadness, without saying a word to anyone, Julie found a sign she had kept in her garage that managed somehow not to get ruined and placed it at her curb under her mailbox. The sign read: "Life Is Good." More on that in a minute.

II.

This flood was no discerner of persons—it took everything from everybody in its path.

Across town, in the Bordeaux neighborhood of North Nashville—neighborhoods where poor Black, White, and immigrant folks live—Miss Mary allowed me, a stranger, to empty the contents of her home: drywall, kitchen cabinets, clothing, photographs. Miss Mary is a widow with high blood pressure, diabetes, and the early stages of dementia. Six months before the flood, her daughter Carole had quit her job with American Airlines in Denver and come home to take care of her mother. After six months, Carole still hadn't found a job.

As I sat in her garage with Miss Mary watching strangers pull out her life's accumulations, she told me that she survived the flood because her daughter had lifted her onto the kitchen counter where they waited, watching the water rise, until the National Guard boat came for them. She told me that Mr. Jack, three houses down, had not been so lucky. An elderly man with limited mobility, no one came to lift him up to safety, so he drowned inside his house before the boat came.

As Mary and Carole sat on the kitchen counter for five hours, Carole watched the small aluminum shed behind her mother's house float down the street. In it was everything she had brought from her move—all her clothes, books, and pictures. The river that ran through the Bordeaux neighborhood that day was so high and moving so fast that no one has yet found that shed.

The pile in front of Miss Mary's house was not very big—she had more building materials in it than possessions. The studs supporting her walls, when we peeled the wet parts away, showed a lot of termite damage.

Miss Mary is poor, by some standards. And Julie is rich, by some standards. But on that day in May, both these women were vulnerable and confused. They were trying to make sense of what had happened. Their lives had been emptied into the streets for the world to see, and maybe to judge.

III.

Back to "Life Is Good." The week after the flood, when I returned to Nashville, Julie told me that she had come to realize the meaning of this calamity. For her, it meant that she now had a chance to do something she knew she had to do spiritually but couldn't do by herself, and that was to "simplify." This physical emptying was a spiritual opening for her—a space in which to repent of some materialism and make more space for God. For people like me—middle class, with many social and economic resources and too much stuff—the message of the flood might well be a call to declutter our lives, remove the idols that fill up the spaces in our hearts and souls where God wants to be.

But imagine if I took this message to Bordeaux and said to Miss Mary and Carole and her neighbors who have struggled to get the few things they had. What if I said to them, "Look at it this way: emptying your house of everything you own and having to start all over again with no resources means that you can now 'simplify.' You can repent of material possessions and create more space for God."

If I were Miss Mary, I think I'd want to punch me in the nose. Maybe, *maybe*, that is the sense she will make of this flood at some point. But it is surely not mine to impose on her. How she processes this flood is God's work within her. No person can tell another what it is that they should empty themselves of. No person can say to another, "Empty yourself of this or that" to better serve God.

IV.

Paul's letter to the church at Philippi, Paul's word to us, beseeches the Philippians to become one people in mind, in love, and in God by emptying themselves as Christ has done in order to be servants of God. They are called to live God's will so completely that they, that we, would give up everything to do what we know is right. Jesus voluntarily emptied himself of all his divine qualities so that he could be a fully human receptacle for God's will. Giving up everything that was divine in him shows the example of being completely prepared for God's will and God's work through our simple human nature. One love comes from one mind, made possible by perpetually emptying our lives to make more room for God. "Let me decrease so that You may increase," as the saying goes.

But I am going to tell you something that is really no secret: this passage in Philippians has been terribly, terribly abused by preachers and teachers and anyone who feels like they can pick up this call for humility, obedience, and servanthood and work it to their advantage. Like I might have done at Miss Mary's, these folks appear in neighborhoods that aren't theirs and preach to people who live there about being servants, about being humble, about being obedient—all things these preachers and teachers have never lived themselves. But let me tell you, this is NOT the word of God in this passage. This is the word of human selfishness, thoughtlessness, and harmful theology.

- So, when servanthood gets preached to women who have never held positions past "breeder women," or mammy, or domestic "help," Dr. Delores Williams says, *the Gospel is not preached.*
- When some are reminded to live as if everyone in the world were better than they in a country where they have never yet been treated as equals—*the Gospel is not preached.*

- When the powerful preach to give up pride when many of us have only known shame—*the Gospel is not preached.*
- When women are told to be silent in church, even when God's word is breaking through our hearts and our tongues—*the Gospel is not preached.*
- When obedience is preached to serve secular culture, when the call is to "wait" but your waiting time has been filled with lynchings and hate crimes, voter suppression, and the construction of what Rev. Dr. Martin Luther King Jr. called a "smothering cage of poverty," when "wait has almost always meant NEVER," then *the Gospel is not preached.*

V.

Preachers and teachers and others who use this passage to limit justice and squelch passions conveniently forget to read on in this passage: "work out your own salvation with fear and trembling; for it is God who is at work in you, enabling *you* both to will and to work for God's good pleasure" (Phil 2:12-13).

In other words, no one can tell us what needs to be cleaned out, what needs to be emptied out of you and me to make more space for God or to better serve God. But there is no doubt that every one of us in this holy place needs to clean house!

Maybe it's the inside of your soul and maybe the inside your garage (and maybe it's both). For my part, I am filled to bursting with worries and anxieties and inferiorities. I worry that my behind is too big and my paycheck is too small. The spaces where God could be, I have filled in with grave doubts about my worthiness. There is hardly any space left to feel God's love for me—maybe a broom closet in the back of my kitchen. To "work for God's good pleasure," I must clear out my fear and open ALL of my house to God. How about you?

- Maybe you have to haul out the shame to make room for pride at being a child of God.
- Or maybe you have to pull out stinking insecurity in order to live the life God calls you to.

- Or maybe you have to wash out the muddy, sticky guilt to make room for forgiveness for yourself and, eventually, the world.
- Or maybe you have to drag out your own comfort and complacency in order to make room for justice and advocacy for those who do not enjoy the privileges and benefits you have.

Whatever it is, it's got to go.

VI.
And the good news is that whatever it is that needs to go, we do not do this heavy lifting alone. Like cleaning up after the flood, God and friends and maybe even strangers will help us move out the things that are damaged or warped or keeping us from being built anew.

The good news is that what the world defines as loss is for us the foundation for gain. But no person, no institution, no government can preach this powerful, life-altering reality idea against us—it is God and God alone who will make it clear to each and every one of us whether it is pride or shame that needs to be cleaned out, whether it's too much voice or too little voice that needs to be cleared out to make way for the power of servant-love.

When the message of your liberation comes through loud and clear in the center of your soul, in the center of your own neighborhood—then the Gospel is preached!

Amen.

Analysis of the Sermon
This sermon is a good example of how a White preacher can use Black and womanist liberation theology in a sermon. You could see in her quotes from both Delores Williams and Martin Luther King Jr., as well as her contrasting stories about the economic strata in America, that Askew held herself accountable to the perspective of the oppressed and marginalized. Therefore, her working gospels were social justice and identity politics.

In parts I and II, Askew used the Invitational strategy of *Tell stories to create empathy* by recounting the flood experience for Julie, whose yard pile evidenced her ability to accumulate material wealth, and Miss Mary, a woman with access to few resources. While Askew created empathy for both women, in part III, she pivoted to upend the authority foundation and the way it's been used and abused to reinforce the American caste system. As we saw in chapters 6 and 7, the womanist and postcolonial perspectives locate authority in the lived experience of the oppressed and marginalized, thus putting subversion as the higher moral good.

In part IV, Askew corrects the bad theology that leads to a religious rationalization of poverty, inequality, and hierarchy. Here, we see the two primary moral foundations of care and fairness. She shows us that harmful theology reinforces an unfair advantage and justifies the continuation of attitudes that support economic systems, which harm some people while giving unfair advantages to others.

Askew also used the Robust strategy of *Be blunt, be bold*, as evident in the bullet points of part IV, which upset the equilibrium of the social, economic, and theological status quo and point out the way the Philippians passage has been used to theologically manipulate those who are already oppressed. Thus, she moved from Invitational to Robust given the nature of the context where her audience knew very well what it is like to experience others deliberately misinterpreting the Bible and theology to oppress them. The shift, however, comes in part V when Askew reveals the theological key in Philippians 2:13 for reclaiming this passage from those who have abused it: "for it is God who is at work in you, enabling you both to will and to work for God's good pleasure." This shift leads to an explanation about what it means to be cleaned up and cleared out—but according to their unique circumstances that only they can name and claim. Here, the liberation foundation comes to the fore—but what that liberation means will depend on the socioeconomic standpoint of the listener.

While there was a high level of trust between Askew and her student who was being ordained, she did not have a relationship with the community in which she was invited to preach. So the stories she told helped to build empathy and connection with her listeners while signaling that she had done significant work to confront her implicit bias and racial stereotypes. Once this connection was established, she was able to bluntly name the way the Philippians passage has been abused, why this is theological malpractice, and how the passage itself contains the key to its reclamation as a liberative text.

Thus, this sermon is a good example of the witness ethic because it counters the domination system's harmful meta-narrative that "self-emptying" should be a universally applied virtue. The sermon itself "cleans up and clears out" bad theology by exposing the consequences of hegemonic power, which locks people into an attitude of acquiescence to subjugation, repression, and inequity. This call for moral agency compels the listeners to make room for God to create something new—whether that is the work of justice (for those who already enjoy privilege and wealth) or the work of claiming one's worth in God's eyes (for those who assumed or been told they were unworthy). In all, the flood cleanup imagery, which was so evocative at the beginning of the sermon, served as an effective bookend at the conclusion. It also functioned as the throughline that allowed for all the strands to be tied together in a powerful theological claim at the end, stating that God is with us in the work of "cleaning up and clearing out."

Conclusion

In this chapter, we worked with Philippians 2:1-13 to see how we can use our ethical foundations, biblical exegesis, theological analysis, and homiletical strategies for a sermon on a social issue. Then, we analyzed two examples of sermons based on the passage, one by Jerry Sumney and one by Emily Askew.

We saw that Sumney applied the passage to the issue of churches divided in the wake of the 2020 election and the resulting coup attempt on January 6, 2021. He wrestled with how to apply Paul's instruction to "be of one mind" in a situation where relationships were being shattered, democracy was threatened, and the very fabric of public life was in tatters. For her part, Askew applied the passage to the theological problem of inequality in American society that is justified by a heresy based on a misapplication of the Philippians text. She contrasted the stories of two individuals whose lives were equally devastated by flooding in Tennessee but who each occupy different positions in terms of socioeconomic privilege. Askew herself contended with what it means to help those in need without imposing on them what "self-emptying" means—especially when this passage is used against those who have already suffered so much loss.

While both preachers based their sermons on their exegesis and theological analysis, they each preached to very different congregations in divergent contexts. In addressing a social issue in a sermon, your preparation and context will be different as well, just as every preacher's will be. In the next chapter, we'll look at case studies of six student preachers who also used the tools and tactics in this book to address social issues in their contexts.

Note

1. See Leah D. Schade, Jerry L. Sumney, and Emily Askew, *Introduction to Preaching: Scripture, Theology, and Sermon Preparation* (Lanham, MD: Rowman & Littlefield, 2023), chapters 12–17.

CHAPTER 10

Case Studies of Preachers Addressing Social Issues

So far, we have looked at data giving us a snapshot of what ministry and preaching about social issues have been like from 2017–2023 in the divisive U.S. social and religious landscape. In chapter 3, the Assessment Tool was presented as an instrument for gauging risk and capacity for preaching about social issues to help preachers determine whether the Gentle, Invitational, or Robust strategy would best serve their context. After that, we established the foundations for addressing social issues, starting with ethical and moral frameworks, followed by biblical and theological fundamentals and then homiletical approaches. We then applied these foundations to three social issues in chapter 8, followed by an analysis of two sermons on social issues in chapter 9.

This chapter will feature case studies demonstrating how preachers have applied the methodologies outlined in this book to craft sermons addressing social issues. These preachers—each of whom gave permission to share their work—represent diverse perspectives, including varying intersections of gender, race, culture, sexual orientation, age, tenure in ministry, and denomination. Moreover, the congregations they served reflect a range of geographic, socioeconomic, demographic, and political contexts. Each of them utilized different tools and tactics described in this book, including some who used the Assessment Tool to gain insights into themselves and their ministry contexts, thus enabling them to employ Gentle, Invitational, and Robust strategies in preaching. These case studies will show that by delving deeply and strategically into the ethical, scriptural, and theological dimensions of contemporary issues, while also utilizing key homiletical strategies, preachers can proclaim God's Word effectively and faithfully. In their own ways, each preacher exercised their prophetic voice, fostered community within the body of Christ, and emboldened their congregations to live out their faith in tangible ways.

A Case Study of a Gentle Approach

"Gathering at the Table"—A Sermon on Matthew 24:29-35

Tamara Mills completed the Assessment Tool to help her think about how best to approach a sermon on an apocalyptic text, Matthew 24:29-35, about the coming of the Son of Man after the time of suffering. Her sermon was for a large Disciples of Christ church in a downtown area of a city in Kentucky. Politically, the church and Mills are aligned left of center, and the congregation had been accepting LGBTQIA+ people for a decade. The congregation is racially homogeneous (White) with a smattering of racial, cultural, and LGBTQIA+ diversity.

According to her results from filling out the Assessment Tool, the total of the three sections suggested that she could use the Robust approach for her sermon. But this was mostly due to the totals of the congregational and relational sections being very high. Mills's personal vulnerability, however, scored lower for several reasons. First, as a seminarian, she does not have the authority and security of a full-time ordained minister. Second, as a female, she knows that she is afforded less legitimacy in the pulpit from the historical church at large (though her congregation has had female associate pastors in the past). And third, as a member of the LGBTQIA+ community, she is more at risk, not in her own congregation, but in society in general. Also, at the time of this sermon, the congregation's senior pastor had retired, so they were in a period of transition and anxiety about their future. Therefore, she decided to go with the Gentle approach.

In this excerpt, note how she paints a picture of her family's kitchen table and draws parallels to the anxieties felt by Matthew's congregation. Thus, she used the *Stand with the congregation, voice the feelings* strategy to lament the current state of the world and acknowledge their anxieties amid troubling times.

Mills's Sermon Excerpt and Analysis

When I was growing up, my family often gathered around my grandparents' dinner table. We drank hot coffee with milk for creamer and ate cherry-flavored Danishes or fresh strawberry cobbler. We laughed with each other and talked about the state of the world. But enjoying each other's company came with a caveat—for each cup of laughter, there was a half cup of worry and hand-wringing. The causes of this hand-wringing were things like failing crops, factory layoffs, and fears about the possibility of war and violence.

As a child, I loved those times around the dinner table. But the fear in Mamaw's kitchen was palpable. The faces of concern were undeniable. The questions we asked rarely had answers. How are we gonna make ends meet? Will I have a job in two weeks' time? Are the Russians gonna bomb us? The tense feeling that the sun would no longer shine or that the moon would lose its light loomed large over my childhood. In the middle of that tension, it was hard to find just a little bit of hope to hold on to.

About two thousand years before my family and I felt this tension at Mamaw's dinner table, Matthew and his church felt tension at their tables too. The people in Matthew's church were mainly Jews who had decided to follow Christ. But with this new faith came hardship. They faced difficulty within their families. They faced difficulty in their jobs. They faced difficulty within their communities. And they faced oppression at the hands of rulers at that time. These people must have looked at each other the same way my family did—with worry and hand-wringing. In the midst of these trials, it must have been hard to find just a little bit of hope to hold on to.

And Matthew knew that his church needed that hope. So, as he was writing his Gospel he wanted to make sure to include passages where Jesus addressed that kind of oppression in order to give his church just a little bit of hope to hold onto.[1]

The Central Purpose for Mills's sermon was to remind listeners that even in a world that seems bleak, Jesus is a source of hope for believers. Did you notice the repeated phrase "just a little bit of hope to hold onto"? This is an example of a "throughline," which gives the listener aural touch points and provides cohesiveness within the sermon.[2]

Later in the sermon, she used a historical–critical lens for her exegesis to explore the significance of the imagery of the fig tree. Her primary moral foundation was care, which she communicated to her unsettled congregation by assuring them of hope: "Not just any kind of hope. Hope that hangs on in the middle of the harshest winters. Hope that hangs on when faced with oppression. Hope that pulls up a chair at Mamaw's dinner table even in the midst of tension and hand-wringing."[3] Thus, she used the witness ethic to counter the doom-and-gloom narrative that is so pervasive in our culture.

At the end of the sermon, she encouraged moral agency by urging her listeners to bring Jesus' light and life as messengers of hope at their own tables and give others "just a little bit of hope to hold onto." (And in a worship service with holy communion, this imagery of hope at the table could be extended to the sacrament.) Thus, she used her throughline to bring the sermon to a satisfying conclusion.

A Case Study of a Gentle to Invitational Approach

"Let Us Be One"—A Sermon on Ephesians 4:1-6

Bridget Hill is a White female licensed minister in the United Church of Christ serving a White congregation in rural Wisconsin. Though the church has a worship attendance of less than one hundred, the membership and finances are stable, and there is a significant percentage of children, youth, and young adults. She completed the Assessment Tool in 2023 in preparation for a sermon on Ephesians 4:1-6, in which Paul calls for the church to be united despite their differences.

Hill had been in ministry at that point for less than five years and less than three years at this church, but she paid close attention to the relationships between and among the congregation. She saw very few signs of congregational stress, unhealthy secret-keeping, or dysfunctional governance. However, the congregation had not yet engaged in healthy dialogue or discussion about contemporary issues. And, because this was a politically mixed group of congregants, Hill knew she needed to take the Invitational approach in her sermon. Her goal was to encourage listeners to focus on the beliefs and faith that unite them rather than the labels society uses to drive people apart.

Hill's Sermon Excerpt and Its Analysis

Hill began by describing the opening of a movie called *Love Actually*, which gave a montage of scenes at Heathrow Airport. A character's voice-over said that in an airport terminal, divisions, political beliefs, colors of skin, genders, levels of education, ages, and sexual orientations recede as people experience love, unity, and oneness when reuniting with their friends and loved ones. Hill then turned to the passage from the letter to the Ephesians focusing on the universal church with Christ at its head and the body in communion. She used the Gentle strategy of *Name the issue and frame it biblically* to describe the strife our society experiences today and how it differs from Paul's vision for the church.

> For every division we establish, there is a person on the other side of it. Yes, there may even be a reason for that division. But still, the person on the other side is a living, breathing human being who has a name and a family. Like you and me, they feel pain, hurt, frustration, joy, and happiness.
>
> Our scripture this morning reminds us that we are connected through one God, who is the Father of all. But for far too long, we have dealt with each other through the lens of our differences. And where has this gotten us? One only needs to turn on the news or look at social media posts to see the judgment and anger.
>
> Recently, I read a local newspaper article about a swastika displayed next to the Democrat's donkey symbol at a local farmer's market. I have seen the phrase "F' Biden" on flags and bumper stickers. I have watched people post memes making fun of Senator Mitch McConnell for "freezing" on camera, laughing at him as he ages. And both sides reference Nazi Germany when speaking of the other.[4]

Later in the sermon, Hill invoked the Invitational strategy of *History, mission, future*. First, she took the listeners step by step through Paul's "recipe" for what is needed to conduct themselves in a way that is worthy of being called Christian. Then, she described the qualities that must characterize the church today: humility, gentleness, patience, bearing with one another in love, and maintaining unity in the bond of peace. As part of that, she made a strong theological claim that all of this is possible because of the "one" element they all share in common: "There is *one* body and *one* Spirit, just as you were called to the *one* hope of your calling, *one* Lord, *one* faith, *one* baptism, *one* God and Father of all, who is above all and through all and in all" (Eph 4:1-6, emphasis added).

Finally, she pointed to a future where "we can honor people for who and what they are because we accept their humanity in the unity of the Spirit." At the end, she mimicked a scene from the *Love Actually* movie where a character holds up large note cards with a series of words to express his feelings for his beloved. On Hill's cards were these words: "With hope—Let us humbly, gently, and patiently—Bear each other in love—In unity with the Spirit—Through the bonds of peace."

Hill's sermon was firmly rooted in the moral foundation of care. While she acknowledged the differences that exist in society, she decried the way labels are used to "defend our positions sometimes with aggression and even violence." So she urged her congregation to seek the moral high ground around their shared values of humility, gentleness, patience, and peace. Thus, she invoked the communicative ethic. Her hope was that this sermon would open the door to future conversation about how her congregation can take a more active role in creating space for deliberation and peace-building.

A Case Study of a Gentle to Invitational Approach

The Sermon–Dialogue–Sermon Process in Cameroon, Africa

My research on preaching in the purple zone has primarily focused on preachers addressing social issues based in the United States. Naturally, we might wonder if these methods work in other countries and contexts. From 2021–2024, I was privileged to work with Father Jude Thaddeus Langeh, a Roman Catholic priest serving the Anglophone community of Saint Charles Lwanga Parish in Yaoundé, Cameroon, to answer that question. Langeh is the major superior of Claretian Missionaries in Cameroon, with twenty parishes under his care and eight weekly worship services serving several different tribes and groups that speak either English (Anglophones) or French (Francophones). Langeh reached out to me through his Doctor of Ministry program with the Aquinas Institute of Theology, where he had learned about the sermon–dialogue–sermon process. He saw the potential for using this process in his culturally, politically, and linguistically divided context in Cameroon, where he wanted to use sermons to help mediate peace. For this project, he worked with the Anglophone community in Nkolbisson.

The stakes are high for Langeh. Not only is he dealing with divisions along the lines of politics and religion but also across cultures, languages, and tribes, all under the weight of postcolonialism. The conflagration of these last three has led to life-threatening situations for him in his ministry. His attempts to reach across the Anglophone–Francophone divide resulted in his being kidnapped, which could have meant his death. The kidnappers, known as the "amba boys," from the Anglophone zone of the country, viewed his efforts for peace as evidence of betrayal. Thus, Langeh's work in adapting the sermon–dialogue–sermon process is not theoretical. His primary question "How can the Church, both laity and clergy, mediate peace, justice, and the reign of God in the socio-political realm of Cameroon?" is literally dealing with life-and-death issues.[5]

Cameroon has a tragic history under colonialism that has resulted in a country splintered into different factions, as Langeh explains:

> The situation in Cameroon has been a challenging one. Many have faced wounds from the slave trade, intertribal wars, jihads, colonialism, interreligious conflicts, and the ongoing socio-political instability. It is a call for all stakeholders to take action. We live in a chaotic world of conflict which has inflicted many wounds on people. At some point, there is a need for a value-oriented system that can break the chain and spiral of violence and conflict. There is an urgent need for strategies to reconcile the human race personally and in the community.[6]

As a Catholic priest, Langeh saw potential for the church in Cameroon to play a much more active role in mediating peace. After reading about the sermon–dialogue–sermon process and working with me on an independent study, he preached his first sermon using the Invitational strategy. He chose Amos 7:12-15 for his sermon, which was one of the Revised Common Lectionary readings for the Sunday that he began his project.

Langeh's Sermon Excerpt

The situation in Amos 7 concerns a confrontation between the prophet Amos and the priest Amaziah at a time when the northern and southern kingdoms of Israel were in conflict over political power, wealth, religion, and culture. In his sermon, Langeh drew parallels to the situation in Cameroon, where factions on many levels are also at odds with each other. Then, he noted that just as Amaziah hurt his fellow Israelites by refusing to collaborate with Amos in carrying out God's call for repentance, so, too, does the church fail its people when its leaders refuse to work with others on behalf of the poor and oppressed. Then, he explained why this story is so instructive for the church in Cameroon caught in an impasse:

> So, what is a society to do when there is an impasse such as this? Sometimes the Bible shows us stories where God's people made the wrong choices, which allows us to imagine what might have happened if they had made better choices. From the look of things, there are uncrossable chasms that cannot be filled regarding the social order and true religion. There is a great gap in the understanding of the role of the priest and the prophet. Our country Cameroon needs prophets and priests who can listen to and execute the commands of YHWH instead of protecting their personal interests. . . .
>
> This text teaches us that sometimes God needs to reprove God's people when injustice, inhumanity, and idolatry are ruling the land. And it is teaching us to be in dialogue with each other about how we can respond in a way that avoids Amaziah's mistakes. The tension between Amaziah and Amos reminds us of the many prophets who suffer and are silenced because of God's word. It took great courage for Amos to move to the northern kingdom to publicly denounce their sins. It also takes courage for the Church to engage contentious public issues. The Church stands in the tension between faith and divisive politics. How do we navigate this tension as a church?[7]

Langeh noted that had they all worked together, the Israelites might have avoided being conquered and exiled into slavery. So, too, he said, priests and laity in Cameroon need to learn to cooperate to help achieve peace in their country. He then issued a challenge for the congregation to see the possibility for collaboration—even with people they consider their enemies:

> In the present sociopolitical crises plaguing our country, this biblical passage from Amos challenges us to live together, collaborate, and

engage in forthright dialogue about the political tensions that surround us. Who is Amos for you, for us, today? Remember, he was from another tribe, but he brought the word of the Lord. Even the brother or sister from another tribe, political affiliation, or region can put me on the right track.

How can we learn from the mistakes of Amaziah and not shut down people based on their tribes and regions? How can we avoid publicly insulting, mocking, and even silencing people?[8]

Langeh concluded the sermon by informing the congregation that the church would be hosting a dialogue about the issue of divisiveness and encouraged them to do this together "because we are rooted in our common values of faith, dialogue, courage, empathic listening, and living together as God's people. We can be a church that collaborates and engages in dialogue through empathic hearing that can engage in healthy conversations about living together as a true family of God."[9]

Sermon Analysis

Langeh's working gospels were threefold: denominational affiliation (Roman Catholic), social justice (informed by postcolonialism and the pragmatic nonviolence of Rev. Dr. Martin Luther King Jr. and Mahatma Ghandi), and identity politics (the complexities of being Cameroonian). He used both a historical–critical hermeneutic for interpreting the Amos passage and a postcolonial lens for applying the text to his parish's context. The sermon drew on three of Haidt's moral foundations: authority, loyalty, and liberty. The first, authority, appealed both to the authority of God's Word and the expected role of the church to mediate peace within its Catholic hierarchy, and to the larger society. Loyalty was a foundation that he used to guide people beyond mere loyalty to one's own tribe and ethnolinguistic group toward a more life-giving faith in God, who desires their collaboration across divisions. These first two foundations served the long-term goal of liberty: freedom from strife, war, violence, and bloodshed so that their country could thrive.

Thus, we see that Langeh used a communicative ethic to build moral consensus around the common desire for peace through dialogue. His sermon pointed to the conflict between Amaziah and Amos as a cautionary tale about what *not* to do when tensions arise. In this way, it sought the moral high ground and invited people to engage in introspection, enabling them to look toward their neighbors and seek peace in their congregation and country. To that end, he used the Gentle strategy of *Name the issue and frame it biblically* and the Invitational strategy of the *sermon–dialogue–sermon process*.

For Langeh, it took more than one sermon to prepare his congregation for the deliberative dialogue. In fact, it took three sermons before he felt they were ready. However, when he did deliver that sermon, the response was heartening. Twenty-four people, ranging in age from eighteen to sixty-five years old, attended, including both Anglophones and Francophones as well as people from different tribes and political parties. They adapted a U.S.-based issue guide called "The Church's Role in a Divided Society"[10] and shared their painful experiences living amid the divisions of Cameroon. As they developed trust with one another, they began thinking of ways that the church could foster more collaboration. They expressed a desire to decentralize the church's clericalism and give more opportunities for women and laity to preach. They also suggested organizing community meals to foster intercultural exchanges. And they asked for more opportunities to dialogue! As a result, in the ensuing years, Langeh trained three others in his parish to conduct the sermon–dialogue–sermon process in different regions and languages that the church serves.

One of the most important things I learned from working with Langeh is that when preaching in a culture and society with multiple layers of division, it may require more than one "rooting" sermon and "prophetic invitation to dialogue" to establish trust and the biblical imperative of engaging in dialogue. Langeh astutely recognized that the preparatory work for the dialogue needed extended time. I believe that because he was patient with this stage of the process and did due diligence with his exegesis and integration of the concepts of preaching peace, the ensuing dialogue was successful.

A Case Study of an Invitational to Robust Approach: A Sermon on Revelation 3:14-22

In 2023, Jeff Birch served as a seminarian pastoral assistant for a federated congregation of the United Church of Christ and the United

Methodist Church in Connecticut. Demographically, the congregation is mostly White, and politically, they lean progressive. However, there is a small group of parishioners who have been resistant to the congregation's move toward a more inclusive and justice-oriented ministry. Nevertheless, they celebrated the Transgender Day of Remembrance and have adopted an Indigenous People Land Acknowledgement Statement. Knowing all of this, and having filled out the Assessment Tool, Birch felt that the congregation was ready to hear a sermon on gun violence using a more Robust approach.

In his homiletical reflection paper, Birch stated his theological belief that "God calls us to follow the example of Jesus and transform ourselves through him into more loving people. I believe that such a transformed love is *active*; it is manifested in positive action to bring justice and liberation."[11] Here, we can see his working gospel of social justice, which informed his intention to preach on Revelation 3:14-22 not only to express the hope that God will win against evil but to compel the "agency that each Christian must employ in bringing that [victory] about."[12] And he wanted to direct that agency to one issue in particular: gun violence.

Birch's sermon was shaped by his concern about the parallels he saw between his church and the church of Laodicea, called out in Revelation for being too comfortable and "lukewarm." "The privileged, mostly White Christians in my congregation are comfortable. As with the Laodiceans, they believe they are rich, they have prospered, and they need nothing (Rev 3:17a)," he explained. "They, no doubt, like many mainline Christians, are content to engage in ministries of food and fellowship and leave more complex issues like gun violence to the realm of secular politics. In my view, this is counter to what God demands of us."[13] Therefore, he crafted the following Central Statements to guide his sermon preparation:

> Central Question: In what ways are we, like the Laodiceans, beguiled by wealth and privilege, and how can we "change our hearts and lives" to embrace the mission of love to which Christ calls us?
> Central Claim: Christ, in his love for all of us, calls us to open the door and see again the needed work for justice with renewed eyes.
> Central Purpose: This sermon calls the congregation to repent from their "lukewarm" apathy about gun violence and reengage with Christ's radical mission of love in the world.[14]

Birch's Sermon Excerpt

Birch began his sermon with two bowls of marbles representing the statistics around gun violence. He explained that a mass shooting is when four people are killed or wounded at one location at roughly the same time. "Just stop and think about that for a moment: four lives, four precious children of God, reduced to a statistic," he said, plinking four marbles into the bowl. He then named locations where mass shootings had happened in the last few weeks, dropping more marbles. Thus, he used a Robust strategy of *Be blunt, be bold* to get the listeners' attention and be frank about the situation around gun violence.

But then he addressed the complacency of their community because none of the mass shootings had happened nearby. This time, he picked up marbles and plinked them into another bowl, thus continuing his "aural throughline." He then turned to the Revelation passage and noted that the author of this apocalyptic book focused on the complacent Laodiceans because "he intended to afflict the comfortable."[15]

> Jesus called the prosperous Laodiceans "wretched, pitiable, poor, blind, and naked." What a shock that must have been! They believed that they had worked hard and become self-sufficient and prosperous. And they had! We know today that they had overcome earthquakes and natural disasters with seeming grit and determination. But they had also become arrogant and complacent. They had failed to look beyond the boundaries of their own prosperous city to see the larger picture.[16]

Birch then explained that Jesus was telling the church then, as he is telling he church now, that what they had done in the past was no longer important. What matters is what they are doing *now*. Jesus was making demands of them that would exact a high cost—the cost of discipleship. But this demand was because Jesus loved them and wanted them to repent of their complacency. "Jesus was knocking at the door. . . . They needed to remember what it meant to be the church," he said.[17]

Birch then pivoted back to the congregation's situation. "We need to recognize that the good life that most of us have can sometimes blind us to the realities of the larger world," he explained. "Jesus is calling us to open that door and see him standing there with all of the victims of gun violence and their families, wanting us to be more than just lukewarm in our response. We need to realize that statistical improvement [plink, plink with the marbles] can be a fig leaf that barely hides the naked truth."[18]

The sermon concluded with a reminder that Christians share responsibility for the well-being of the nation in which they are citizens, which includes putting love into action. "Love is active and proactive," he said. "It is our hands and feet and voices that Christ calls us to use in God's service. God stands against evil in the world, and in Christ, we stand in God's righteousness."[19]

Sermon Analysis
Birch collaborated with members of his ministry support team while he was writing the sermon. Thus, he had the support of key leaders in the congregation when he tackled the challenging topic of gun violence. Later, he planned to encourage the congregation to take on actionable goals, such as writing letters to elected officials, talking with candidates for political office, and launching a social media campaign about gun reform. Thus, he utilized the Robust strategy of *Collaborate before, during, after*.

He used a historical-critical lens for his scriptural exegesis and utilized three moral foundations for his sermon: loyalty, authority, and care. He appealed to the congregation's loyalty to Christ as well as Christ's authority to move them away from their comfortable, lukewarm faith into a proactive response to gun violence. This, in turn, would put love (care) into action in a concrete way. Thus, Birch's sermon would fit in the category of liberation ethics in that he educated them about gun violence to urge them to work for social change on that issue. Ultimately, his hope is that the church will organize for a justice-oriented response to gun violence in the same way that they have addressed transgender and Indigenous rights.

Case Studies in Invitational to Robust Approaches

Two Sermons on the Story of Vashti in the Book of Esther

This section will include excerpts of sermons from two of my former students who experimented with embodied preaching informed by a postcolonial perspective, which inspired them to address social issues in creative and moving ways. Just as Jerry Sumney and Emily Askew used the same biblical text for two different social issues in chapter 9, these students used the same story about Queen Vashti in the book of Esther, which resulted in two different sermons on the topics of misogyny, rape culture, sexism, and racism.[20]

Queen Vashti Example 1: Inspiring the Moral Agency of Women in a Patriarchal Society

Preachers who serve predominantly White, Western congregations can draw on the perspectives and wisdom from postcolonial preachers when addressing social issues. One of my students, Mariah Newell, is a White woman who served as a youth minister in a White congregation in Texas (she now serves as associate minister for kids and youth). She discovered that a postcolonial perspective gave her three goals in preaching about social issues: "naming, manifesting, and dreaming."[21] Naming involves calling out the systems that are creating the injustice in order to raise awareness in the congregation. Manifesting is enacting the biblical call for God's justice, which is amplified by those who suffer from injustice today. And dreaming "invites the congregation into God's eschatological vision for the world and our communities," Newell explained.[22]

The more she learned about postcolonial preaching, the more she realized that "this kind of preaching provides prophetic care and holy disruption within a diverse community, but also invites a racially homogeneous congregation to begin to recognize the diversity that exists beyond skin color."[23] She began to understand that "while we often talk about diversity in terms of visible differentiations between persons, even within seemingly less 'diverse' congregations, diversity *is* present. Most congregations are not 'one type' of individuals. There are many stories, life experiences, and theologies which inform congregants who are listening to the sermon," she noted.[24] "All people are connected to a network of individuals which embody the diversity that may not be readily visible by looking in the sanctuary on Sunday morning. By naming, manifesting, and dreaming, I as a preacher can be a faithful steward of God's words to preach justice and awaken my community to God's vision for humanity."[25]

For her sermon in the course, Newell chose to tell the story of Queen Vashti in Esther 1:10-20. Her working gospels were social justice and identity politics (feminist liberation). Her Robust approach utilized a *Be blunt, be bold* strategy as well as the invitational strategy of *Tell stories to create empathy*. Using a monologue format, Newell spoke as the character of Vashti, telling the story of her objectification in the king's court and the danger she faced for refusing him.

Newell's Sermon Excerpt
In this excerpt from the end of the sermon, she indirectly addresses the social issues of domestic abuse and rape. Note her theological framing throughout this segment:

> I know I am one of the fortunate ones. I am standing. I am alive to tell my story. We women know so many others who are trapped or who were killed for an act like mine. I don't believe God favored me more than the women before me who bravely took a stand, but I do believe, whatever my outcome might have been, that God stood with me, and God endured with them.
>
> My husband's actions and the actions of men like him are inexcusable. The image of God is vibrant within me, within you, and within all women. We are not simply bodies, sex toys, or objects to be manipulated by the wants of men.
>
> They say that he banished me from his court. But let me tell you: I refused to ever see him again. My life and safety are precious to God. Your life and your safety are also precious to God. . . .
>
> I did hear about the new Queen. Her name is Esther. I am proud of her bravery. She stood up to the King like I did. She saved her people.
>
> I believe my words made a space for her. And I believe your words will make a space for someone else.
>
> God makes a space for you and me and for our stories. Because our lives matter to God. Our bodies matter to God. For that I say, thanks be to God.[26]

Sermon Analysis

In Newell's sermon, the influences of postcolonial preaching were evident through her bodily movement and vulnerability to make a connection with her listeners. She enacted Vashti in a "burlesque-esque" way, as Lis Valle-Ruiz would call it (see chapter 7), through both speech and prophetic symbolic action, including removing the crown from her head during the sermon. It was a movement of deliberate choice that demonstrated her agency within a patriarchal system and rape culture. In terms of ethical approaches in homiletics, this sermon would fit within the witness ethic because of its countercultural message against the norms of patriarchy and the meta-narratives of toxic masculinity. Two lines in particular demonstrate the way in which she cultivated a virtue ethic for women: "Your life and your safety are also precious to God" and "I believe your words will make a space for someone else."

When it comes to Haidt's moral foundations, care and liberty were primary for this sermon, while—in the spirit of postcolonial homiletics—Newell inverted two other foundations: loyalty/betrayal and authority/subversion. Betrayal of the king became the more noble action, while subversion of the patriarchal system was the key to Vashti's and many other women's survival. One other moral foundation that comes into play is sanctity/degradation in that Newell asserts that women's bodies "are not simply bodies, sex toys, or objects to be manipulated by the wants of men" but, rather, sacred in and of themselves because they are "precious to God."

Queen Vashti Example 2: "A Displaced Crown"

Dikiea Elery, a Black woman serving a predominantly Black Disciples of Christ (Christian Church) congregation in Kentucky, also preached on the story of Queen Vashti. As a Black female pastor, Elery deals with both implicit and explicit questioning of her authority and legitimacy. Thus, she wanted to "use the resources of embodiment in preaching to empower those who lack privilege to be active in their struggle for justice and equality."[27] Specifically, she wanted to give voice to the oppressed in her context of ministry so that it "opens a lane for conversation" involving the lived experiences of Black people in general and the struggles of Black women in particular.[28]

Elery's Sermon Excerpt

For her assignment, Elery developed a dramatic sermon and monologue called "A Displaced Crown," which is about the parallels of her life as a Black woman in ministry and the struggles of Queen Vashti. She had in mind the predominant interpretation she heard growing up in church that Vashti was a poor role model for women because she disobeyed her husband. "Queen Vashti's reputation is that she was disrespectful, disobedient, insubordinate, selfish, and an embarrassing disgrace because she humiliated her husband, the king," she explained.[29]

She then pointed out the parallels between Vashti's life and the life of a Black woman in ministry using the image of a crown. While the crown is supposed to be a symbol of honor, nobility, privilege, blessing, access, membership, and authority, in reality it is "too heavy to be worn on the head of a woman who desires justice, equality, and dignity." Therefore, it is a "displaced crown" of degradation, humiliation, discrimination, limitation, oppression, silence, disrespect, denial, and exclusion.[30]

"The demands and costs of this crown far outweigh the benefits of it, and so it must be laid down or traded in for the rightful crown that is to be worn by any child of God," she explained in the first part of the sermon.[31] Then she invited her listeners to imagine how Queen Vashti might have felt upon receiving her husband's request to dance before his male guests. The crown that had previously been one of honor and respect was now one of degradation and objectification:

> It was no longer a crown of safety but a crown that made her vulnerable. Imagine standing naked with only a crown: the intense gaze of men who were merry with wine, the weight of expectation and egos that could top skyscrapers, the fear of the violence that could ensue if one of them or all of them decided that they wanted more than just a dance.[32]

Before transitioning to the monologue, which was in the form of a liturgical dance, she noted that Vashti was not allowed to speak in this story. Her words are not included in the text. So, too, this part of the sermon would be wordless. Elery invites listeners to enter the room where Queen Vashti is welcoming the regal women gathered for the festivities. She then dons a crown as the song "Oceans (Where Feet May Fall)" plays in the background.[33]

At first, the Queen happily entertains her guests, chatting and laughing. But then she opens the door to the messengers with a look of concern and reacts with shock, anger, and indignation, crossing her arms and hands protectively across her body. Then, she pushes back against the messengers, refusing them. Overcome with emotion at what she was asked to do, she alternates between praying with outstretched hands and covering her crying face. She then collapses on the steps of the chancel, visibly distraught, and pounds the floor with her hand. She rips the crown from her head and slams it on the floor beside her. Then, she picks it up one more time, cradling it in her hands, obviously saying goodbye.

But then, she puts the crown back down, wipes away her tears, and stands up. She reaches down to the step below the discarded crown and picks up an invisible crown. She picks it up, raises it to the top of her head, adjusts it, and turns to face the congregation. With regal grandeur, she walks down the aisle, her dignity intact.

Elery briefly returns to finish the sermon, no longer as the person of Queen Vashti but as herself, a Black female pastor, who reminds them of the courage it takes to cast off a displaced crown and position oneself to receive a godly crown. "May we go forth wearing the crown God ordained for us," she concludes.[34]

Sermon Analysis
Elery's sermon was informed by her working gospels of social justice and identity politics, specifically as a Black woman. She utilized a womanist hermeneutic that reclaimed Vashti's story from one of disgraceful disobedience to that of courageous dignity. In this way, like Newell, she flipped the script on the moral foundations of authority/subversion and loyalty/betrayal. Protecting her own body from degradation and claiming her personhood as a child of God drew on the sanctity, care, and liberty foundations. Also, like Newell's sermon, Elery's utilized a witness ethic that stands against the injustice of misogyny. And they both used the robust strategy of *Be blunt, be bold* as well as the invitational strategy of *Tell stories to create empathy*.

But Elery's wordless liturgical dance monologue was more akin to Lis Valle-Ruiz's silent proclamation of Sophia Divinatrix, which we explored in chapter 7. Like Valle-Ruiz, Elery preached through "negation," using her body to tell the story of voiceless Vashti and reclaim her "crown" of dignity from a patriarchal system both outside and within the church. Similarly to Valle-Ruiz, Elery's sermon was part theater, part dance, and part pantomime. It showed through symbolic action, rather than just public speech, a vision of a possible future: a Black woman claiming her own crown and personhood independent of the patriarchy that tries to define and control her.[35]

Valle-Ruiz said that Sophia Divinatrix "invites preachers to use less words and more body, to step out of the pulpit and out of the worship service and into where the people are."[36] This is exactly what Elery did. She was "was sharing her testimony and inviting others to go out sharing power to build different ways of interrelating in the world."[37]

Conclusion

In this chapter, we saw examples of six preachers who used the different tools and tactics in this book to help them craft sermons addressing social issues. These preachers have demonstrated that addressing contemporary topics in sermons involves careful and discerning consideration of one's social and demographic intersections as well as the context of the congregation and how the minister functions therein. With this in mind, a preacher can think methodically about how ethics, Scripture, and theology guide our understanding of important contemporary issues.

I hope these examples of preachers applying the tools and tactics outlined in this book move you to find different ways to address social issues in your preaching as well. As ministers, we are called to engage with our congregations and communities in meaningful ways, addressing the pressing social issues of our time with courage, conviction, and creativity. By adopting the various homiletical approaches that are appropriate for your context, you can effectively communicate the biblical and theological foundations of contemporary issues. This, in turn, can motivate your congregation to embody the transformative power of the gospel in a world fraught with division and strife. With support from ministerial colleagues, mentors, accountability partners, and family members, you can prophetically challenge and encourage your congregation to be the church in a divided and broken world. We are, indeed, "ambassadors for Christ" (2 Corinthians 5:18-20), and your preaching can inspire these emissaries of God's reconciliation, reparation, and restoration.

Notes

1. Tamara Mills, "Sermon on Matthew 24:29-35," unpublished sermon, Lexington Theological Seminary, February 2023. Used with permission.

2. Alyce McKenzie developed the concept of the "throughline" for preaching from novelists and screenwriters. The throughline refers to the flow of thought of the movie, or in this case, the sermon. She explains: "The throughline is the plotline that answers the question, 'What happens to the protagonist?' In a sermon, it's called the focus or the theme. It's what the sermon is about, summed up in one sentence. Novelists differ in the way they work, but many say they figure out the last scene of their novel first and then plot the whole novel toward it." Alyce McKenzie, *Novel Preaching: Tips from Great Writers on Crafting Creative Sermons* (Louisville, KY: Westminster John Knox, 2010), 53.

3. Mills, "Sermon."

4. Bridget Hill, "Let Us Be One," unpublished sermon, Lexington Theological Seminary, September 2023. Used with permission.

5. Jude Thaddeus Langeh, "Preaching Peace in a Culturally and Politically Divided Context: Church Mediating Peace in Cameroon," D.Min. thesis, Aquinas Institute of Theology, 2023, 3.

6. Langeh, 26.

7. Jude Thaddeus Langeh, "Homily Based on Amos 7:10-17," unpublished sermon delivered at Saint Charles Lwanga Parish, Nkolbisson, Yaoundé, Cameroon, July 11, 2021. Used with permission.

8. Langeh, "Homily."

9. Langeh.

10. Leah D. Schade, Erin Oeth, and Gregg Kaufman, "The Church's Role in a Divided Society," Baylor University Public Deliberation Initiative, 2019.

11. Jeff Birch, "A Homiletical Reflection on Revelation 3:14-22," unpublished paper, Lexington Theological Seminary, February 2023. Used with permission.

12. Birch.

13. Birch.
14. Jeff Birch, "Sermon on Revelation 3:14-22," unpublished sermon, Lexington Theological Seminary, February 2023. Used with permission.
15. Birch.
16. Birch.
17. Birch.
18. Birch.
19. Birch.
20. An excellent resource for sermons that address gender-based and domestic violence is John S. McClure and Nancy J. Ramsay, eds., *Telling the Truth: Preaching about Sexual and Domestic Violence* (Cleveland, OH: United Church Press, 1998).
21. Mariah Newell, "Final Paper: Preaching as Performance," unpublished paper, Lexington Theological Seminary, April 27, 2021. Used with permission.
22. Newell.
23. Newell.
24. Newell.
25. Newell.
26. Mariah Newell, "Vashti Sermon," unpublished sermon, April 9, 2021. Used with permission.
27. Dikiea Elery, "Preaching as Performance: Final Paper," unpublished paper, Lexington Theological Seminary, April 2021. Used with permission.
28. Elery.
29. Dikiea Elery, "A Displaced Crown," unpublished sermon, Lexington Theological Seminary, May 2021. Used with permission.
30. Elery.
31. Elery.
32. Elery.
33. Hillsong United, "Oceans (Where Feet May Fall)," on *Zion*, Hillsong Music, 2013.
34. Elery, "Displaced Crown."
35. See Lis Valle-Ruiz, "Non-Preaching? Unmasking (White) Preaching through Negation," in *Unmasking White Preaching: Racial Hegemony, Resistance, and Possibilities in Homiletics*, ed. Lis Valle-Ruiz and Andrew Wymer, 205–220 (Lanham, MD: Lexington Books, 2022).
36. Valle-Ruiz, 216.
37. Valle-Ruiz, 216.

CHAPTER 11

Practical Advice for Preaching and Social Issues

We want to keep the Body of Christ together. We strive for unity in our diversity and try to build bridges across difference as we address the issues of public concern. To that end, this book has offered tools and tactics for preachers to do this work as they are addressing the social issues that are affecting their parishioners' lives, the communities in which they live, the ecosystems that sustain them, the societies that structure life around them, and the global forces that affect us all. These methods, approaches, strategies, and tactics can, in a sense, "inoculate" the Body of Christ against the "viruses" of divisiveness and polarization.

This ministry is done through deep listening to understand people's stories of how they come to believe what they do. It involves ethically, biblically, and theologically rooting a social issue and engaging in healthy civil discourse. In these pages, I have urged clergy and parishioners to focus on building relationships, finding common values, establishing trust, and practicing Spirit-led compassion. Engaging in dialogue and honoring people's stories can sometimes lead to changed hearts and minds, by the grace of God.

But, as I've surveyed, taught, trained, interviewed, and had informal conversations with thousands of clergy and laity about ways to navigate political divisiveness in the church, I've also learned that sometimes people leave the congregation no matter how hard we try to keep everyone together. And I've come to see that there are times when it's OK for parishioners—or clergy—to depart if the relationship does not serve the mission of the church or align with Jesus' vision of the Beloved Community and Realm of God.

So, in this chapter, I'll begin with some advice about how to avoid the worst-case scenario of leave-taking by keeping ourselves and our congregation in a relationship that is healthy, transparent, accountable, and trustworthy—even when there are disagreements. Then, I'll explore how to respond when a well-intentioned sermon results in negative pushback from sermon listeners. After that, for those who are considering leave-taking over ethical, biblical, theological, or political differences—whether on the part of parishioners or pastors—I'll offer suggestions for appropriately and gracefully parting ways. I'll include anecdotes of parishioners and pastors who have chosen to leave and what insights they learned about how to have healthy closure. We'll see that in some instances, unexpected revitalization and enthusiasm for ministry can result from leave-taking. Finally, I'll wrap up the chapter—and the book—with some words of inspiration and encouragement for your journey in preaching and ministry about social issues.

Advice for Avoiding Pitfalls and Strengthening Relationships for Preaching about Social Issues

Lisa L. Thompson reminds us that every sermon is an act of risk-taking if the preacher is faithful in their preaching ministry. This is because "we are attempting to say something fully life sustaining in a world that often affirms death over life. Before we can ever take such a risk, we ourselves have to believe that something more is possible and that it is a holy possibility demanding a holy risk."[1]

There are some things that preachers do, however, that unintentionally create more risk for themselves than is necessary. These are what we might call "unforced errors," to use a sports metaphor. An unforced error refers to a mistake made by a player that is not the result of an opponent's skill or game play. These are careless blunders that are entirely the fault of the person making them rather than being caused by external factors. Here is a list of unforced errors that can happen when preaching about social issues and what to do to avoid or fix them.

Unforced Errors in Preaching about Social Issues and How to Avoid or Remedy Them

- *Preaching about social issues too frequently.* Preaching challenging messages taxes both the preacher and congregation. There is only so much bandwidth for doing deep dives, taking on controversial topics, and engaging in intense dialogue. So, first, be sure to gauge your own and your congregation's energy level before a sermon about a contemporary topic. Also, vary the subjects, styles, and tones of your sermon week to week so that there is a mixture of messages that alternate between comforting, teaching, challenging, and exhorting.
- *Inadequate planning for preaching about a social issue.* Occasionally, there are times of crisis and emergency when a preacher does not have time to go through the steps of preparing themselves and their congregation for addressing a controversial topic in a sermon. But, aside from those rare occasions, a preacher needs to do their homework and lay the groundwork for preaching about a subject of communal concern. This means doing things like educating yourself about the issue, talking with or reading from the work of experts in the field, having preparatory discussions with the congregation's governing body, or hosting listening sessions with the congregation to hear multiple perspectives. Especially, if you want the congregation to take part in long-term discussions over time, think about how and over what time period the topic should be introduced and taken up by the church.
- *Insufficient study of the scriptural text, biblical scholars, and theologians.* Merely spouting one's opinion about a social issue, or using eisegesis to justify one's opinion, or using a text only as a jumping-off point to dive into a contemporary issue without grounding it in exegetical study does a disservice to the text, to your congregation, and to your reputation as a preacher. So commit to studying at least three reputable commentaries, biblical scholars, or theologians about a text that will be the basis of your sermon about a social issue. This will help ensure that you are staying firmly rooted in the Bible and theology as you are addressing social issues.
- *Preaching only "law" with no "gospel" (judgment without hope).* Societal matters arise because there are problems that need

people's attention. Often, these problems involve some level of discomfort, anger, pain, and even despair, and these are important to name. But a sermon that focuses on only those "pain points" or sins (law) without offering any recourse to hope and action (gospel) will leave listeners frustrated, defensive, hurt, and perhaps even obstinate, depending on the preacher's tone and message. So, if you're going to address a social issue, be sure to open paths for people to repent (if that's what's needed), repair what is broken, make amends, and participate in healing. Give them a place to land with their feelings and responses to the sermon through talk-back sessions, community dialogues, service opportunities, connection events, or one-on-one conversations.

In addition to avoiding pitfalls, here are things you can do that will keep your sermons about social issues spiritually grounded, liturgically connected, collegially supported, and responsive to the emotional and felt needs of your congregation.

Spiritual, Liturgical, Collegial, and Pastoral Practices to Support Preaching about Social Issues

- *Remember to use the power of prayer and silence in your preparation.* When we feel rushed and pressured, we can be tempted to charge ahead with a sermon about a social issue without grounding ourselves in prayer or prayerful silence. But clearing space in our hearts and minds for that "still, small voice" (1 Kings 19:12) and "the peace that passes all understanding" (Philippians 4:7) will keep a preacher open to God's guidance, attuned to Jesus' presence, and focused on the leading of the Spirit.
- *Connect to worship, ritual, and liturgy.* Remember that the sermon is part of the worship service and, as such, should serve the larger purpose of helping worshippers focus on God and God's relationship to the congregation, the larger society, and all of Creation. This means that preachers should think about how the elements of the service support the topic as well as how the sermon can be linked to the rituals and liturgical elements therein. For example, choose hymns and write prayers that speak to the theme of the sermon. Perhaps write a ritual of confession and forgiveness or

a litany of repentance about the topic. Also, consider the ways in which baptism or Holy Communion can serve as rituals that reinforce values associated with the issue. For baptism, this might include our common baptismal vocation, being washed of our systemic sin through the baptismal waters or dying to our egotistical selves and rising with Christ. For communion, the themes of joining together at the table, sharing the bread and cup, experiencing the forgiveness of sin, and being fed in order to feed others are possibilities for connecting with a sermon on a social issue.

- *Cultivate peer-to-peer or mentoring relationships.* Even with the best preparation and a seemingly successful sermon, more is needed to sustain the work of addressing social issues in one's ministry. Says John S. McClure, "Many of us need some form of ongoing reflection, accountability, and feedback to ensure that our preaching remains on the right path."[2] He suggests peer coaching, where colleagues learn about each other's situations and what each of them is trying to accomplish in their ministry settings in order to give substantive feedback, suggest different approaches, and give space for critical reflection. A preaching mentor can also provide opportunities for structured feedback, critical reflection, and prayerful support for the task of addressing social issues in sermons.

- *Provide time and space for processing emotions, thoughts, and feedback with sermon listeners.* Before, during, and after a sermon about a controversial social issue or any sermon that addresses a sensitive matter, offer time to meet, either one-on-one or in small groups, to talk about how folks are feeling about the issue so that these emotions can be processed together in a spirit of prayer. These conversations can provide a kind of release valve so that tensions, questions, and curiosity can be expressed in a healthy way.

- *Focus on belonging.* No matter what contemporary topic you might address in a sermon, such as citizenship, environment, LGBTQIA+ rights, or racism, a core matter to focus on is the universal human need for *belonging*. As Thompson describes it, "Belonging is about a state of being connected and in relationship without breach. Belonging conjures a sense of being in relationship with someone or something. It's just as much about a sense of home as it is having one's presence and place affirmed in the midst of another."³ Understanding this yearning for belonging and naming it as a core human need is another way to create bridges between people who are working from different moral foundations, occupying opposing worldviews, or utilizing different working gospels. Articulating, describing, and demonstrating the importance of belonging, along with "our mutual dependence on one another and the entire creation for ongoing survival," can open minds, soften hearts, and unclench fists in order to receive and be changed by God's love, grace, and mercy.⁴

How to Respond to Negative Pushback to a Sermon about a Social Issue

Despite your best efforts to preach about social issues with integrity, sensitivity, humility, and prudence, you may still encounter resistance from listeners who have a knee-jerk reaction to hearing about certain topics mentioned in the pulpit. Merely posing questions about these matters or referencing specific current events in your sermon can carry the potential for a rapid and adverse response. This has happened to me on more than one occasion. The first time, it caught me off guard, and I felt like I didn't respond as well as I would have liked. So I talked with preaching colleagues and a trusted mentor to process what happened and think through options for how I might be less flustered and more centered the next time it happened, because I knew there would be a next time. I was committed to addressing the topics that mattered in our world, so I needed to be able to draw on a set of responses that would enable me—and the person who took issue with the sermon—to be our best selves.

To that end, I began compiling a list of steps I could take when someone approached me to criticize my sermon. I've now practiced these steps on numerous occasions, coached other pastors and my preaching students with them, and included them in my book *Preaching in the Purple Zone*.⁵ I'm sharing them here, slightly revised and with additional thoughts and suggestions, because I believe they can be helpful to preachers who receive pushback when they address issues of public concern in their sermons.

Twelve Steps for Responding to Criticism about a Sermon Regarding Social Issues

1. *Breathe and pause.* When the body feels threatened or attacked, which is how it may feel when someone comes at you to criticize your sermon, the brain releases a surge of stress hormones that prepare the body for a fight-flight-or-freeze response. They speed the heart rate, heighten blood pressure, tighten the stomach, reduce the capacity to think rationally, and decrease breath capacity. So pausing and taking a deep breath allows the body to activate a relaxation response and counter those stress hormones. Taking just one deep breath will center you, give you a moment before responding, calm your nerves, and allow you to gather your thoughts. And your first thought should be to . . .
2. *Say thank you.* It may sound counterintuitive to thank the person for sharing their thoughts and concerns with you. Why would you thank someone who has just criticized you? First, saying thank you dials back negative emotions for both of you. Second, you are recognizing that they have given you an opportunity to engage in dialogue by sharing their criticism with you directly instead of complaining to others behind your back. So, whether you think the criticism was unfair, unwarranted, or spot on, you can respond with something like "Thank you for sharing your concern with me. You could have walked away without saying anything to me and stewed about it. You would have been angry with me, and I would not have known why. So I appreciate your sharing this with me directly."
3. *Ask to set up a time to meet with the person.* Often, sermon critiques come at inopportune times, such as in the handshake line after the service or when you're heading out the door to your next appointment. Or they come through email, text, or letters that might be filled with "rants." So, after thanking the person for coming to you with their concerns, the next step is to ask to meet with them in person. Meeting in person is preferable to an email exchange, where body language and in-person communication are missing. Also, asking to meet at a separate time communicates your willingness to engage with them and give them your

full attention without interruption. When choosing a location, it's probably best to avoid meeting at your office. Choose neutral ground, such as a coffee shop. A word of caution, however; if you do not trust the goodwill of this person or are feeling unsafe meeting alone for any reason, ask if a neutral third party can be part of your meeting. The board president, head of the staff–parish relations committee, or another mutually agreed-upon person whom you both trust are all good options.

4. *Ask questions that get to the emotional level rather than debating content.* People can intellectually disagree about anything you say in the pulpit. But just below the surface are the feelings and unconscious intuitions that need to be brought out in the open. So, when a person criticizes what they heard you say (even if they misunderstood you), resist the urge to defend your points or debate them. Instead, ask "How did you feel when you listened to the sermon? What emotions did you experience?" Emotions are neither good nor bad—they are part of being human. Once the person expresses that they felt angry, or sad, or hurt, or alarmed, you can express empathy. "If that happened to me when I listened to a sermon, I would feel that way too." Acknowledge those feelings and thank them for honestly sharing them with you. Then, you can move on to the principles and values.

5. *Discern their moral foundations.* Jonathan Haidt advises those who want to understand someone with an opposing viewpoint to *follow the sacredness*.[6] In other words, ask questions that can help you determine which of the six moral foundations are most important to them (i.e., care, fairness, loyalty, authority, sanctity, or liberty), such as "Can you tell how you came to this position? Can you tell me a story that illustrates why this is a concern for you?" Invite them to share their journey with you. Then, affirm that the values undergirding their position are good ones to have. For example, you might say, "It sounds like fairness is important to you. It's important to me too!" Once they feel that you understand where they're coming from, the disagreement can shift to a more respectful and constructive place.

6. *Identify the common biblical and Christian ground.* Once the relational aspects of the exchange are in a stable and nontoxic place,

you can look at the biblical passage and the sermon together. Start off by pointing to the common ground you share: you're both Christians and want to follow God's will, you're both serving this church and want what's best for this congregation, and you're both good people who have a heart for following Jesus. Remind them that there are lots of stories in the Bible of God's people disagreeing with each other yet when they trusted the guidance of the Holy Spirit, they often found a way forward and perhaps you and they can too.

7. *Clarify the biblical and theological principles and tenets.* As you're examining the sermon, ask the person to show you where they think you veered from the teachings of Jesus or went against the theology of the church. Here's where it's important to remember the underlying paradigms and moral foundations that might be shaping their beliefs and how they heard your sermon. Keep in mind what you've learned in this book about the two moral worldviews (i.e., Strict Father and Nurturing Parent), the working gospels (i.e., American sentimentalism, American exceptionalism, prosperity, denominational affiliation, evangelical, social justice, and identity politics), and moral foundations (i.e., care/harm, fairness/cheating, liberty/oppression, loyalty/betrayal, authority/subversion, and sanctity/degradation). This might illuminate the underlying issues.

8. *Use reflective listening.* Listen to the person without trying to defend yourself. Ask clarifying questions and then paraphrase what you heard them say: "What I hear you saying is . . . Do I have that right?" Assuring the person that they have been heard and accurately understood is critical for establishing trust and maintaining the pastoral relationship.

9. *If they are open, share what's at stake for you.* Ask if they're willing to hear *you* on a deeper level as well. "Would you like to know why I decided to preach about this?" Explain how you prayerfully discerned the call to preach on the topic in question. Share how you considered the Bible and biblical scholars, looked at different perspectives, and listened to a variety of voices. Tell them what moral foundations you saw in the text regarding this issue that are important to you.

10. *Determine if it's appropriate to apologize.* If you realize you made a mistake or hurt the person's feelings, don't be afraid to say you're sorry. For example, I once preached a sermon in which I inadvertently perpetuated some harmful stereotypes about older adults. When a parishioner pointed this out, I realized my mistake, apologized, and thanked her for bringing it to my attention. But don't apologize if someone is offended by the gospel itself. You can thank them for sharing their concern and perspective, but Jesus' teachings do not require an apology.
11. *Return to their feelings, seek a way forward.* As the conversation comes to a close, it's good to check in on an emotional level one more time. "How are you feeling now that we've had a chance to talk about this?" Again, acknowledge those feelings without defensiveness or judgment. Then comes the task of ending the exchange so that the person's dignity—as well as your own—is intact. You can ask "How can we move forward from here?" or "What would you like to see happen moving forward?"
12. *Conclude with dignity.* Ideally, the conversation will end in a better place than it started. If that happens, you can share your appreciation for the fact that your relationship is stronger now and that even if you disagree on some things, you've found points of commonality and built trust. You may even come up with some ideas for how to take further steps together. However, if the conversation ends at an impasse (or escalates in a negative way), you can suggest that you both give the conversation a pause; take some time to think, read, and pray separately; and then circle back in a week or two. Or if you feel that the person is not engaging in good faith—or you are feeling browbeaten, bullied, or truly threatened—simply say, "Thank you for expressing your concern but this is something we'll just have to disagree about for the time being." Regardless, you can tell them that you learned a lot from the conversation, which will be both a truthful and dignified way to end the conversation for both of you.

What to Do When It All Falls Apart[7]

What happens when these tools and tactics don't work? What happens when people refuse to engage in constructive conversation? When they walk out of sermons? Threaten to withhold their offerings? Threaten to leave the church? If this has happened in your congregation, you're not alone. Recall from chapter 2 that sometimes congregations are too brittle, tensions are too high, worldviews are too incompatible, and differences are simply irreconcilable to maintain unity.

When this happens, it raises difficult questions. How do we handle those who want to silence the pastor's voice? Or stop a congregation from engaging in social issues? How do we call out harmful behaviors while remaining pastoral? Do we simply preach the gospel and let the chips fall where they may—even if people become angry? At what point, do we let them go with God and concentrate on doing the work of the church without them?

While I don't have all the answers to these questions, I believe we need to discuss them—as well as some cherished assumptions—openly and forthrightly among our colleagues, in our church leadership meetings, and with our denominational leaders.

Are We Really Supposed to Be One Big, Happy Family?

As I discussed in chapter 2, many pastors avoid addressing social issues in sermons or teaching for fear of disrupting the unity of the church. Parishioners themselves sometimes say things like, "Our church is like a family, so we need to stay together." Here, we can detect the loyalty foundation from Haidt's list. In this case, if the preacher addresses sensitive contemporary topics that cause discomfort, a parishioner may accuse the pastor of hurting or dividing the church.

It's worth pointing out that as much as we want the Body of Christ to hold together, Jesus warned against the seductive trope of the family. His teaching in Luke 12:49-53 tells us that following him may put us at odds with one's family members, fellow employees, elected leaders, and even fellow Christians. But it can be especially difficult for congregants who cling to the notion of being a "family" in Christ, as Jesus cautioned: "You will be betrayed even by parents and brothers, by relatives and friends; and they will put some of you to death. You will be hated by all because of my name. But not a hair of your head will perish. By your endurance you will gain your souls" (Luke 21:16-19).

Endurance is exactly what is required of clergy who dare to speak prophetically in this divisive climate. The stress of trying to hold things together takes a tremendous toll on a minister's physical, emotional, mental, and spiritual health. And sometimes, despite our best efforts to build bridges of understanding, people will still leave. And it can get ugly.

Undoubtedly, there can be tremendous pain and loss when people leave a congregation over politics. Most of the time, we keep these kinds of disagreements quiet. Maintaining harmony and peaceful relationships allows us to continue to pack the food bags for the pantry ministry, serve together on the altar guild, fix the church's leaky roof, or engage in pleasant chitchat over coffee and cookies after the service.

But, despite our desire for "niceness," sometimes the Bible confronts us with values that are counter to a White supremacist, nationalist, militaristic, xenophobic, homophobic, misogynistic, anti-environmental, or ableist agenda. Even without mentioning a specific president or elected official, a sermon that preaches the values of welcoming the immigrant, obeying the commandment not to murder, lifting up "the least of these," or valuing Black lives can be mistakenly perceived as promoting a "political agenda." This indicates that something deeper is going on. The idols know they are on notice. When confronted with the teachings of Jesus—with the cross and resurrection—they bristle because they are being challenged.

For example, Pastor A (names in this chapter are withheld to protect privacy) served a congregation that walked on eggshells wanting to appease a parishioner who wanted their ministry to fit with her conservative political viewpoint. "After a sermon that touched on racial justice issues, the woman resigned from her leadership position in protest. The next month, she came to a council meeting to disrupt and complain about the current nationwide focus on racial justice. She wanted our church to leave the denomination." Pastor A's story is one of many that ministers have told me over the past few years (which she and others in this chapter have given me permission to share).

In a group I cofounded in 2020, called the Clergy Emergency League (CEL) (https://www.clergyemergencyleague.com/), I asked ministers in our Facebook group to describe instances where congregants left because of their prophetic preaching. In just a few hours, forty ministers had responded. They posted about pushback they received from sermons mentioning or directly addressing LGBTQIA+ inclusivity, Black

Lives Matter, immigration, systemic racism, White supremacy, immigrant children in cages, war, police brutality, gun violence, and other issues of justice and equality, all of which led to parishioners leaving.

Threat Multipliers

As I explained in chapters 2 and 3, there are certain demographic markers that make some preachers more vulnerable to congregational criticism and antagonism than others. For example, preaching while being female is a threat multiplier.[8] Female pastors face added complications when preaching prophetically. Not only are they afforded less respect; they also face intimidation and even physical threats more often than their male colleagues. Additionally, female clergy are often placed in smaller churches that can ill afford the loss of parishioners angry about a justice-oriented sermon. And, when these churches are in right-leaning "red zones," female clergy are at even greater risk of threats and intimidation.

Pastor B, for example, described the pain she and her congregation endured during a year of conversations about becoming a Reconciling in Christ (RIC) congregation (a program welcoming LGBTQIA+ folks). "The secretary and a group of members lied, sabotaged me, and made phone calls to people telling them they should leave the church. And they constantly insinuated that it was because I was a woman and not fit for the position. It was so painful. They stayed long enough to vote against RIC." Nevertheless, the motion passed anyway, and the opposition group left the church. "We are now healthier than any church I've ever served," she said.

Another threat multiplier is preaching as a minoritized body in a congregation where those distinctions are immediately evident. This can include a queer preacher in a church of mostly cisgender heterosexuals; a preacher with a visible disability in a church with mostly able-bodied individuals; or a Black, Indigenous, Latino/a, Asian, or other racially or culturally minoritized preacher in a mostly homogeneous, White, English-speaking congregation.

"Many minoritized bodies choose to remain in contexts that have not been hospitable to their presence, historically, and at times have been downright hostile," observes Lisa L. Thompson. "Granted these are not the only options. One may determine it is best to use their voice elsewhere, which is a valid decision."[9] In other words, a minoritized preacher must discern whether their mental, physical, emotional, and physical well-being can withstand the constant barrage of suspicion, questioning of their ability, and challenge to their authority. However, "[t]hose who remain and render a message in places that would prefer their invisibility, dare to preach with a distinct and creatively tactical imagination for the sake of their deepest convictions—ingenuity. Preaching is an act of risk-taking that relies on ingenuity," says Thompson.[10]

Remember Your Ordination and Baptismal Vows

Many parishioners are not aware of (or have conveniently forgotten) that clergy commit to ordination vows that compel them to speak prophetically. For example, when I was ordained in the Evangelical Lutheran Church in America (ELCA), I took a vow that requires me to preach and teach in accordance with the Holy Scriptures, lead by example, and "give faithful witness in the world through word and deed."[11]

On a more fundamental level, a Christian's baptismal vow calls them to speak against evil and resist demonic powers in the world. For Lutherans, there is a profession of faith that asks the candidate (or their parents/sponsors) to declare their faith in Christ Jesus, reject sin, and confess the faith of the church. This includes "the devil and all the forces that defy God, the powers of this world that rebel against God, and the ways of sin that draw us away from God."[12] Further, we are to "live among God's faithful people; hear the word of God and share in the Lord's Supper; proclaim the good news of God in Christ through word and deed; serve all people following the example of Jesus; and strive for justice and peace in all the earth."[13]

Your baptismal and ordination vows may read differently, depending on your denomination. However, if you have folks in your congregation who complain, threaten, or attempt intimidation because of your preaching about social issues, it may be time to pull out these vows and look at them together. Or you could review them with your congregational leadership or write a series of reflections on them in the church newsletter. You might even preach a sermon series on ordination and baptismal vows so that people know that addressing social issues is part of your call to ministry.

When Parishioners Leave, Sometimes It Opens Room for New Growth

Even with all the steps you take to create a healthy, discerning church, there may be times when people will leave over "politics" no matter what you do. Simply put, when people try to silence clergy and muzzle their prophetic voices, the church can be held hostage, so sometimes the leaving turns out to be a good thing in the long run.

When we stop allowing certain opinions to derail our efforts of engaging in the important issues of our time, the Spirit can find new ways to create community and excitement for Christ-centered ministry. "Folks leaving in anger over prophetic preaching or issues of justice and equality have self-work to do," Pastor C reflected in the CEL clergy group. "And their leaving seems to relieve the congregation of the toxicity they have been carrying either under the surface or right out in the open."

Others affirmed this experience of relief when certain parishioners left their congregation. "The Holy Spirit opened the windows, and it was like a breath of fresh air," said one pastor. Said another, "I felt so relieved when they left. And then the church began to grow. The ones who have come since then are faithful, creative, and loving. God is doing a new thing!"

Drawing Boundaries and Pruning the Vine

Pastor A noted that "one of the reasons some people leave churches is emotional abuse by people who want the church to fit their idea rather than being open to following the Spirit. When they see this abuse happening, it can turn them off from church, knowing it could happen to them at any time." In other words, churches can lose members if they allow abusive behavior. However, when the pastor maintains their biblical and theological commitments and the abuser/disrupter leaves, it can be liberating to pastor and congregation alike.

For example, Pastor A recounted what happened after the council president left her church. "I prayed for weeks that God would show us what we could do about racial justice in our little parish. After worship one Sunday, one of our elder saints came to talk with me. 'Pastor, I think we need to do a book study about race.' A council member got funds to buy books, and eighteen of us are doing the study! I love God's surprises!" She made it a point to note that the elder came to her with this idea the week *after* the council president resigned.

From a biblical perspective, perhaps this is the "pruning of the vine," which Jesus speaks of in John 15. "God removes every branch in me that bears no fruit. Every branch that bears fruit God prunes to make it bear more fruit" (15:2). Pruning is part of a healthy process of removing dead branches and making room for new growth. This allows the plant to produce healthier and more abundant fruit. This is not to say that we should equate people with fruitless branches; that would be dehumanizing. Rather, what is being pruned are unhealthy actions or structures that bear no fruit. People may choose to leave in the process, but as Pastor B noted, "It's God who does the pruning. That which is pruned can be transformed into new life over time."

So, if you are fretting about folks leaving because of your prophetic preaching, ask yourself, might the congregation be freed up to pursue justice when the threat of internal retaliation is gone? "People can leave, and, conversely, transformation can happen when we speak truth. Of course, it's hard work and can be costly," observed Pastor D. She recounted the situation of some folks leaving after her sermons on inclusivity and being welcoming of those of different races and cultures. However, the remaining parishioners discovered their own prophetic courage—enough to hang a Black Lives Matter banner outside the church in a conservative community.

Should I Stay or Should I Go?

What if there are people in the congregation who want to make *you* leave? Sometimes it's not the parishioners who depart, but, rather, the pastor is forced out because of their prophetic ministry. Whether through subversive tactics or explicit efforts, some clergy face the loss of their pulpits if enough congregants align against them. What do you do if you and the congregation come to a crisis point? There are two primary things to consider if you are thinking about leaving: (1) How might your mental, physical, emotional, and spiritual health be affected whether you either stay or resign? (2) What support can you count on from your denominational office, pastoral colleagues, spiritual director/counselor, and family/friends?

Whether you are forced out of your position or choose to leave, talking with a professional counselor will be incredibly helpful. The damage of these kinds of conflicts can lead to what some call "post-traumatic church syndrome," which will follow you to whatever church you next serve. However, despite the suffering, we are also assured of the resurrection and new life. So a counselor can give you space and time to explore important questions. Just imagine what might happen if you were in a church without the naysayers and those who insist that the church should not engage in social issues? What might be possible for your preaching ministry with the muzzle tossed aside? What if people were excited to learn about how they as a church could take part in the work of God's Blessed Community? Might your congregation actually draw in new folks when they see that your church is not just talk but also action?

In my own ministry, there have been times when people left because of my prophetic preaching, even when I tried to be as diplomatic as possible. There were also a few parishioners who called for me to either be fired or resign (neither of which happened). But there were also folks who started attending and even joined the church because they heard about the work we were doing in the community to advocate for justice. Their presence opened the way for even more receptivity to God's transformative justice.

What I've learned from talking with pastors and congregants is that the presence of conflict does not necessarily mean the absence of God and that sometimes the leaving is necessary for there to be healing and for the work of ministry to go forward. Negative pushback can be painful to endure, but this is part of what it means to live out our vocation as Christians and clergy.

At the same time, prophetic courage can be contagious! As Pastor E said in describing the aftermath of her preaching about confronting racism, there are two ways to look at the loss of the members who leave. "Did we take a big hit? Or was God clearing a path for ministry? For us it was the latter. We saw the hate, and we used it to inspire us to do more. So no more holding back! We're now moving forward. Sometimes we take leaps. Sometimes baby steps. But always forward."

Final Thoughts and Words of Inspiration

Even though there are risks that come with addressing social issues in preaching, I hope that this book has given you tools and tactics to build your capacity and increase your confidence for this work. I want to leave you with some words of inspiration as you continue in this ministry of preaching. The source may seem surprising, but the spirit and passion of these words resonate strongly with me and perhaps will for you as well.

Welsh actor and social activist, Michael Sheen,[14] delivered a stirring speech at a St. David's Day march on March 1, 2015, to celebrate the National Health Service (NHS) and its founder, Aneurin Bevan.[15] Sheen lambasted cuts to the NHS and called for politicians to find their ethical courage. He also called for citizens to reclaim a society that ensures the well-being and flourishing of all.

> What sort of society do we want to be? What is our vision for ourselves? What are the qualities and the principles that we aspire towards and choose to defend?
>
> Because it is a choice. Do we want to be a society that is fractured, divided, disconnected? Do we want to be a society that is suspicious and mistrustful of its own people? A society that is exploitative, that sees people as commodities, as numbers? Mere instruments of profit, to be used while they have use, drained of whatever they can offer, and when they are seen as no longer useful, just abandoned, cut adrift? Preferably unseen and never again heard from?
>
> Or do we want to be a society where each person is recognised? Where all are equal in worth and value. And where that value is not purely a monetary one. A society that is supportive, that is inclusive and compassionate. Where it is acknowledged that not all can prosper. Where those who are most vulnerable, most in need of help, are not seen as lazy, or scrounging, or robbing the rest of us for whatever they can get. Where we do not turn our backs on those facing hard times. We do not abandon them or exploit their weakness. Because they are us. If not now, then at some point, and inevitably, they are us.[16]

Though this speech was for a secular context, Sheen's words speak to a basic premise of this book, which is that the needs of the most vulnerable in our society, as well as the current breakdown of civic engagement, call for a renewed vision of our highest moral and ethical aspirations. Preachers can name the qualities and principles that should guide a congregation's discernment around social issues and remind listeners that things such as inclusivity, compassion, and helping those in need are integral to the very nature of the God whom Christians worship.

Sheen goes on to call for people to face and embrace hard truths *together* because doing so makes us stronger individually and as a society. He says that in today's political climate, politicians (and, I would add, some pastors) are "careful, tentative, scared of saying what they feel for fear of alienating" people. But this only leads to "bland neutrality," which keeps our values and our best selves "behind closed doors."

> So when people are too scared to say what they really mean, when they're too careful to speak from their hearts, when integrity is too much of a risk, it's no surprise that people feel disengaged with politics.
>
> There is never an excuse to not speak up for what you think is right. You must stand up for what you believe. But first of all—by God, believe in something.
>
> To those across the whole party political spectrum, and to anyone in any position of power or authority, I ask you to search your heart, and look at who and what you serve.[17]

In the same spirit, I want to encourage you as a preacher to have the courage to say what you really mean, speak from your heart, and speak with integrity. As we've learned in this book, there are many ways to speak up for what you think is right, what you believe—and, more importantly—what the Bible and our theological convictions call us to believe and act on. It all depends on your personal strengths and risks, your preaching context, and the relationship you have with your congregation. While there may be different working gospels and we may draw on various moral foundations for our sermons, each of us must *believe in something*. And, indeed, we must search our hearts and look at who and what we serve.

Conclusion

Embracing authenticity and integrity in preaching is paramount. It requires the courage to speak genuinely from the heart, aligning our words with our beliefs and our ethical foundations, theological convictions, and the teachings of the Bible. As Thompson reminds us:

> Preaching does not exist for the sake of itself. It is a creative practice and exists for the hopes of something more. We urge preaching alongside its holy hopes to make way for sacred reverberations in our communities and world. Preaching hopes to render evident what is most true and holy—namely, proclamation that is recognizable by the entire community, as it possesses contemporary veracity and sustains the lives of those gathered. A message that makes way for such possibilities has the potential to reshape and push a community forward in a holistic manner.[18]

As highlighted throughout this book, the avenues for advocating what we perceive as right are diverse and tailored to our individual strengths, circumstances, and connections with our congregations. Thus, as preachers addressing social issues, we must examine our convictions and earnestly fulfill our role as stewards of faith and agents of positive change in our communities. Despite our differences, our core remains steadfast: a commitment to God's vision of flourishing for all people and for Creation.

Notes

1. Lisa L. Thompson, *Ingenuity: Preaching as an Outsider* (Nashville, TN: Abingdon Press, 2018), 176.

2. John S. McClure, *Ethical Approaches to Preaching: Choosing the Best Way to Preach about Difficult Issues* (Eugene, OR: Cascade Books, 2021), 120.

3. Lisa L. Thompson, *Preaching the Headlines: Possibilities and Pitfalls* (Minneapolis, MN: Fortress Press, 2021), 79.

4. Thompson, 79.

5. Leah D. Schade, *Preaching in the Purple Zone: Ministry in the Red-Blue Divide* (Lanham, MD: Rowman & Littlefield Publishers/Alban Books, 2019), 187–90.

6. Jonathan Haidt, *The Righteous Mind: Why Good People Disagree about Religion and Politics* (New York: Vintage Books, 2012), 364.

7. Portions of this section originated with a blog piece I wrote, "What to do When Parishioners Leave—Because of Politics," *Patheos* (Blog), August 27, 2020, https://www.patheos.com/blogs/ecopreacher/2020/08/what-to-do-when-parishioners-leave-because-politics/.

8. An excellent book examining the challenges to women pastors is Karoline Lewis, *She: Five Keys to Unlock the Power of Women in Ministry* (Nashville, TN: Abingdon Press, 2016).

9. Thompson, *Ingenuity*, 175.

10. Thompson, 175.

11. Evangelical Lutheran Church in America, "Ordination to the Ministry of Word and Sacrament," in *Evangelical Lutheran Worship Occasional Services for the Assembly* (Minneapolis, MN: Augsburg Fortress, 2009, 2019).

12. Evangelical Lutheran Church in America, "Holy Baptism," in *Evangelical Lutheran Worship* (Minneapolis, MN: Augsburg Fortress, 2006), 229.

13. Evangelical Lutheran Church in America, "Affirmation of Baptism," in *Evangelical Lutheran Worship* (Minneapolis, MN: Augsburg Fortress, 2006), 236.

14. Michael Sheen is an award-winning actor of stage and screen and is best known for his role in a trilogy of films as UK prime minister Tony Blair, David Frost in *Frost/Nixon*, William Masters in the television series *Masters of Sex*, and Aziraphale in the television series *Good Omens*. He has supported numerous charities, causes, and social justice projects. See Nadia Khomami, "Michael Sheen Declares Himself a 'Not-for-Profit Actor,'" *The Guardian*, published December 6, 2021, accessed February 15, 2024, https://www.theguardian.com/film/2021/dec/06/michael-sheen-not-for-profit-actor-activist.

15. The National Health Service is a government agency in Great Britain that provides free comprehensive public health services for all citizens financed primarily through taxes. See Encyclopedia Britannica, "National Health Service," accessed February 13, 2024, https://www.britannica.com/topic/National-Health-Service.

16. Michael Sheen, "Full Text of Michael Sheen's Speech," *The Guardian*, published March 2, 2015, accessed February 13, 2024, https://www.theguardian.com/culture/2015/mar/02/full-text-of-michael-sheens-speech.

17. Sheen.

18. Thompson, *Ingenuity*, 173.

Bibliography

Agosto, Efrain. "Islands, Borders, and Migration: Reading Paul in Light of the Crisis in Puerto Rico." In *Latinxs, the Bible, and Migration*. Edited by Efraín Agosto and Jacqueline M. Hidalgo, 149–160. Cham, Switzerland: Palgrave Macmillan, 2018.

Agosto, Efraín, and Jacqueline M. Hidalgo, eds. "Introduction." In *Latinxs, the Bible, and Migration*. Cham, Switzerland: Palgrave Macmillan, 2018.

Alberta, Tim. *The Kingdom, the Power, and the Glory: American Evangelicals in an Age of Extremism*. New York, NY: Harper, 2023.

Allen, O. Wesley Jr. *The Homiletic of All Believers: A Conversational Approach*. Louisville, KY: Westminster John Knox Press, 2005.

Allen, Ronald J. "Preaching on Social Issues." *Encounter* 59, no. 1/2 (1998).

———. *Preaching the Topical Sermon*. Louisville, KY: Westminster John Knox Press, 1992.

Allen, Ronald J., and O. Wesley Allen Jr. *The Sermon without End: A Conversational Approach to Preaching*. Nashville, TN: Abingdon Press, 2015.

Allen, Ronald J., John S. McClure, and O. Wesley Allen Jr., eds. *Under the Oak Tree: The Church as Community of Conversation in a Conflicted and Pluralistic World*. Eugene, OR: Cascade Books.

Baer, Hans, and Merrill Singer. *African American Religion in the Twentieth Century: Varieties of Protest and Accommodation*. Knoxville, TN: University of Tennessee Press.

Brooks, David. "How America Got Mean." *The Atlantic*. Published August 14, 2023. Accessed January 11, 2024. https://www.theatlantic.com/magazine/archive/2023/09/us-culture-moral-education-formation/674765/.

Brueggemann, Walter. "The Preacher, the Text and the People." *Theology Today* 47 (October 1990): 237–47.

Calderón Pilarski, Ahida. "Gendering (Im)migration in the Pentateuch's Legal Codes: A Reading from a Latina Perspective." In *Latinxs, the Bible, and Migration*. Edited by Efraín Agosto and Jacqueline M. Hidalgo, 43–66. Cham, Switzerland: Palgrave Macmillan, 2018.

Conde-Frazier, Elizabeth, "Evangélicas Reading Scriptures: Readings from within and Beyond the Tradition." In *Latina Evangélicas: A Theological Survey from the Margins*. Edited by Loida I. Martell-Otero, Zaida Maldonado Pérez, and Elizabeth Conde-Frazier, 73-89. Eugene, OR: Cascade Books, 2013.

Cooper-White, Pamela. *The Psychology of Christian Nationalism: Why People Are Drawn in and How to Talk across the Divide*. Minneapolis, MN: Fortress Press, 2022.

Cressman, Lisa. *The Gospel People Don't Want to Hear: Preaching Challenging Messages*. Minneapolis: Fortress Press, 2020.

Detrow, Scott, Gabriel J. Sánchez, and Sarah Handel. "He Was a Top Church Official Who Criticized Trump. He Says Christianity Is in Crisis." NPR. Published August 8, 2023. Accessed August 13, 2023. https://www.npr.org/2023/08/08/1192663920/southern-baptist-convention-donald-trump-christianity.

Djupe, Paul A., and J. R. Neiheisel. "Clergy Deliberation on Gay Rights and Homosexuality." *Polity* 40, no. 4 (2008): 411–35.

Djupe, Paul A., and L. Olson. "Public Deliberation about Gay Rights in Religious Contexts: Commitment to Deliberative Norms and Practice in ELCA Congregations." *Journal of Public Deliberation* 9, no. 1 (2013): 1–27.

Du Mez, Kristen Kobes. *Jesus and John Wayne: How White Evangelicals Corrupted a Faith and Fractured a Nation*. New York, NY: Liveright Publishing Corp., 2020.

Evangelical Lutheran Church in America. "Affirmation of Baptism." In *Evangelical Lutheran Worship*. Minneapolis, MN: Augsburg Fortress, 2006.

Evangelical Lutheran Church in America. "Holy Baptism." In *Evangelical Lutheran Worship*. Minneapolis, MN: Augsburg Fortress, 2006.

Evangelical Lutheran Church in America. "Ordination to the Ministry of Word and Sacrament." In *Evangelical Lutheran Worship Occasional Services for the Assembly*. Minneapolis, MN: Augsburg Fortress, 2009, 2019.

Evangelical Lutheran Church in America. "Talking Together as Christians about Tough Social Issues." Published 1999. https://download.elca.org/ELCA%20Resource%20Repository/Talking_Together_as_Christians_About_Tough_Social_Issues.pdf.

Gabbatt, Adam. "Losing Their Religion: Why US Churches Are on the Decline." *The Guardian*. Published January 22, 2023. Accessed August 15, 2023. https://www.theguardian.com/us-news/2023/jan/22/us-churches-closing-religion-covid-christianity.

Gafney, Wilda C. *Womanist Midrash: A Reintroduction to the Women of the Torah and the Throne*. Louisville, KY: Westminster John Knox Press, 2017.

———. *A Women's Lectionary for the Whole Church: Year W* (2021), *Year A* (2021), *Year B* (2023), *Year C* (2024). New York, NY: Church Publishing.

Gardner, Tyshawn. *Social Crisis Preaching: Biblical Proclamation in Troubling Times*. Brentwood, TN: B&H Publishing, 2023.

Garnett, Matthew F., Sally C. Curtin, and Deborah M. Stone. "Suicide Mortality in the United States, 2000–2020." Centers for Disease Control and Prevention. Published March 2022. https://www.cdc.gov/nchs/data/databriefs/db433.pdf.

Gilbert, Kenyatta. *The Journey and Promise of African American Preaching*. Minneapolis, MN: Fortress Press, 2011.

Gorski, Philip S., and Samuel L. Perry. *The Flag and the Cross: White Christian Nationalism and the Threat to American Democracy*. New York, NY: Oxford University Press, 2022.

Grant, Jacqueline. *White Women's Christ and Black Women's Jesus: Feminist Christology and Womanist Response*. Chișinău, Moldova: Scholars Press, 1989.

Greene, Joshua. *Moral Tribes: Emotion, Reason, and the Gap between Us and Them*. New York, NY: Penguin, 2013.

Guthrie, Clifton F. "Quantitative Empirical Studies in Preaching: A Review of Methods and Findings." *Journal of Communication and Religion* 30 (2007): 317–47.

Haidt, Jonathan. *The Righteous Mind: Why Good People Are Divided by Politics and Religion*. New York, NY: Vintage Books, 2012.

Harper, Amanda Wilson. "Strengthening Congregational Communities: Social Justice Engagement through Deliberative Dialogue." *Social Work & Christianity* 47, no. 3 (2020): 85–99.

Helsel, Carolyn. *Anxious to Talk about It: Helping White Christians Talk Faithfully about Racism*. St. Louis, MO: Chalice Press, 2017.

———. *Preaching about Racism: A Guide for Faith Leaders*. St. Louis, MO: Chalice Press, 2018.

Hess, Jacob. "Perspective: The Braver Angels Plan to Heal America." *Deseret News*. Published March 9, 2022. Accessed January 27, 2024. https://www.deseret.com/2022/3/9/22949616/perspective-the-braver-angels-miracle-polarization-democrats-republicans-dialogue-politics-election.

Heyward, Carter. *The 7 Deadly Sins of Christian Nationalism: A Call to Action.* Lanham, MD: Rowman & Littlefield, 2022.

Hidalgo, Jacqueline M. "The Bible as Homing Device among Cubans at Claremont's Calvary Chapel." In *Latinxs, the Bible, and Migration.* Edited by Efraín Agosto and Jacqueline M. Hidalgo, 21–42. Cham, Switzerland: Palgrave Macmillan, 2018.

Jones, Jeffrey M. "U.S. Church Attendance Still Lower than Pre-Pandemic." Gallup. Published June 26, 2023. Accessed January 5, 2024. https://news.gallup.com/poll/507692/church-attendance-lower-pre-pandemic.aspx.

Kim, Eunjoo Mary. *Preaching Jesus: Postcolonial Approaches.* Lanham, MD: Rowman & Littlefield, 2024.

Kim, Yung Suk. *How to Read the Gospels.* Lanham, MD: Rowman & Littlefield, 2024.

Kim-Cragg, HyeRan. *Postcolonial Preaching: Creating a Ripple Effect.* Lanham, MD: Lexington Books, 2021.

Krogstad, Jens Manuel, Khadijah Edwards, and Mark Hugo Lopez. "Latinos and the 2022 Midterm Elections." Pew Research Center. Accessed February 1, 2024. https://www.pewresearch.org/race-ethnicity/2022/09/29/latinos-and-the-2022-midterm-elections/.

Krogstad, Jens Manuel, and Mark Hugo Lopez. "Most Latinos Say U.S. Immigration System Needs Big Changes." Pew Research Center. Published April 20, 2021. Accessed February 1, 2024. https://www.pewresearch.org/short-reads/2021/04/20/most-latinos-say-u-s-immigration-system-needs-big-changes/.

Lakoff, George. *Moral Politics: How Liberals and Conservatives Think.* 3rd ed. Chicago: University of Chicago Press, 2016.

LaRue, Cleophus J. "African American Preaching Perspectives." In *The New Interpreters Handbook of Preaching.* Edited by Paul Scott Wilson, 293–97. Nashville, TN: Abingdon Press, 2008.

Lewis, Karoline. *She: Five Keys to Unlock the Power of Women in Ministry.* Nashville, TN: Abingdon Press, 2016.

Lincoln, C. Eric, and Lawrence H. Mamiya. *The Black Church in the African American Experience.* Durham, NC: Duke University Press.

McClure, John S. *Ethical Approaches to Preaching: Choosing the Best Way to Preach about Difficult Issues.* Eugene, OR: Cascade Books, 2021.

———. *Preaching Words: 144 Key Terms in Homiletics.* Louisville, KY: Westminster John Knox Press, 2007.

———. *The Roundtable Pulpit: Where Leadership and Preaching Meet.* Nashville, TN: Abingdon, 1995.

McClure, John S., and Nancy J. Ramsay, eds. *Telling the Truth: Preaching about Sexual and Domestic Violence.* Cleveland, OH: United Church Press, 1998.

McGhee, Heather. *The Sum of Us: What Racism Costs Everyone and How We Can Prosper Together.* New York, NY: One World, 2022.

McKenzie, Alyce. *Novel Preaching: Tips from Great Writers on Crafting Creative Sermons.* Louisville, KY: Westminster John Knox Press, 2010.

National Issues Forum Institute. "Climate Choices: How Should We Meet the Challenges of a Warming Planet?" Accessed May 23, 2024. https://www.nifi.org/en/issue-guide/climate-choices.

Pew Research Center. "Modeling the Future of Religion in America." Published September 13, 2022. Accessed August 15, 2023. https://www.pewresearch.org/religion/2022/09/13/modeling-the-future-of-religion-in-america/.

Pew Research Center Religious Landscape Study. "Latinos Who Are Conservative." Published 2014. Accessed February 1, 2024. https://www.pewresearch.org/religion/religious-landscape-study/political-ideology/conservative/racial-and-ethnic-composition/latino/.

Public Religion Research Institute. "A Christian Nation? Understanding the Threat of Christian Nationalism to American Democracy and Culture." Published February 2, 2023. Accessed August 14, 2023. https://www.prri.org/research/a-christian-nation-understanding-the-threat-of-christian-nationalism-to-american-democracy-and-culture/.

Public Religion Research Institute. "Clergy and Congregations in a Time of Transformation: Findings from the 2022–2023 Mainline Protestant Clergy Survey." Published September 13, 2023. Accessed January 5, 2024. https://www.prri.org/research/clergy-and-congregations-in-a-time-of-transformation-findings-from-the-2022-2023-mainline-protestant-clergy-survey/.

Putnam, Robert D. *Bowling Alone: The Collapse and Revival of American Community.* New York: Simon & Schuster, 2000.

Putnam, Robert D., and D. E. Campbell. *American Grace: How Religion Divides and Unites Us.* New York: Simon & Schuster, 2010.

Resner, André. "Do You See This Woman? A Little Exercise in Homiletical Theology." In *Theologies of the Gospel in Context: The Crux of Homiletical Theology.* Edited by David Schnasa Jacobsen, 19–24. Eugene, OR: Cascade, 2017.

———. *Living In-Between: Lament, Justice, and the Presence of the Gospel.* Eugene, OR: Wipf and Stock, 2015.

———. "Reading the Bible for Preaching the Gospel." In *Collected Papers of the 2008 Annual Meeting of the Academy of Homiletics,* 2008.

Rose, Lucy Atkinson. *Sharing the Word: Preaching in the Roundtable Church*. Louisville, KY: Westminster John Knox Press, 1997.

Schade, Leah D. "Countering White Christian Nationalism: Reflections for a Lenten Sermon Series Based on Readings from the Revised Common Lectionary, Year A, 2023." In *Jesus and Justice in Public: A Study-Action Guide*. Wisconsin Council of Churches, 2023.

Schade, Leah D. *Preaching in the Purple Zone: Ministry in the Red-Blue Divide*. Lanham, MD: Rowman & Littlefield/Alban Books, 2019.

Schade, Leah D. "White Mainline Protestant Preachers Addressing Racial Issues: 2017 vs. 2021." In *Unmasking White Preaching: Racial Hegemony, Resistance, and Possibilities in Homiletics*, ed. Lis Valle-Ruiz and Andrew Wymer, 69–84. Lanham, MD: Lexington Books, 2022.

Schade, Leah D., Jerry L. Sumney, and Emily Askew. *Introduction to Preaching: Scripture, Theology, and Sermon Preparation*. Lanham, MD: Rowman & Littlefield, 2023.

Segovia, Fernando F. "Approaching the Bible in Latino/a Theology: Doing Theological Construction and Biblical Criticism in an Ethnic-Racial Key." In *Latino/a Theology and the Bible: Ethnic-Racial Reflections on Interpretation*. Edited by Francisco Lozada Jr. and Fernando F. Segovia, 3–26. Lanham, MD: Lexington Books/Fortress Academic, 2021.

Sheppard, Phillis-Isabella, Dawn Ottoni-Wilhelm, and Ronald J. Allen, eds. *Preaching Prophetic Care: Building Bridges to Justice: Essays in Honor of Dale P. Andrews*. Eugene, OR: Pickwick Publications, 2018.

Smith, Christine M., ed. *Preaching Justice: Ethnic and Cultural Perspectives*. Cleveland, OH: United Church Press, 1998. Reissued by Wipf and Stock, 2008.

Snider, Phil, ed. *Preaching as Resistance: Voices of Hope, Justice, & Solidarity*. St. Louis, MO: Chalice Press, 2018.

St. Clair, Raquel "Womanist Criticism," in *The New Interpreters Handbook of Preaching*, ed. Paul Scott Wilson, 170–72. Nashville, TN: Abingdon Press, 2008.

Stroud, Dean G. *Preaching in Hitler's Shadow: Sermons of Resistance in the Third Reich*. Grand Rapids, MI: Wm. B. Eerdmans Publishing Co., 2013.

Sumney, Jerry L. *The Politics of Faith: The Bible, Government, and Public Policy*. Minneapolis, MN: Fortress Press, 2020.

Thomas, Frank A. *How to Preach a Dangerous Sermon*. Nashville, TN: Abingdon Press, 2018.

———. *Surviving a Dangerous Sermon*. Nashville, TN: Abingdon, 2020.

———. *The God of the Dangerous Sermon*. Nashville, TN: Abingdon, 2021.

Thompson, Lisa L. *Ingenuity: Preaching as an Outsider*. Nashville, TN: Abingdon Press, 2018.

———. *Preaching the Headlines: Possibilities and Pitfalls.* Minneapolis, MN: Fortress Press, 2021.

Tisdale, Leonora Tubbs. *Prophetic Preaching: A Pastoral Approach.* Louisville, KY: Westminster John Knox Press, 2010.

Valle-Ruiz, Lis. "Non-Preaching? Unmasking (White) Preaching through Negation." In *Unmasking White Preaching: Racial Hegemony, Resistance, and Possibilities in Homiletics.* Edited by Lis Valle-Ruiz and Andrew Wymer, 205–20. Lanham, MD: Lexington Books, 2022.

Voelz, Richard W. *Preaching to Teach: Inspire People to Think and Act.* Nashville, TN: Abingdon Press, 2019.

Walker, Alice. *In Search of Our Mothers' Gardens: Womanist Prose.* San Diego: Harcourt Brace Jovanovich, 1984.

Wehner, Peter. "The Evangelical Church Is Breaking Apart." *The Atlantic.* Published October 24, 2021. Accessed August 10, 2023. https://www.theatlantic.com/ideas/archive/2021/10/evangelical-trump-christians-politics/620469/.

Whitehead, Andrew L. *American Idolatry: How Christian Nationalism Betrays the Gospel and Threatens the Church.* Grand Rapids, MI: Brazos Press, 2023.

Whitehead, Andrew L., and Scott L. Perry. *Taking America Back for God: Christian Nationalism in the United States.* New York, NY: Oxford University Press, 2020.

Williams, Delores S. *Sisters in the Wilderness: The Challenge of Womanist God-Talk.* Maryknoll, NY: Orbis Books, 1993.

Williams, Melvin. *Community in a Black Pentecostal Church: An Anthropological Study.* Long Grove, IL: Waveland Press, Inc.

Wisconsin Council of Churches. *Jesus and Justice in Public: A Study-Action Guide.* 2023.

World Economic Forum. "Here's How Immigrants Have Boosted the U.S. Economy." Published September 17, 2020. Accessed January 13, 2024. https://www.weforum.org/agenda/2020/09/immigrants-expand-the-us-economy/.

Scripture Index

Hebrew Scriptures (Old Testament)		Matthew 19:21	109
Genesis 16:1-16	118–119	Matthew 21:12-13	109
Genesis 18:1-15	90	Matthew 22:15-22	109
Genesis 21:9-21	118	Matthew 24:29-35	198–200
Genesis Chapters 37-46	157	Matthew 25:31-46	109, 110
Leviticus 19:33-34	153–54	Matthew 26:47-56	72–74
Deuteronomy 7:3-6, 23:2	154	Matthew 27:15-31	171
Deuteronomy 26:5-9	157	Mark 8:1-13	109
1 Kings 19:12	222	Mark 8:35	63
Ezra 9:1-2	154	Luke 4:18	109
Nehemiah Chapter 13	154	Luke 12:49-53	229
Esther 1:10-20	211–215	Luke 19:1-10	145
Psalm 137	113	Luke 21:16-19	229
Isaiah 58:12	72	John 14:15-21	144
Ezekiel 37:1-14	171	John 15:2	234
Amos 7:12-15	203–206	John 21:15, 16	3
		Acts 2:43-47	80
Christian Scriptures		Acts 4:32-37, 5:1-11	80
(New Testament)		Acts chapter 5	108–109
Matthew 2:13-23	156	Acts 6:1-7	80
Matthew 4:1-11	171	Acts chapters 6-11	80
Matthew 10:16	78	Acts 16:16-40	130
Matthew 15:32-39	109	Acts 17:22-34	90

Romans 8:18-25	69–70	Philippians 2:6-11	178
Romans 13:1-7	110	Philippians 2:7	74
2 Corinthians 5:18-20	83, 216	Philippians 2:12-13	186, 190, 193
Ephesians 4:1-6	200–202		
Philippians 2:1-13	176–195	Philippians 4:2	177–78
Philippians 2:2	177, 178	Philippians 4:7	222
Philippians 2:3	183	Revelation 3:14-22	206–209

Topical Index

Page references for figures are italicized.

African American preaching. *See* homiletics, African American
Agosto, Efrain, 113–14
Allen, O. Wesley, Jr., 135, 137
Allen, Ronald J., 1–2, 127, 135, 137
ambassadors for Christ, 83–84, 90, 95, 102, 216. *See also* Scripture Index, 2 Corinthians 5:18-20
Amos and Amaziah, 203–205
Andrews, Dale, xii, 11
Askew, Emily, 186–96
assessment tool for preaching about social issues, 40–61
authenticity, importance of, 79, 90, 155, 167, 237
authority:
    in biblical interpretation, 99, 112, 114–15, 116, 120, 136, 158, 205;
    in preaching, 3, 13, 29, 106, 114–15, 134, 135, 136, 205, 209, 212–14, 232;
    in exercising power, 88, 91, 92, 93, 96, 145–46, 165, 193, 212–14;
    moral foundation. *See* Moral Foundation Theory: authority/subversion
authoritarianism, 162

baptism, baptismal vows, 8, 223, 232–33
belonging, 98, 128, 165, 168, 223–24
Bible:
    as political document, 108–113, 175;
    ethics and, 107–111, 226–27;
    exegesis and interpretation, 106—23;
    historical-critical exegesis, 107–111, 185;
    Latino/a hermeneutics, 111–115, 123n16, 152–53;
    migration in, 112–115;

public policy and, 2, 17, 27, 33, 63–64, 77, 107–111, 113–15, 153, 160;
social issues and, 106–111, 112–115, 118–121, 122–23, 175, 181–86, 190–94, 200–202, 203–206, 207–209, 211–16, 226–27, 237–38;
womanist interpretation, 115–21, 158, 212–15
Braver Angels, 90
Brooks, David, 83–86, 100–101, 129

Cameroon, sociopolitical and religious dynamics, 202–206
Central Statements (Central Question, Central Claim, Central Purpose), 179–80, 187, 207
Christian nationalism, x, xi, 19, 24, 25, 81n15, 161–63, *164*, 165–68, *169*, 170–72, 174n26, 230;
definition of, 162–63.
See also preaching and social issues, topics: Christian nationalism.
Christianity, Christians:
colonialism, 144–45. *See also* colonialism;
decline of, 23;
responding to contemporary issues, 13, 17, 31, 34, 73, 80n2, 83, 92, 98–99, 102, 105–106–110, 112, 114, 129–30, 138, 139, 183–84, 201, 207–209, 227, 229, 232, 235;
White Christians, *See* Christian nationalism

Church:
African American and Black, 45, 138–42, 212–15;
church and state, 24, 110;
desire for unity, 23–24, 30, 77, 97, 172, 185, 201–202, 202–206, 219, 229;
Disciples of Christ, Christian Church, 9, 33–34, 198, 212;
divisiveness within, 4, 20, 23, 24, 26–27, 30, 33, 35, 36n14, 40, 100, 105, 129, 135–36, 161, 182–86, 202–206, 219, 229;
Evangelical, 22, 25, 91, 92, 105, 139, 140, 152, 169, 170;
Lutheran (ELCA), 7–9, 92, 232–33;
politics and, xvi, 2–3, 5–12, 17–18, 22–23, 24, 25–27, 33–34, 36n14, 39–40, 43, 46, 48, 63, 8687, 94–96, 100, 105, 106–110, 113, 128, 138–41, 154, 159, 169–72, 175, 180–86, 198, 200–202, 202–206, 219, 220, 230, 233;
Roman Catholic Church, 152–53, 202–206;
United Methodist Church, 26, 34–35, 207.
See also congregations
civil discourse. *See* dialogue
clergy:
gender and sexual orientation, 21, 29, 32, 40, 42, 44–45, 231–32;
intimidation of, 5–6, 25, 31–32, 36n18, 85, 105, 231–35;
leaving churches, 27, 234–36;
mentoring, 223;
navigating politics. *See* church, politics and;

need for training, support to engage social issues, 33–34, 43, 234–36;
ordination vows of, 232–33;
political leanings, 23, *24*, 25;
race and culture of, 45–46, 50;
stress, burnout, 19–20, 27, 31, 43, 50, 234–36;
colonialism, 111, 114, 142–147, 193, 203–206. *See also* homiletics, post-colonial
Conde-Frazier, Elizabeth, 112
congregations:
"brittleness" and stress within, 19–20, 26–27, 32, 43, 46–47, 50, 57, 59, 60, 64–65, 175, 185, 228–32. *See also* church, divisiveness within;
conflict, conflict resolution, dysfunction within, 31, 40, 43, 46, 47, 53, 57, 86, 105, 175, 177, 203–206, 235;
diminishing attendance, 22–23, 35n9;
deliberation within, 33, 47–48, 68, 100, 136, 155–57, 167, 202–206. *See also* dialogue; sermon-dialogue-sermon method;
emotional abuse within, 233–34;
engaging social issues, 33–34, 46–51, 91–92, 106–111, 111–23, 135–37, 138–42, 143–47, 184–85, 235;
fears of closing, 22–23;
governance, 47;
health, vitality, and resilience, 44, 46–48;
leaving because of politics, 24–25, 233–35;
political contrasts/conflicts with clergy, 23, *24*, 25, 46–47, 48, 91–92, 105;
race and culture of, 45–46;
relationships with surrounding community, 48, 113–14, 115, 119, 136–37, 138–40, 202–206, 235;
relationships within membership, 46–49, 132–33, 154–57, 165–168, 220–30;
trust within, 47–49, 57, 59, 60, 64, 65, 67, 70, 71, 74–76, 79, 100, 154, 157, 160, 167–68, 175, 206, 219, 227, 228. *See also* church
conservative ideology or worldview, 7–9, 42, 48, 87–88, 92, 94, 95, 97, 98–99, 128, 152, 162, 165, 168, 169–70, 174n27, 230. *See also* moral worldview, Strict Father
conspiracy theories. *See* disinformation, misinformation, propaganda, conspiracy theories
Cooper-White, Pamela, 162–68, *169*
courage in addressing social issues, 12, 14, 20, 27–28, 40, 67, 71, 78, 163, 204–205, 215, 234, 235–38
COVID-19 pandemic, 19, 22, 23, 33, 39, 40, 144
Cressman, Lisa, 3, 5, 19, 46, 63, 70–71

deliberative dialogue, 81n5, 155–57, 167, 204–206;
preaching and, 68, 69, 90, 100, 131–37, 154–57, 204–206, 222

democracy, 81n5;
  dysfunction or undermining of, x, 16, 85, 164, 194
disinformation, conspiracy theories, propaganda 19, 105, 161, 165, 174n27
divisiveness, 12, 20, 24, 26, 33, 83, 87, 94, 103n10, 105, 129, 135–36, 155, 161, 164–66, 169, 172, 174n26, 177–178, 180–86, 194, 197, 203–206, 216, 219, 229, 236. *See also,* church: divisiveness within; polarization
Durkheim, Emile, 97

elections. *See* preaching and elections
emotions and social issues, 2, 3, 11, 48, 23, 51, 60, 64, 77, 94, 97, 105–106, 132, 159, 160, 167–71, 173n26, 174n27, 201, 222, 223, 225, 226, 228, 233
empathy, in preaching and ministry, 11, 60, 67, 69, 79, 87, 88, 90, 115, 129, 131, 137, 160, 167, 170–171, 192, 193, 205, 211, 214, 226
equity, equality, inequality, 3, 4, 9–10, 12, 64, 87, 89, 91, 107, 108, 109, 112, 123, 130, 139, 159, 178, 187–95, 212–13, 231, 233, 236
exegesis and preaching, 64–65, 66, 69, 80n2, 106–11, 120, 135, 141, 144, 176–78, 179, 185, 194, 195, 200, 209
extremism, 26, 32, 85, 96–97, 165, 170, 184

Esther, 140, 211. *See also* Vashti, Queen.
ethical approaches in preaching, 128–37;
  communicative ethic, 128—29, 133–36, 138, 158, 161, 170, 186, 202;
  hospitality ethic 131–36, 153, 154, 168;
  liberation ethic, 130–31, 140–42, 144, 158, 170, 209;
  witness ethic, 129–30, 140–42, 144, 146, 171, 200, 214
ethics, 84, 235–36;
  Bible and, 107, 181–85;
  culture and, 94;
  emotions, feelings and, 94, 159–60, 166–68, 174n26;
  nuance within, 93, 100;
  moral reasoning and developing virtues, 94–95.
  See also Haidt, Jonathan; moral foundations theory; morality
Eucharist. *See* Holy Communion

faith and politics, xi, 2–3, 17–18, 23–25, 34–35, 63, 86, 92, 94–99, 105, 106–111, 128, 153, 159, 169–71, 175, 200–202, 202–206, 207–209, 233.
  See also Bible, as political document, public policy and, social issues and; politics, church and; politics, preaching and

Gafney, Wilda C., 115–16, 120–21, 142
Gardner, Tyshawn, 51, 67, 71, 75, 77, 138–40, 147, 158
Gilbert, Kenyatta, 10, 16n9

Gore, Al, 7–9. *See also* preaching and social issues (topics): climate change.
Grant, Jacquelyn, 116–17

Hagar, 117–19, 125n43, 142
Haidt, Jonathan, 13, 84, 86, 94–100, 165, 168, 226. *See also* ethics; moral foundations theory; morality
hate crimes, groups, speech, 5, 6, 77, 85, 166, 184, 191
Helsel, Carolyn, 158–61
Heritage Foundation, 7–8
hermeneutics. *See* Bible, exegesis and interpretation
Heyward, Carter, 162
Hidalgo, Jacqualine M., 114
Holy Communion, 200, 201, 223
homiletics, 11, 13–14, 127–47;
African American, 138–42;
Asian, 143–45;
conversational and collaborative, 133–37, 154, 157, 159, 161, 186, 202–206;
Latina, 145–46;
post-colonial, 143–46, 202–206, 210–217;
womanist, 140–42
humility, importance of, 71, 74–76, 85, 129, 176–77, 182–83, 186, 190, 201, 202, 224

ideology, political and racial, 23–25, 86, 111, 158, 161, 163, 170–71, 172. *See also,* conservative ideology or worldview; progressive ideology or worldview
idolatry, 169–70, 189, 204, 230
inequality. *See* equality

integrity, importance of, 74–79, 166, 224, 237–38

Jesus Christ, 3, 8, 142, 169–71, 176, 178–79, 183–85, 190–91, 199–200, 201–202, 206–209, 220, 222, 227, 232;
cross, crucifixion, resurrection, 83, 90, 91, 109, 138–39, 146, 230;
is political, 10, 17, 28, 107–109, 113, 142, 145, 156, 207, 229;
teachings of, 24–26, 28, 63, 73–74, 105–106, 109–110, 144–45, 169, 170, 227, 228–30, 234
justice, injustice, 3, 9–12, 14, 20, 24, 29–30, 32, 33, 39, 42, 65, 69, 72–74, 91–92, 93, 108, 110, 116, 120, 128, 130–31, 134, 139, 145, 158, 161, 166, 170–71, 187, 191–92, 194, 203–206, 207–209, 210–15, 230–35

Kim-Cragg, HyeRan, 143–45
King, Jr., Martin Luther, 128, 191, 192, 205

Lakoff, George, 87
LaRue, Cleophus J., 138
Latino/a perspectives and scholars. *See* Bible, Latino/a interpretation
law and gospel, 71–72, 221–22
liberal or progressive ideology or worldview, 23, 24, 25, 48, 87, 88–89, 93, 97, 98, 99, 140, 207. *See also* worldview, Nurturant Parent

listening, importance of, 9, 32, 49, 60, 64–65, 67, 72, 74–76, 79, 90, 101–102, 115, 122–23, 132, 133–34, 144, 155, 157–61, 165–68, 186, 205, 219, 221, 223, 226–27

liturgy and social issues. *See* worship and social issues

Living Room Conversations, 155–157

love:
- of or for God and Jesus, 3, 11, 25, 79, 85, 106, 176–78, 187, 190, 191, 201–202, 207, 208, 220, 224;
- for others, 66, 79, 85, 86, 97–98, 106, 114, 153, 168, 170, 176–78, 183, 184, 190, 192, 201—202, 207, 209;
- preaching message of, 32, 79, 105, 106, 170, 184, 187, 201–202, 207–209, 224

marginalized voice, listening to, 10, 106, 107, 111–12, 114, 116, 120, 121, 122–23, 130, 134, 149n58, 157, 192, 193

McClure, John, 128–37, 223

McGhee, Heather, 160

media, role in politics and faith, ix, 2, 63, 105, 165, 201

Moore, Russell, 24–25

morality:
- "groupishness" and, 95–97;
- loss of in America, 84–87, 100–101;
- moral and social capital, virtues, 99–100, 236–37;
- moral diversity, 86, 94, 100, 153–54, 224;

moral and virtue formation, 75, 85–86, 87, 94, 100–102, 129, 131, 202, 224, 236–37;

moral imagination and vision, 74, 86, 87, 101, 131–32, 147, 171, 236–37;

moral agency, discernment, intuitions, and reasoning, 84, 94–95, 97, 154, 166–70, 200, 205–206, 210, 227;

religion and, 85–86, 94–102, 107, 128–36, 139, 143–46, 153–54, 158–61, 162–72, 194, 205–206, 226–27.

See also ethics; Haidt, Jonathan

Moral Foundations Theory, 95, 96, 97–99, 226;
- application to preaching, 109–110, 115, 116, 128–36, 137, 139, 143–46, 152, 157–58, 158—61, 164–71, 175, 184–86, 193–94, 200;
- authority/subversion, 96, 97, 98, 99, 110, 115, 116, 145–46, 154, 164, 165, 193, 205–206, 209, 212, 214;
- care/harm, 95–96, 98, 109, 116, 129, 130, 140, 141–42, 144, 146, 152, 154, 156–57, 165, 170, 185, 193, 200, 202, 209, 212, 214;
- fairness/cheating, 88, 96–97, 109, 116, 129, 130, 152, 154, 156–57, 165, 193;
- liberty/oppression, 97, 109, 116–17, 129, 130–31, 139, 141, 143–44, 147, 152, 154, 157, 158, 162, 165, 170, 171, 192, 193, 205–206, 209, 212, 214;

loyalty/betrayal, 96, 97, 145, 146, 152, 154, 163, 165, 205, 209, 212, 214, 229;
sanctity/degradation, 96–97, 98–99, 145–46, 152, 154, 165, 212, 214
moral worldviews, 84, 86–90, 91–94, 98–99, 106, 128, 152, 153, 169, 224, 229;
Nurturant Parent, 87, 88–89, 92, 93;
Strict Father, 87–88, 92, 93, 152, 169;

Nashville, flooding, 188–93
nuance, in addressing social issues, 92, 93, 94, 100, 140, 151

partisan, non-partisan, 3, 20, 24, 68, 180
pastoral care and conversations, importance of, 11, 12, 102, 114, 143, 166, 222–24, 227, 229
patriotism, 163
Paul, teachings and writings of, 69, 83, 90, 102, 110, 113, 130, 172, 176–85, 186–91, 194, 200–202
peace, 74, 123, 138, 202, 203–206, 222
Pilarski, Ahida Calderón, 114
polarization, 1, 2, 5, 11, 19, 20, 83, 219. See also church: divisiveness within; divisiveness.
politics:
church and, 2–3, 7, 11, 12, 17–20, 23, 24, 25, 26, 28–29, 34–35, 39–40, 46, 48, 105, 106–111, 159, 162, 169–71, 175, 181–82, 198, 200, 202–206, 207, 209, 219–220, 230–31, 233;
definition, 2–3;
faith and. See faith, and politics;
preaching and, 2–3, 19–20, 27–28, 36n14, 40, 43, 48, 86, 128, 130, 138, 140–41, 143, 154, 159, 169–71, 180, 181–85, 200–202, 202–206, 207–209. See also Bible, as political document, public policy and, social issues and; politics, church and; politics, preaching and; church, politics and
power dynamics and social issues, 4, 10, 25, 73, 87, 89, 108, 111, 118, 121, 122, 129–30, 139, 143–44, 162, 165, 170, 171, 183–84, 191–92, 194, 203–204, 232, 237
postcolonialism, 111–12, 143–46, 147, 193, 203, 205, 209–10, 212;
Latina, 112, 145–46;
See also, colonialism
prayer, importance of, 74–75, 222, 223, 228
preaching:
African American, Black, 16n9, 45, 138–42, 212–15;
collaborative/conversational, 72, 73–74, 131–33, 154, 157, 159, 161, 202–206;
congregational context and, 4, 42–51, 76–77, 138–40, 153, 185–86, 193, 202–206;
criticism or negative pushback about, 5–6, 18, 20, 24–26,

30–32, 36n14, 42, 78, 165, 220, 224–35, 231;
elections and, 18–19, 33, 180–86, 194;
embodiment and, 121, 141, 145–46, 147, 158, 212–15, 231–32;
gender and, 21, 29, 42, 44–45, 116, 143, 158, 217n20;
narrative or story, use of, 45, 60, 67–68, 69, 70, 71, 72, 74, 90, 113, 115, 116, 122, 129, 130, 131, 137, 139, 157, 159, 160, 170, 171, 186, 192, 193, 194, 204, 210, 211, 213–15, 219, 226, 227;
politics. *See* politics, preaching and;
prophetic. *See* prophetic preaching;
research about, 18–35;
theatre and, 146, 210–215;
theology and, 28, 65, 66, 72, 74, 83, 99, 106, 109–10, 112, 113, 117, 119, 120–21, 122–23, 127, 128, 135–37, 138–42, 178, 179, 190–95, 202, 207–209, 210–15, 221, 227, 237–38;
topical, 127–28;
vulnerabilities, risks, and capacity, xii, 12, 26, 27–30, 40–43, 46–47, 49–51, 52–60, 61, 64, 175, 198, 212, 220, 225, 231–32, 236–37
preaching and social issues [*for specific topics, see* social issues (topics)]:
approaches and strategies for, 60–61, 64–74, 80, 89–90, 109, 115, 119, 153–58, 159–61, 164–71, *181*, 185–86, 192–94;
assessing capacity for, 41–60;
avoiding and remedying mistakes, 220–26;
biblical foundations for, 83–84, 107–123, 176–78;
case studies and examples, 178–94, 198–215;
challenges for clergy, 17–21, 23–25, 27–32, 36n14, 39–40, 41–49, 63–64, 106–106, 219–20, 231–32, 234–36;
ethical foundations for, 86–100, 128–32, *133*, 134–37;
homiletical foundations for, 127–47;
necessity of, ix–xii, 1–5, 17–18, 84–86, 87, 101–102, 122–23;
negative pushback about, 224–31, 233–34;
parishioners' views about, 32–35, 224–35;
preparing for, 74–79, 221–24;
societal challenges of, 5–9, 26–27;
support for clergy, 32, 36n19, 222–24, 232–33, 236–38;
progressive ideology or worldview. *See* liberal or progressive ideology or worldview
propaganda. *See* disinformation, misinformation
prophetic preaching, xii, 4, 10–12, 16n9, 20, 27, 32, 40, 45, 65, 68–69, 79, 135–36, 137, 143, 145–47, 159, 161, 198, 212, 216, 229, 230, 231, 232–35
prophetic care, xii, 11, 210
prophets, biblical, 3, 108, 145, 203–204
Purple Zone preaching, 7–9, 11, 12, 18, 32, 48, 68, 135–36, 159, 202, 224

Putnam, Robert, 99

reconciliation, ministry of, 65, 74, 75, 83–84, 95, 102, 172, 186, 203, 218. *See also* Scripture Index, 2 Corinthians 5:18-20
red-blue political divide, 12, 23–26, 135. *See also* church: divisiveness within; Purple Zone preaching
Resner, André, 91
respect/disrespect in addressing social issues, 42, 67, 75, 86, 89, 90, 94, 101, 132, 154–55, 166–67, 213, 226, 231
Rose, Lucy Atkinson, 134

Segovia, Fernando, 111
sermon-dialogue-sermon method, 18, 33–34, 60, 68, 69–70, 77, 132, 135–36, 155–57, 202–206
sermon strategies for addressing social issues:
   Gentle, 64–67, 90, 109, 129–33, 136, 145, 153–54, 159–60, 164–68, 185–86, 198–200, 200–202, 206;
   Invitational, 67–70, 90, 115, 129–33, 145, 154–57, 160, 164–68, 170, 193, 200–202, 206, 209–215;
   Robust, 70–74, 90, 119, 129–33, 136–37, 139–40, 142, 146, 157–58, 160–61, 170–71, 186, 193, 206–209, 209–215
Sheen, Michael, 236–37, 239n14
social crisis preaching, 75, 77, 138–40, 158. *See also* Gardner, Tyshawn

social issues:
   definition, 1–2;
   emotions and, 65, 159–60, 226–28;
   preaching and. *See* preaching and social issues
social issues (topics):
   abortion, women's reproductive health, x, 4, 140;
   Christian nationalism, x, xi, 24, 25, 161–63, *164*, 165–68, *169*, 170–72, 174n26, 174n27;
   domestic, gender-based, or sexual violence, 114–15, 117–19, 120, 142, 211–15, 217n20;
   economic issues, capitalism, poverty, ix, 17, 45, 107, 108, 109, 111, 113, 118, 143–44, 152, 160, 162, 172n1, 184, 187–94, 191;
   environment, climate change, 6–9, 48, 69–70, 98–99, 144–45;
   government, 88–89, 107–11;
   gun violence, x, 4, 72–74, 207–209;
   drugs, opioid crisis, 77;
   immigration, 4, 17, 66–67, 112–15, 152–58, 170, 171, 172n1;
   Indigenous issues, 143–45;
   LGBTQIA+, 5, 42, 45, 56, 68–69, 198, 231;
   misogyny, rape culture, sexism, 116–17, 140, 210–215;
   patriarchy, 120, 140, 143, 144, 147, 162–63, 165, 210–215;
   police violence, 5, 39, 73;
   political divisiveness, 180–86, 200–202, 202–206;
   race, racism and racial justice, 5, 45, 56, 85, 115–21, 128, 137–42, 145–47, 158–61, 191–92, 212–215, 230–31, 233, 235;

sexism, sexual abuse, 114–15, 116–18, 140, 141–42, 210–15; whiteness, 121, 145–47, 162–171

social justice. *See* justice, injustice

stress, clergy and congregations, 19–20, 26–27, 31–32, 43, 47, 50, 57, 60, 64–65, 67–69, 70–72, 79, 175, 185, 225, 229–35. *See also* congregations, "brittleness"

Sumney, Jerry, 107–111

systemic issues, systemic sin, 1, 11, 79, 89, 108–110, 112, 115, 118, 123, 129–131, 141, 143, 146, 160, 193–94, 203, 210, 212, 215, 223

theology:
African American/Black, 138–40;
harmful, 190–94;
Latino/a, 111—15, 145–46;
Postcolonial, 143–46;
womanist, 115–21, 140–42, 158, 193, 212–15

Thomas, Frank A., 18, 84, 86–94, 100;
dangerous sermon, 20, 84, 86–87, 100

Thompson, Lisa L., ix–xii, 3, 4, 12, 63, 77, 78–79, 122, 125n43, 140–42, 158, 220, 223–24, 231–32, 238

Tisdale, Leonora Tubbs, 10, 65, 79

trust:
as moral virtue, 96–100;
lack of in society, 85, 236;
necessity for preaching, 47, 48–49, 57, 59, 60, 65, 67, 71, 74–75, 79, 154, 157, 160, 167–68, 175, 206, 219–20, 227–28

unity. *See* church, desire for unity

Valle-Ruiz, Lis, 145–47, 212, 215
Vashti, Queen, 210–215

Walker, Alice, 116
Wehner, Peter, 105
Wesleyan Quadrilateral, 134
Whitehead, Andrew, 81n15, 162, 164, 169–71
whiteness, white privilege, 29, 39, 41–42, 45, 50, 93, 117, 121, 143–46, 158–61, 165, 170, 207
white supremacy, 88, 93, 111, 145–46, 162–65, 170, 171, 230, 231,
Williams, Delores, 117–19, 192, 193
womanism, 115–16. *See also* Bible, womanist interpretation
working gospels, 91–94, 95, 138–40, 227;
American exceptionalism, 91, 92, 170;
American sentimentalism, 91, 92, 169;
denominational affiliation, 91, 93, 205–206;
Evangelicalism, 91, 92, 138, 169;
identity politics, 91, 111, 116, 138, 143, 170, 193, 205–206;
prosperity gospel, 91, 92, 170;
social justice, 91, 93, 107, 116, 138, 143, 185, 193, 205–206, 214
worship, and social issues, 98, 145, 200, 222

www.ingramcontent.com/pod-product-compliance
Lightning Source LLC
Chambersburg PA
CBHW050104170426
43198CB00014B/2457